Birds of
Forest, Yard, and Thicket

Also by John Eastman

Enjoying Birds in Michigan (Ed.)

The Book of Forest and Thicket

The Book of Swamp and Bog

Birds of
Forest, Yard, and Thicket

John Eastman
Illustrated by Amelia Hansen

STACKPOLE
BOOKS

Published by
STACKPOLE BOOKS
5067 Ritter Road
Mechanicsburg, PA 17055

Printed in the United States of America

First Edition

10 9 8 7 6 5 4 3 2 1

Cover design by Wendy A. Reynolds

Library of Congress Cataloging-in-Publication Data

Eastman, John (John Andrew)
    Birds of forest, yard, and thicket / John Eastman ;
illustrated by Amelia Hansen. — 1st ed.
        p.   cm.
    ISBN 0-8117-2680-0
    1. Birds—East (U.S.)   2. Forest ecology—East (U.S.)
I. Title.
QL683.E27E37   1997   96-33617
598.2974—dc20   CIP

To the memory of my friend
William J. Mills, Jr.

And to my teachers and mentors who have inspired me by example and enthusiasm: Raymond J. Adams, Jr., Richard Brewer, Jack Ellis, James Granlund, John P. Hubbard, and Harrison B. Tordoff.

"If you keep a green bough in your heart, the singing bird will come."
—Chinese adage

Contents

Acknowledgments

The talents of illustrator Amelia Hansen not only meticulously enhance the value of this book but form an integral part of it. In this, our third joint effort, I am again privileged to be associated with this brilliant artist as both collaborator and friend.

The impressive avian research facilities of the Kalamazoo Nature Center were graciously placed at our disposal by staff personnel. I am fortunate to have enlisted the time and critical expertise of three notable bird researchers. Raymond J. Adams, Jr., one of this nation's outstanding field ornithologists, is research director of the Kalamazoo Nature Center; Dr. Richard Brewer, professor emeritus of biology at Western Michigan University, is a well-known author, ornithologist, and ecologist; and James Granlund, curator of birds at the Kalamazoo Nature Center, is a science teacher, skilled field and museum ornithologist, and author. Each has read the text of this book and offered useful suggestions and comments, for which I am profoundly grateful. The final result, of course, does not necessarily reflect, indicate, or imply their approval of everything I have written. For that, I alone accept full blame and responsibility.

My friend Jacqueline Ladwein helped find and photograph many nests in the field. The steadfast enthusiasm and companionship of this teacher, naturalist, and fine field observer have enhanced my own outdoor work and pleasure for many years. Likewise I appreciate the many days and hours spent afield with Calvin J. Everly, a science teacher whose knowledge, eyesight, and bottomless humor have enlivened the ultimate quest.

I thank the owners of certain original Hansen drawings, who have granted us permission to use them in this book. Their names are given in the relevant captions. Sarah Reding and Dr. Willard M. Rose were also helpful in this regard. Dr. Richard Brewer kindly permitted the use of Hansen illustrations from *The Atlas of Breeding Birds of Michigan*, by Brewer, McPeek, and Adams (East Lansing: Michigan State University Press, 1991).

Curtis and Shirley McComis have granted me particular favors, for which I will always be grateful. I also thank Stephen Allen, Sally Atwater, Valerie Gittings, and Joyce Bond for their numerous contributions to this effort.

The original work of many American bird researchers, both named and unnamed in the following pages, has contributed vitally to this book. Though I know few of them personally, their dedication, scholarship, and professional skills provide the foundation and superstructure for each species account herein.

The one most vital to me is, as always, Susan Woolley Stoddard, a person accomplished in many endeavors—quilter, world traveler, lover of life, participant in all my works, and my loving companion of almost two decades.

Introduction

This book focuses on sixty-eight of the most common and familiar bird species of eastern North America—birds that most of us can see in the appropriate season without traveling too far from home. Accounts treat each species from an ecological perspective—that is, as community dwellers coequal with their plant and animal associates in the total complex of their habitats and environments. This perspective follows the general pattern of my two previous volumes relating to plants, *The Book of Forest and Thicket* (1992) and *The Book of Swamp and Bog* (1995).

Birds, of course, require a somewhat different approach. Unlike plants, they place high on the consumer end of the food chain. They are mobile, and many of their actions result from volition within the broad context of genetically based behaviors. Yet their evolutionary adaptations in anatomy (bills, wing shapes, types of feet) and behaviors (flight and foraging patterns, migrations, reproductive strategies) express close interactions with specific aspects of their surroundings. To observe a bird in its natural habitat is to observe a totality, to catch a sense of the entire ecological mosaic that each bird contains and reveals in its being. Whether we are sharp enough to perceive a bird in this way is another matter, and one that I hope this book may help address.

Another primary aim is to convey some discoveries of recent research, especially findings of the past two decades. Current bird research is continually updating our knowledge, revising our conclusions, in some cases even subverting gospel. My foremost sources have included professional bird journals such as *The Auk, Wilson Bulletin,* and others; book-length monographs on a single species or family; several recent state and regional bird atlases; and not least, records of my own bird observations plus much shared knowledge and opinion from respected birding friends and associates.

Sixty-eight species represent only about a tenth of the bird species that breed in North America. Some three hundred fifty species regularly occur east of the Mississippi and north of the Ohio River, the regional focus of this book. Many of these are birds that reside in habitats outside the scope of this book, such as waterfowl, shorebirds, seabirds, and birds of marsh, open country, and plains. Even with the birds of forest, yard, and thicket habitats, I have opted for closer looks over total inclusiveness. Rather than give perfunctory accounts of *all* such birds—a job already accomplished by many excellent state and regional bird guides—I have focused on the so-called core species of these habitats.

My particular selection of these is arbitrary. Aside from the cruel choices dictated by space limitations, some species present awkward problems for the habitat pigeonholer. I have, for example, omitted great blue herons and bald eagles, birds that could be classified either as forest dwellers based on their nesting habitats or as wetland residents based on their foraging habitats. Likewise I have omitted such open-country foragers as eastern kingbirds, tree swallows, and eastern bluebirds, which could often qualify as edge nesters. In deciding such cases, I have usually chosen foraging habitat as the foremost criterion, since feeding areas are the places where most species are easiest to observe. Another author may have handled these distinctions differently or selected other birds for inclusion or omission; I readily grant that other valid options abound.

Experienced bird observers will note two striking departures from conventional treatment of birds in this book. One is important; the other I consider trivial.

The most significant change occurs in the taxonomic sequencing of birds (as reflected in the Contents). Until recently, the American Ornithologists' Union (AOU), arbiter of North American bird naming and taxonomy, has always classified bird species on the basis of their general physical and adaptive characteristics. During the 1980s, however, a revolutionary new taxonomic system was presented by biologists Charles G. Sibley, Jon E. Ahlquist, and Burt L. Monroe, Jr. ("A Classification of the Living Birds of the World Based on DNA–DNA Hybridization Studies." *The Auk* 105:40 [1988]). These researchers based their classification on DNA hybridization techniques; simply stated, the DNA molecules of bird species are compared and taxonomic classification is based on genetic rather than physical and adaptive similarities. This new system, many ornithologists agree, has given us a biologically more accurate (and much different) picture of bird relationships than previously existed. It confirms that physical resemblances between birds may in many cases result from convergent evolution of nonrelated species, producing unreliable indicators of genetic kinship.

Quite predictably, the changes wrought by the new system have been greeted by controversy. Not all birders are ready to accept such a radical revision of their long-familiar standardized checklists. And some ornithologists argue that bird classification must be based on combinations of genetic and other characters. (One of the new system's foremost contributions lies in its uniform set of criteria versus the present "shotgun" approach to classification.) Yet even if acceptance of the Sibley-Ahlquist system in whole or in part must await the next generation of birders, its effects have already been repercussive; and it is not very hazardous at this point to forecast consequent total revision of the current AOU checklist. (Helping mediate matters, no doubt, is the fact that some of the new system's key proponents are also AOU chieftains.) Conservatively, the system's originators make no claim that their classification is a final "true reflection of the phylogeny of living birds, but we believe that it represents progress toward that elusive goal." Taxonomy is always tentative. Yet evidence is now amply sufficient to justify use of the new classification in popular bird guides such as this one, which is, I believe, one of the first to embrace full use of it. Thus the arrangement of species herein, as well as English and Latin nomenclature, abandons current AOU formats, accepting instead the authority of *A World Checklist of Birds,* by Burt L. Monroe, Jr., and Charles G. Sibley (New Haven: Yale University Press, 1993).

Much less significant is my decision to lowercase all English bird names (except in account headings), a practice contrary to the heated insistence of many bird biographers. I am familiar with all the arguments for capitalizing bird names; I simply disagree with them. Especially in a book that focuses on birds as living elements of the total ecology—as organisms vital but not superior in any way to other species of the environmental complex—it would seem to me peculiar business for a naturalist to make such distinctions. "Let us surrender to the dictionary," as Anselm Atkins advises; "until we do, we ornithologists, with our Important Capitals, continue to look Curiously Provincial."

I have divided each species account into several sections. Each account begins with the bird's English and Latin names, as given in *A World Checklist of Birds.* Family and order designations follow. Where two or more species of a single family are given accounts, an introductory paragraph on the family precedes the accounts. A brief description of the bird's appearance and sounds follows its names.

Close relatives identifies the bird's nearest kin.

Behaviors describes the bird's characteristic actions, focusing on what an observer may actually see. Included here are the bird's breeding distribution and migrational habits. Descriptions of specific seasonal behaviors and activities follow under seasonal subheadings.

Spring is when migrants arrive, singing peaks, and most North American birds form pair bonds and begin nesting. Many yearling birds return in spring to areas near their birth sites, and most previously mated adult birds return to their previous breeding territories.

Many birds remain monogamous breeders throughout a season and some throughout their lives. Seasonal monogamy most often "comes with the territory"—that is, a female bird selects a desirable territory and almost incidentally accepts the male that "owns" it. Yet some sixty species (at last count) of North American songbirds are known to engage in at least occasional breeding, or extrapair copulations, outside the primary nuptial bond. Nesting data are framed in a standardized paragraph of this seasonal section.

In *summer,* most birds complete nesting activities; song diminishes and juvenile birds disperse. Feathers litter the ground in late summer, when the annual plumage molt occurs in most species, and many migrant birds assemble in flocks.

Fall is another highly stressful season of migration. Some species migrate only to the southern United States; others move much farther, to Central and South America. Some of the Neotropical migrants that travel farthest move from North American fall to South American spring, but they do not renew breeding activities at their destinations.

Winter for most birds is a season of feeding, either in flocks or solitarily, depending on the species. For certain species that winter in the north, this may be a season of great hardship and mortality if food becomes scarce, as it often does. Winter distribution of migrants is also described in this section.

Ecology focuses on specific details of the bird's relationships to other organisms and to its seasonal environments. Sequenced paragraphs discuss the bird's habitats, nesting, food, competitors, predators, and brood parasites. Not detailed in most accounts are the bird's external and internal parasites. Almost all birds carry them, and many bird species carry the same genera or species of parasite. The most common skin and feather parasites include fowl mites (*Ornithonyssus),* bird lice (Philopteridae), larval louse or hippoboscid flies (*Lynchia),* and larval blow flies (*Protocalliphora).* Many birds also carry internal parasites, such as roundworms, tapeworms, and flukes. Avian pox, a common virus disease, results from *Poxvirus avium* infection. "I suspect that parasites have been very influential in the evolution of birds," one ecologist writes.

Focus, a catchall section, presents information on origins of the bird's name, the bird's place in native or cultural history, details of certain adaptations it may show, elaborations on previous sections—anything interesting that fits nowhere else.

Closer looks gives references to books or other sources that offer more detailed information than my accounts can provide.

Latin names of plant and animal organisms other than birds are kept to a minimum, included only for specific organisms that bear special ecological relevance to the bird.

Several recurrent terms may need defining:

Birding is the methodical field activity of observing birds; *birders* are people who engage in this activity, either as a pastime or for data collection.

Pishing is a simple method used by birders to attract birds closer for easier observation. It consists of making repetitious hissing or sibilant sounds (as in "psst psst psst"). These sounds seem to excite birds' curiosity or, in some cases, alarm. Some birds, such as black-capped chickadees and common yellowthroats, almost invariably respond to these sounds. Others, such as American redstarts, respond irregularly, and still others grandly ignore the whole business. Pishing usually works best during the breeding season, when birds are territorial and alert to any unusual sounds or activities in their vicinity. *Squeaking*—kissing the back of the hand loudly, rapidly, and repeatedly—sometimes more effectively fetches a bird than pishing.

Incubation is egg heating by the parent bird, accomplished by sitting on the eggs for long intervals over days or weeks; in most (though not all) North American species, incubation is done exclusively by females. Incubating females usually develop brood patches, temporarily bare areas of abdominal skin by which they transfer body heat to the eggs. Some species begin incubation when the first egg is laid, resulting in differential hatching times. In most species, however, incubation starts after the laying of the last egg in a set, or clutch, and hatching occurs more or less simultaneously.

Fledging refers to the nestling's development of feathers and its act of leaving the nest, thereby becoming a *fledgling* until it can feed independently; then it is a *juvenile*. Used as a subhead in the boxed paragraph in the *Spring* section of accounts, *fledging* refers to the number of days between hatching and nest departure.

A *juvenile,* or immature, bird feeds independently but has not yet developed its first winter (usually adultlike) plumage, a molt that occurs concurrently with the feather molt of adult birds in late summer or fall. (I do not use the term *juvenal,* by which some authors refer to the juvenile bird's plumage.)

Edge is a habitat term, referring to a zone of transitional vegetation (usually shrubs, small trees, and thickets) between forest and open land. Most roadside and hedgerow vegetation is also labeled edge.

Mixed forests are wooded stands containing both deciduous (such as oak, aspen, cherry) and coniferous (such as pine, spruce, hemlock) trees.

Territory is, in its broadest definition, the area defended by a singing male or bonded pair of birds. Territories vary in size among species and also among members of the same species. Territory size often depends on abundance of the species and quality of habitat in a given area. Birds establish their territories by singing and by defensive behaviors against intruders of the same or competing species. Most songbird breeding territories enclose both nesting and feeding sites. Many birds, however, must leave their territories to feed, drink, or bathe; a loose designation for these extraterritorial areas is *home range*. Colonial pairs usually defend much smaller territories than solitary nesters, though a few of the latter, such as mourning doves and common ravens, also maintain extremely small territories. Nonbreeding territories in some species may include defended food sources, night roosts, and winter foraging sites.

A resident bird's *home range* is the total space it inhabits in a given area; home range encloses the territory but is not defended. Home ranges of separate pairs of a species often overlap.

The general decline of many forest songbird species over the past few decades has caused ecologists to reevaluate some previously held concepts of habitat. Some years ago, when I was an employed wildlife biologist, field professionals and conservationists alike emphasized the supreme value of edge habitats—abundant mixtures and mosaics of vegetation—as the sites most conducive for maintaining the largest diversity of wildlife (especially game species). Edges reflected their own plant diversity in the fauna, offering virtually something for everyone. Edge creation, usually accomplished by mowing, chopping, or burning, became the dominant gospel of wildlife habitat management. "Over the years," ecologist Richard Brewer wrote, "the premier technique for managing almost any [species] has come to be cutting holes in the forest."

Today, however, we are learning that universal edge is not a cure-all for maintaining biological diversity. We have discovered that species such as pileated woodpeckers, wood thrushes, scarlet tanagers, and many warblers are *area sensitive*—that is, they require extensive stands of unbroken forest for optimal habitats. Forest fragmentation not only depletes these forest-interior habitats but also increases access for predators, most of which are edge-dwelling species. Nest-parasitizing brown-headed cowbirds and nest-competitive European starlings, also edge dwellers that easily invade fragmented forests, owe much of their phenomenal increase over the past decades to the chopped-up landscapes we have created. Clearly our love affair with edge—whether created by well-meaning conservationists or as by-products of agricultural practices, suburban development, oil and gas exploration, timber harvesting, and various multiple-use schemes—is, in many areas, devastating our forest bird populations. Clear-cutting is an obvious threat to forest habitats. Equal enemies of biological diversity, however, include those foresters who claim to be serving wildlife and the environment by salvage harvesting—selectively thinning and removing dead and diseased trees from large forest tracts. As every ecologist knows, this so-called waste element of the forest complex is also vital, especially to cavity-nesting birds. Added to these known stresses are two still unknowns: the effects of rain forest destruction and the use of DDT and other pesticides in the Neotropics, where many of our migrant songbirds spend most of their lives.

How big must a forest be to maintain forest-interior bird populations? Various estimates and methods of calculation give a range of answers; some are presented in the species accounts that follow. Ornithologist James Granlund suggests an island analogy to forest fragmentation: "the larger the island, the greater its diversity." Another prominent ornithologist suggests that forest songbird decline could be reversed by establishing a network of forests no smaller than twenty thousand acres apiece. Although few environmentalists can be optimistic enough to believe that such an enlightened conservation ethic is near at hand, certain signs may indicate progress. For one, the scientific basis for such an ethic is now well established. For another, people who care about a decent quality of life, not only for themselves but as a legacy, are becoming increasingly vocal and involved in environmental issues.

Aldo Leopold once challenged a generation with the conservation ethic of "thinking like a mountain." With what we now know, we can begin "thinking like a forest." Perhaps such forethought embodies the only kind of patriotism that will finally mean much to our progeny.

For many of us, birds provided a first irresistible lure to the world of nature observation. The phenomenal growth of birding in recent years, as both serious pursuit and pleasant avocation, attests to the increasing popularity of an outdoor activity that can be engaged in by oneself or with others. Birders come in all shapes, sizes, ages, and degrees of intensity. Some specialize in certain families or species, virtually ignoring all others; others seek to observe the largest possible diversity of birds. For some, birding has become a highly competitive, even frantic sport, a quest to identify as many species as possible in a day, in a certain area, in a lifetime. While such gaming is not my own cup of tea, it has unquestionably publicized birding, provided general information on bird abundance, and enlarged the company of birders. In one way or another, attention to birds is being paid, and birding rewards exist at all levels. For anyone keen to get started, local birding groups now exist almost everywhere, glad to take novices under their wing, as it were.

I earnestly hope that this book will send you afield, help you observe, and aid your interpretations of what you see and hear. If it fuels your curiosity—or, even better, if it finally proves inadequate to it—I shall be pleased.

1

PHEASANT FAMILY (Phasianidae), order Galliformes

This family (often called gamebirds) includes the pheasants, partridges, grouse, turkeys, and Old World quails—all ground-dwelling, chickenlike birds. Adding the prairie-chickens and ptarmigans (both grouse), northeastern species number nine; almost two hundred species range worldwide. Genes of the common fowl, a subspecies of the red junglefowl *(Gallus gallus)* of Asia, appear in many domestic "breeds of chicken." Most gamebirds do not migrate and are incapable of sustained flight; their pectoral muscles (the white meat) can generate brief, powerful wingbursts but are easily fatigued. Many show spectacular plumages, the most notable being the peacock (male common peafowl, *Pavo cristatus*), an Asian pheasant. Various species also display wattles and inflatable neck sacs.

PHEASANT FAMILY (Phasianidae)

Ruffed Grouse *(Bonasa umbellus)*

Both sexes are brownish with ragged head crests, dark neck "ruffs," and fan-shaped tails showing a broad, black band near the tip. The band on female tails is usually discontinuous on the central feathers; the male band is unbroken. Two color forms, or morphs, occur: Grouse with rusty red tails are more common in the bird's southern range; gray-tailed birds mainly occur in the north.

Close relatives. The nine North American grouse include spruce grouse *(Dendragapus canadensis)*, ptarmigans *(Lagopus)*, prairie-chickens (*Tympanuchus*), and the sharp-tailed grouse (*T. phasianellus*).

Behaviors. Hunters know the ruffed grouse as partridge or pat, the most widely distributed gamebird on the continent; in the East, however, its range extends south only to the Carolinas and southern Appalachians. This bird is most often seen as it flushes from cover with a startling whir of wings. Its sudden burst of flight usually carries it only a short distance before it lands on the ground or a tree branch. Alarmed or disturbed birds, especially females with young, emit a variety of clucking or whining sounds. Ruffed grouse forage from the ground and both low and high branches. They often dust themselves in patches of dry, sandy soil, creating small ground depressions that show scratch marks and wing prints. Dust bathing probably helps relieve them of skin and feather parasites.

Spring. Especially in early morning and evening, listen for the distinctive drumming of the male birds—a pulsating series of thumps that begins slowly, then quickens in tempo to a whir. These low-pitched sounds, repeated at regular intervals (usually three to five minutes), vary in intensity and often sound more distant than they are (a quarter mile is about the farthest that human ears can hear them). Grouse perform on what are called drumming stages, usually one or more moss-covered logs in dense, brushy cover. Drumming not only proclaims the male's territory to other male grouse but also attracts females. The same bird often uses the same log in successive years. Signs of a current drumming log include grouse droppings and leaf fanning—bare spaces on either side from which the bird's wingbeats have blown away leaves and other

Fan-shaped tails, either gray or reddish, identify ruffed grouse. Note the broken black band, indicating that this is a female; tail bands of most males are continuous.

Grouse drumming logs are usually large, often showing an advanced stage of decay. Grouse droppings (inset) at drumming sites somewhat resemble porcupine scat.

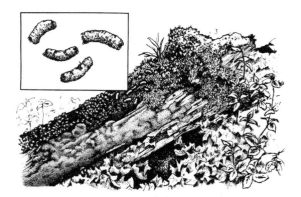

debris. In optimal habitat, drumming grouse seldom space themselves closer together than about five hundred feet. When a female approaches, the male struts, erecting his crest and ruff feathers, and the birds mate. Yet no genuine pair bond is formed. The female goes off to nest, while the male continues drumming and attracting available females throughout the season. Drumming occurs sporadically year-round but most frequently in early spring.

If you should happen to discover a grouse nest during incubation, the female will probably abandon it and renest elsewhere. Grouse chicks are *precocial;* that is, they can leave the nest within hours after hatching, following the female as she forages. The young feed on small insects and spiders as they trail behind. Until they can fly, the female broods them beneath her body at night. During this period, the female vigorously performs distraction displays if the group is disturbed. Many times in the spring woods I have been startled by several loud warning clucks, followed by the headlong rush of a female grouse directly at me. Flapping and squawking as if injured, she veers to one side, making herself as conspicuous as possible while her brood silently huddles.

EGGS AND YOUNG: nine to twelve; eggs buff colored, brown spotted. INCUBATION: by female; about twenty-four days. FEEDING OF YOUNG: none. FLEDGING: young leave nest shortly after hatching, fly in about twelve days.

Summer. Female and young usually occupy a home range of a quarter mile to a half mile across. The juveniles soon graduate to a vegetarian diet, roosting in trees at night. Adult birds begin their annual feather molt in July and become highly secretive; they may be flightless for a brief period until the new flight feathers become fully grown. The outer two primary feathers of a juvenile bird show pointed tips, in contrast to the rounded tips of those of older birds. As summer advances, adult males may join the family groups and forage with them.

Fall. Juveniles usually remain with the female until early fall. Soon, however, most broods disperse; many birds travel more than a mile and become solitary. Adult birds usually remain on the home range. In October, grouse begin growing their "snowshoes"—comblike, horny scales on the edges of each toe, which double the toe surface, allowing the birds to walk atop snow. Grouse lose these appendages in spring.

Winter. Coveys of foraging and roosting grouse (not necessarily family groups) often form in late fall and winter. In winter, grouse often roost in the dense lower branches of conifers, which provide tentlike shelter from snow and wind. When a foot or more of snow covers the ground, however, many grouse seek shelter in the snow itself, often flying directly into it. They remain buried for the night—or much longer if a blizzard rages; sometimes the bird's breath melts a small breathing hole in the snow. Usually they emerge by flying directly out of their well-insulated cover, in which the temperature may range up to 50 degrees higher than at the surface.

Ecology. Ruffed grouse favor edge habitats, such as overgrown, shrubby pastures or orchards; wetland margins; or early successional stages of regenerating forest. The foremost plant associate in the northern range is aspen; elsewhere the birds occupy a variety of mixed hardwood habitats. Common feeding and cover sites, especially in the fall, also include overgrown apple orchards and thickets of alder, gray dogwood, hawthorn, greenbrier, and blackberry.

The nest, a slight hollow scraped in the ground and lined with dry leaves, is usually placed at a tree base, under a windfall, or against a log, well camouflaged by low vegetation, often near a forest path or road.

Ruffed grouse consume insects and other invertebrates during their first weeks of life, but infrequently thereafter. Much of their survival success owes to their wide range of plant foods. In spring, they relish newly sprouted leaves of aspens, birches, cherries, apple, willows, greenbriers, clovers, dandelion, wild strawberry, wintergreen, and Christmas fern, among others. As fruits ripen in summer and fall, grouse consume quantities of dogwood and greenbrier berries, wild grapes, hawthorn fruits, cherries, blueberries, viburnum fruits, apple fruit and seeds, blackberries, beechnuts, and acorns. Aldo Leopold noted that oak galls were favored autumn foods. In winter, the primary grouse food is buds, especially the catkin buds of male aspens, plus seeds of staghorn sumac and other shrubs.

Two main ground-foraging competitors, especially in winter, are white-tailed deer and snowshoe hares.

The foremost grouse egg predators are probably opossums and raccoons. Striped skunks, weasels, red foxes, eastern chipmunks, and red and gray squirrels also raid the nests. Northern black racers, black rat snakes, and fox snakes may consume entire egg clutches at once. Accipiter hawks often prey on the chicks. The chief natural predators of adult grouse are probably hawks, great horned owls, and red foxes. On one predation site, I found a neat pile of aspen buds surrounded by a few grouse feathers. An owl had consumed almost everything except the crop contents. Grouse drumming attracts predators, but since owls cannot hear such low-frequency sounds, they capture few grouse at drumming logs.

Focus. Ruffed grouse abundance fluctuates in about ten-year cycles. After analyzing many state census records, one authority stated that peak grouse years often end in the number two, lowest years in the number seven. Peak-year densities in ideal fall habitats may number two hundred or more birds per square mile.

American natives valued grouse for food, and hunted and snared them, but found them relatively uncommon. Since presettlement times, the results of land clearing and agriculture have increased grouse habitats. Because of the sharp skills required to shoot a ruffed grouse, its human predators consider themselves an elite fraternity among gun toters. Licensed hunters seldom take more than 30 percent of a fall grouse population in any given area.

Aldo Leopold, using a Latin word meaning "essence," or "spirit," called the muffled throb of ruffed grouse wings "the numenon of the northwoods." Thoreau likened it to "little drumsticks on our tympanum . . . a throbbing or fluttering in our veins or brows or the chambers of the ear." The drumming sound emanates from the bird's cupped wings as it beats them forward and upward, tail braced against the drumming log. Slapping the hands against the chest will sometimes evoke response from a drumming grouse. Male grouse have been known to attack tractors and other engines and been attracted to sounds of wood chopping.

The ruffed grouse is Pennsylvania's state bird.

Closer looks. Atwater, S., and J. Schnell, eds. *The Wildlife Series: Ruffed Grouse.* Harrisburg, PA: Stackpole Books, 1989.

Rue, L. L. *The World of the Ruffed Grouse.* Philadelphia: Lippincott, 1973.

Ruffed Grouse Society, 451 McCormick Road, Coraopolis, PA 15108.

PHEASANT FAMILY (Phasianidae)

Wild Turkey *(Meleagris gallopavo)*

This streamlined version of the barnyard turkey has a bluish, naked head with wartlike *caruncles,* a bulbous dewlap on the neck, bronze-colored plumage, and rusty tail tips. A fleshy appendage called the *snood* projects from the top of the bill. In males, called toms or gobblers, a beard of long, bristlelike feathers dangles from the breast and a sharp spur projects from the rear of each leg. Hens are smaller, with a smaller snood, and only occasionally have a beard. Wild turkeys gobble and utter numerous other sounds, mostly during the breeding season.

Close relative. The only other turkey species is *Agriocharis ocellata,* the ocellated turkey, native to Mexico and Central America. Domesticated turkeys all derive from the wild turkey.

Behaviors. North America's largest gamebird sometimes reaches a weight of twenty-five pounds or more. A ground feeder, often in flocks, it prefers to run—often reaching a speed of fifteen miles per hour or more—rather than fly from danger, but its burst of powerful flight may carry it a mile or so. At night turkeys usually roost in trees, often near the top. Today wild turkey range spans the continent from southern Canada to Mexico, and the bird far exceeds its original distribution, though not its former abundance.

Spring. The tom's appearance and behavior become conspicuous in early spring. Sometimes in small male groups dominated by one tom, but more often solitary, he gobbles from a tree roost, beginning before dawn and often continuing throughout the morning. Tom wanders widely, his "territory" being his own proximity. He attracts hens to himself, first by his loud gobbling, then by a close-range strutting display with erect plumage and tail, dragging his wings and uttering low-pitched "chumps" or humming sounds, known as the "pulmonic puff." His head and neck display "mood colors," brightening to vivid hues of red, blue, and white in a matter of seconds when a hen or another tom approaches. Toms often fight with bills and leg spurs as they compete for mates. They are *polygynous,* often following one or more hens around and mating with as many as they can attract. The tom's come-hither gobble call is only one of some

Belligerent toms strut and display in spring, sometimes hardly feeding for days at a time. The chest beard remains unmolted in summer. (Courtesy of Kalamazoo Nature Center.)

thirty calls voiced by wild turkeys. Other commonly heard notes include the alarm "putt" when a predator is spotted; the hen's loud, nasal "keow!" or love call, which sounds at a distance like a yelping dog and is also used as a contact call; and assorted clucks and chatters. Despite the ingenuity of various turkey-calling devices used by hunters, either sex sometimes responds to completely unturkeylike sounds—a car horn, human voice, or slamming door, for example. I once conversed with a yelping turkey for several minutes by knocking a dead branch against a log.

After mating, the hen goes off by herself, scratches a shallow depression in the ground, usually beneath a shrub, windfall, or low branches, and begins to nest. Each time she leaves the nest before incubation begins, she covers the eggs with leaves, thus collecting nesting materials after, and not before, laying begins. Disturbance before hatching often causes the hen to abandon her eggs; unless incubation is well advanced, she usually renests in another place. Soon after hatching, the young birds, called *poults,* are led from the nest by the hen, who broods them on the ground. They soon begin roosting above ground and thenceforth always roost in trees at night.

EGGS AND YOUNG: ten to twelve; eggs buff, dotted with reddish-brown. INCUBATION: by female; about a month. FEEDING OF YOUNG: none. FLEDGING: poults begin flying and roosting above ground in about two weeks.

Summer. Wild turkeys now assemble into gregarious flocks of three types. *Family flocks,* consisting of brood hens and their poults, often merge to form groups of thirty or more birds. These groups may daily forage over an area of several hundred acres. *Adult broodless hens* also form flocks, some of them joining the family flocks. *Regrouped toms* form flocks of a dozen or so males.

A more adultlike plumage soon replaces the brown juvenile feathers of the poults. Adult turkeys undergo their annual molt, a gradual feather replacement that does not prevent them from flying.

Toms do not molt their long beard feathers. In turkey country, this is the season when you may find long, well-worn wing primary feathers lying about. The poults play and chase, perform mock adult fighting and mating activities, wallow in dust baths, and feed extensively.

Fall. As the poults grow to adult size, another breakdown in group composition occurs. The immature males, or *jakes,* form bachelor flocks by themselves; most jakes do not compete with older toms for mates until their second year. The family flocks now consist of young and adult hens only. About 40 percent of fall turkey populations consists of young hens or jakes, and the sex ratio is evenly split. In all flocks of either sex, conflicts among individual birds establish a peck order or hierarchy; a dominant bird achieves social superiority over all others in the flock, with each bird occupying a step-

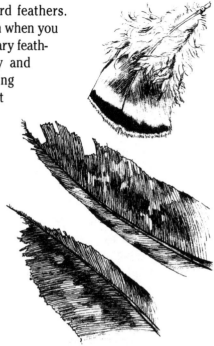

The turkey's long wing primaries, often found on the ground during the summer plumage molt, show evidence of hard wear. Breast contour feathers (top) are much smaller and are iridescent.

like rank beneath it. Demonstrations of subservience by lower-ranking birds may include beak nuzzling into the breast plumage of a dominant bird. Jakes and young hens now undergo a fall molt and acquire their first adult winter plumage.

Winter. Now the turkey flocks often split into smaller groups that withdraw into sheltered places such as gullies, wooded creek-bottoms, or south-facing slopes. The birds feed and loaf, remaining fairly sedentary. During severe weather, they may roost for a week or longer without feeding. Turkeys are well adapted to survive winter weather, however, and can scratch through snow a foot deep.

Yet snow depth probably limits turkey range, and they sometimes succumb to starvation at this season. Toms develop a thick layer of fat called the breast sponge, believed to supply their energy needs during spring courtship activities, when they often "forget" to feed.

Ecology. Wild turkeys favor mature deciduous and mixed woodlands, but their habitats change somewhat with the seasons. In spring and summer, they frequent forest edges and openings. In the fall, flocks withdraw into the deeper woods, where mast crops (nuts) are most abundant. In winter, turkeys often shelter in or near stands of pine. Often they feed near springs or in areas where white-tailed deer have pawed the snow. Their flexible food habits and adaptable use of several habitat types account for much of this bird's success as a species.

Nests are frequently located near the edge of a woodland road or clearing.

Wild turkeys feed omnivorously, their diet largely dictated by the seasons. Poults consume high amounts of insect protein in spring; grasshoppers and march fly larvae (Bibionidae) are favored items, along with spiders, snails, and crayfish. The adult turkey diet, however, consists of at least 90 percent plant foods in all seasons—leaves, bulbs, tubers, buds, flowers, seeds, and fruits. Low forest herbs, such as sprouting ferns and violets, provide spring forage. The main summer foods are probably grasses and upland sedges, both leaves and seeds, reflecting turkey habitats at this season. Oak acorns are staple foods year-round, becoming most abundant in the fall; the American chestnut, before its virtual extinction from North American forests, was a major mast source for turkeys. Turkeys also relish beechnuts, flowering dogwood fruits, wild grapes, blackberries, and corn, along with many other fruits and seeds. In winter, they feed on residual fruits, sumac seeds, succulent bulbs, evergreen fern leaflets, dried spore stalks of sensitive fern, and clubmoss spore stalks.

Turkeys compete for mast foods with many other bird and mammal species—woodpeckers, crows, jays, squirrels, and white-tailed deer, to name just a few. A poor mast year results in increased competition for food, and creatures such as turkeys that cannot travel extensive distances for food may be severely disadvantaged. Offsetting this is the turkey's ability, like ruffed grouse, to derive nourishment from almost any plant source.

American crows, opossums, raccoons, and striped skunks destroy up to half of the wild turkey nests each spring; in most cases, the hen renests. Hawks and owls are ever watchful for poults, as are bobcats and red foxes. Great horned owls prey on roosting turkeys at night, especially where protective overhead branches are lacking. A snake, as one observer reports, "will sometimes send a turkey into near hysteria." When European settlers arrived in America, they found wild turkeys unafraid of humans; natural selection has since eliminated such turkey trust.

Turkey poults commonly suffer a mild case of fowl pox skin lesions, a virus disease carried mainly by mosquitoes. A more serious disease, apparently spread from domestic turkey flocks, is enterohepatitis, or blackhead disease, caused by a protozoan (*Histomonas meleagridis*). Infected birds become listless and droopy and are usually taken by predators before they die.

Focus. The only thing that can possibly be mistaken for a courting turkey, say old turkey hunters, is a politician. Politician Ben Franklin proposed the wild turkey as our national bird—the tom's head is red, white, and blue, after all—but he was outvoted in favor of what my friend Jack Olsen labels a "garbage bird," the carrion-eating bald eagle.

Domestic turkeys bear little resemblance to their wild brethren; docile and heavy, the farm and commercial breeds depend totally on humans for their existence. These genetically engineered and inbred "meat machines" are largely reproduced by artificial insemination.

How the name *turkey* originated can only be guessed. The likeliest story is that when explorer Hernando Cortés brought Mexican-domesticated turkeys back to Spain in 1520, people confused them with guinea fowl (*Numida meleagris*), barnyard birds from Turkey; they labeled both birds turkeys, and the name for one of them stuck.

Domesticating turkeys was probably a simpler job than later efforts to return them to the wild, and a hunter friend of mine even swears that all wild turkeys "want to be domesticated." Imprinting of the ancestral birds on humans probably enabled the Aztecs to domesticate a now-extinct subspecies of wild turkey. Following Cortés's gift to his country, flocks of descendant birds were soon being raised all over Europe. The Pilgrim colonists brought farm turkeys with them—the first Thanksgiving was hardly their first taste of the bird—and the four native wild turkeys given to them by their Indian hosts on that occasion didn't look much different than the ones in their pens. At least some tribes regarded wild turkeys as hardly worth a man's time; the birds were so abundant and unwary that hunting them was assigned to children. "Could it be possible," speculated naturalist John Madson, "that the Indians brought turkeys to the Pilgrims' first Thanksgiving feast just to get rid of them?" In America, roast turkey replaced roast goose as the main course of holiday feasts. Turkey quills also replaced goose quills as writing instruments; the Declaration of Independence and U.S. Constitution were probably written and signed with turkey feathers. Franklin thus partially triumphed after all.

Estimates of the precolonial North American wild turkey population range from seven million to forty million. By 1920, however, market hunting and habitat depletion had completely eliminated wild turkeys in almost half of the thirty-eight states that encompassed their original range, reducing their total population to one-tenth or less of their pristine levels. Today conservationists proudly label the wild turkey's comeback as one of their biggest success stories, but trial and error marked the first efforts to reestablish populations. Game biologists soon discovered that pen-reared wild turkeys couldn't make it in the wild. Genetic contamination—the mixture of genes from domestic turkey flocks—plus exposure to various poultry diseases weakened their adaptive capacities. Restocking programs eventually focused on transplanting turkeys from wild populations. Today about four million wild turkeys exist, and their numbers continue to increase in all the states they originally occupied plus several others. Although human intervention certainly played a large part in turkey restoration, at least equally important was the reversion after 1940 of

Turkeys forage by scratching, as this jake is doing. Its leg spurs may become fierce weapons during the breeding season. (Courtesy of Kalamazoo Nature Center.)

much farmland acreage to edge and forest habitats—plus the wild turkey's inherent hardiness and adaptability.

Most adult wild turkeys die before age two, but occasionally birds survive ten years or more. Turkey sign is easily recognized. The four-inch-long, three-toed tracks resemble those of sandhill cranes in form and size, but habitats of the two species do not often coincide. V-shaped scratch marks indicate the turkey's four-stroke sequence: It rakes back one foot (usually the right) all the way, rakes back twice with the other, then repeats the first-foot scratch. Droppings are often found beneath the roost trees. Tom droppings are J-shaped; hen droppings are typically spiral or bulbous piles.

Closer looks. Dickson, J. G., ed. *The Wild Turkey: Biology and Management.* Harrisburg, PA: Stackpole Books, 1992.

Lewis, J. C. *The World of the Wild Turkey.* Philadelphia: Lippincott, 1973.

National Wild Turkey Federation, P.O. Box 530, Edgefield, SC 29824.

2

WOODPECKER FAMILY (Picidae), order Piciformes

Adaptations for their tree habitats include *zygodactyl* feet (two toes front, two rear) and stiff, bracing tails. Their stout, chisellike bills, extremely long tongues, strong neck muscles, and bone-reinforced skulls equip them for hammering into wood and extracting insects. All are tree-cavity nesters, and their flight is undulating, or bouncy.

The woodpecker tongue is an extraordinary mechanism. Its base connects to a V-shaped cartilage, or *hyoid,* which curves up the back of the skull to the top of the head. Anchored at the base of the bill, this apparatus extends the tongue by uncoiling from the head crown. The tongue tip, horny and barbed with back-projecting spines, enables the birds to snag insects.

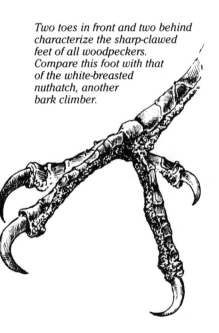

Two toes in front and two behind characterize the sharp-clawed feet of all woodpeckers. Compare this foot with that of the white-breasted nuthatch, another bark climber.

Melanin pigments in the black, stout-shafted tail feathers—virtually a third foot—increase their strength and durability as props. Drumming on resonant surfaces is a characteristic woodpecker courtship and territorial behavior. A loudly drumming woodpecker is not excavating for food or a nest cavity; loud drumming is analogous to the singing of songbirds, done to attract a mate and to claim a territory. Any resonating surface (usually a hollow tree, but also metal eaves, house siding, or garbage cans) may be habitually used as a drumming station, often by either sex.

Nine woodpecker species breed in the Northeast, some twelve others in the western United States. More than two hundred species exist worldwide.

Closer looks. Kilham, L. *Woodpeckers of Eastern North America.* New York: Dover, 1992.

Lawrence, L. deK. *A Comparative Life-history Study of Four Species of Woodpeckers.* Lawrence, KS: American Ornithologists' Union, Ornithological Monographs No. 5, 1967.

WOODPECKER FAMILY (Picidae)

Red-headed and Red-bellied Woodpeckers
(*Melanerpes erythrocephalus* and *M. carolinus*)

Both sexes of adult red-headed woodpeckers have all-red heads, jet black backs, white bellies, and conspicuous white wing patches; juveniles have brownish heads, backs, and white wing patches. In red-bellied males, red crowns extend over the nape; in females, the red covers only the nape; juveniles of both sexes are brown headed, devoid of red. The zebra-striped back of red-bellies is distinctive in all sexes and age groups. Orange hues of male red-belly underparts, whence the bird derives its inaccurate name, may represent display coloration, since these birds spend much of their foraging time upside down. Red-bellies measure about an inch longer (to ten and one-half inches) than red-heads. The churring calls of both species sound somewhat alike, though red-heads usually sound louder, shriller, and more emphatic.

Close relatives. Nearest North American relatives include the gila woodpecker (*M. uropygialis*), golden-fronted woodpecker (*M. aurifrons*), acorn woodpecker (*M. formicivorus*), and Lewis' woodpecker (*M. lewis*), all western species.

Behaviors. Distinctive red-head traits include fly catching, sallying briefly from a perch to capture winged insects. Red-bellies frequently forage upward on tree trunks, and both species also feed occasionally on the ground. Northern red-head populations often migrate southward depending on food availability. Both woodpeckers reside in the eastern United States from Canada to the Gulf, but red-heads range farther north and west (to the Rockies) than red-bellies. The latter's range continues to expand northward from southern states.

Spring. Both species exhibit conspicuous territorial behaviors as they begin breeding activities in May and June—chasing, calling, reciprocal tapping, and drumming. Red-heads drum in well-spaced bursts; red-bellies drum in short bursts often preceded by a few slower taps. But both species drum less frequently than other woodpeckers. Both also excavate their own nest cavities in dead trees. Red-heads, however, often use natural cavities or their own previous cavities and tend to nest somewhat later than red-bellies.

EGGS AND YOUNG: four or five; eggs white. INCUBATION: by both sexes (males at night); about two weeks. FEEDING OF YOUNG: by both sexes; insects. FLEDGING: about one month.

Summer. In most areas, these woodpeckers nest only once a year. Young birds fledge and feed in family groups beginning in early summer; the groups split in September concurrently with the annual molt of adult birds.

Fall, Winter. Juveniles molt into their first adult plumage throughout fall and winter. Individuals of both species establish and defend fall and winter territories, which enclose roost and feeding locales. One researcher suggests that the same coloration of both sexes in red-heads relates to fall territories. Such similarity permits red-head females to hold their own with males, which might otherwise force the females into inferior feeding areas. Sexually distinct male red-bellies are dominant over females, but this species exhibits less territorial defensiveness in the fall than the more aggressive red-heads.

Ecology. Both species reside in woodlands, but red-heads are said to favor drier country—open stands, old burns, or edges containing solitary dead trees and snags. My own observations run counter to this, however; the largest red-head population near my home occupies a flooded creekbottom. For nesting, red-bellies usually prefer denser forest, often in river lowlands; after breeding, they tend to inhabit parks and suburbs with large trees. The two species often occupy closely adjacent territories, especially in fall and winter.

For nest cavities, red-heads favor isolated, long-dead, barkless trees and snags. They also use utility poles and fence posts. Often they begin excavating at a preexisting crack. Red-bellies usually select dead limbs of living trees or recently dead trees that retain the bark. Red-head nest cavities average forty feet in height; red-belly cavities are usually low. The unlined cavities average about a foot deep.

Both species are vegetarians to a larger extent than all other eastern woodpeckers. Acorns and beechnuts (mast) become staples during fall and winter, and mast abundance probably governs whether the birds remain in a locale over winter or shift elsewhere. Both birds also relish corn and wild fruits; red-bellies occasionally raid Florida orange groves. Mulberries and Virginia creeper and poison-ivy berries are particular favorites. Both species store acorns, berries, insects, and other foods in the fall, hammering them into bark furrows, tree crevices, and various other apertures; red-heads often seal up their caches with plugs of moist splintered wood. After a period of hasty collection and storage, the birds often remove some of their caches, distributing their contents over wider areas. Such caches provide the main winter food supply, and the birds jealously guard them from intruders. Red-heads also feed at sapsucker wells during winter and spring and create their own sap wells by scaling off bark and consuming fragments of the cambium layer beneath. Insect foods become important in spring and summer diets. The birds consume ants, wood-boring beetle larvae, grasshoppers, wood roaches, and caterpillars in abundance, and red-heads frequently capture large flying insects, seeming to prefer bright-colored ones.

Food competitors, especially for acorn and beech mast, include other woodpeckers, blue jays, European starlings, squirrels, and many other birds and mammals. Competition between the two woodpecker species for nest cavities is minimal because of the birds' differing site preferences, but squirrels, smaller woodpecker species, American kestrels, great crested flycatchers, and European starlings may usurp old or freshly excavated holes. Starling competition for nest cavities probably accounts for some degree of red-head declines over the past fifty years. One study, however, showed that red-heads often instigate nest cavity conflicts with starlings, which usually nest earlier than red-heads, and that the less aggressive red-bellies are much more frequent victims of starling aggression.

The northern black racer, a tree-climbing snake, sometimes invades woodpecker nest cavities and consumes eggs and young. Cache robbers include other woodpeckers, blue jays, European starlings, and squirrels. But human cleanup of standing dead timber from woodlots is probably the foremost antiwoodpecker act, guaranteed to deplete their local populations. Dutch elm disease, which virtually wiped out American elm trees in many localities during the 1950s and '60s, indirectly benefited red-head populations by providing dead timber for nesting cavities. Subsequent uses of DDT and other pesticides for elm disease control, however, erased many of the benefits along with many birds.

Focus. Alexander Wilson, the Scottish cofounder of American ornithology, shot a red-headed woodpecker in Delaware the first day he stepped off the boat in 1794. The sight of the gorgeous bird inspired him to begin compiling his classic *American Ornithology* (1808–14), the first comprehensive attempt to describe New World species. Naturalist John Burroughs reported red-heads as more numerous than American robins in Washington, D.C., during the late 1800s, an abundance long since vanished. Red-head populations have fluctuated widely, but the trend over the past century has been downward. Habitat depletion, woodland sanitation, and starling abundance are the reasons usually suggested for their decline. Red-bellies, though, are on the increase; like so many southern native birds in the past fifty years, they continue to push northward in distribution.

Yellow-bellied Sapsucker
(*Sphyrapicus varius*)

A white wing patch, bright red forehead patch, and dull yellowish belly mark adult sapsuckers. Sexes differ only in the throat patch, which is red in males and white in females. Juveniles lack the head coloring. Sapsucker drumming is a rapid series of thumps slowing to several slower, arrhythmic knocks. These birds emit a whining, catbirdlike, mewing note and a squealing "cheerrr."

Close relatives. Western North American sapsuckers include Williamson's sapsucker (*S. thyroideus*), red-breasted sapsucker (*S. ruber*), and red-naped sapsucker (*S. nuchalis*).

Behaviors. Sapsuckers don't really suck sap—they lap it from parallel rows of small pits they drill on living tree trunks. Such pitted areas always indicate sapsucker presence. Sapsuckers are also skillful fly catchers, sailing out briefly to snatch an insect. The sapsucker's long tongue is brushlike and blots up sap by capillary action. This bird, the red-headed woodpecker, and the northern flicker are the only true migrants among northeastern woodpeckers.

Spring. Sapsucker breeding range is the relatively narrow strip of northern hardwood forest that spans the continent. Males usually arrive in early April, several days before females. The monogamous pair bond is a function of territory, since both members return to their previous nesting area. Courtship activities—loud drumming, ritual tapping, bobbing motions, and snipelike wing-winnowing sounds—precede mating, which occurs in May and June. The territory, extending one hundred feet or less around the nest tree, is centered in the home range, which may include several acres enclosing sap well trees. Nestlings squeal and chatter almost constantly in the tree cavities; such "talking trees" make sapsucker nests relatively easy for a sharp-eared listener to find.

EGGS AND YOUNG: five or six. INCUBATION: by both sexes; twelve or thirteen days. FEEDING OF YOUNG: by both sexes; sap, fruits, insects, sometimes regurgitated. FLEDGING: about four weeks.

Summer. Young birds fledge by mid-July. About a week before they do, parent birds begin a brief period of renewed courtship drumming and displays but do not renest. Sapsucker families, bound to their territories by one or two sap trees where they regularly feed, remain together through summer. The annual molt begins soon after the nestlings fledge, continuing into early fall. Juvenile birds have acquired most of their adult plumage by the time they migrate. Many sapsuckers begin moving southward by late summer.

Fall. Sapsuckers migrate through the fall. Banding studies have shown that females travel farther south than males, an example of *differential migration.*

Winter. Sapsucker winter range extends from the central tier of states southward to Panama and the Bahamas. Although this sapsucker is sometimes called the most migratory of woodpeckers, small numbers often remain in southern locales of the breeding range through winter.

Ecology. Sapsuckers inhabit forests and woodlots, preferring hardwood or mixed stands often near water and forest openings. Mature aspen groves are frequent habitats.

Sapsuckers almost always excavate new nest cavities each year, frequently in trees showing their previous cavities. Cavities average about twenty-five feet high, often on the south side of large aspen trees infested with the hoof-shaped brackets of false tinder fungus (*Phellinus tremulae*). This fungus softens and decays the heartwood, making it easy to excavate; the surrounding hard shell of sapwood protects the nest cavity. Other fungus-infected trees often used by these birds include birches, American beech, and maples. Vacated sapsucker cavities near a functional nest hole are often reoccupied by gray, red, or flying squirrels, whose presence many sapsuckers seem to tolerate.

Except during the breeding season, sapsuckers feed mainly from the sap wells they excavate. They first feed on the soft inner bark exposed by drilling, then return at intervals to feed from the flowing pits. The birds defend their sap trees from other birds and mammals.

Sap well excavation follows a progressive pattern: First a bird drills a horizontal *primary band* of squarish holes, sometimes encircling the trunk. If sap flows, the bird then drills more holes above the primary band, eventually creating vertical columns of pits. *Bast bands* are series of ragged holes where the birds drill for inner bark, mainly in winter and spring. *Spiral sap bands* wind around the uppermost twigs. More than two hundred native tree species may be drilled for sap. Preferred above all are white birches, which have a sap sugar content of 20 percent. Other favored trees include Scotch pine, basswood, apple, and hickories. The birds often select scarred or injured trees, which often accumulate abundant nutrients near the point of injury as tissue healing begins. Except in early spring, the sap consumed is *phloem* sap, the nutrient-rich liquid being transported *down* the tree from the leaves. Although the sap in winter-dormant northern trees remains stationary, thawing days and freezing nights cause some sap movement, and the birds tend to drill on the sunny side of trunks. Conifers have sap storage cells and are favored in freezing weather.

Sap wells drilled by yellow-bellied sapsuckers provide the chief food source for these woodpeckers at most times of the year. An irregular pattern, as shown here, probably indicates exploratory rather than frequent drilling.

Sapsuckers never entirely abandon their sap wells in either summer or winter ranges. But during the breeding season, when protein is needed, their main diet shifts to insects—carpenter ants, crane flies, mayflies, beetles, moths (including destructive spruce budworms and forest tent caterpillars), yellowjackets, and hornets. Many of these are probably captured at the flowing sap wells. In the fall, sapsuckers also consume berries and other fruits.

Since most woodpeckers do not excavate nest cavities in trees that contain previously used holes, the sapsucker's tolerance for such sites, shared mostly with squirrels, gives them a competitive edge over other cavity nesters. European starlings are probably their foremost competitors for cavities.

Sap well users, however, include a host of opportunists that exploit a food resource made accessible by the birds. In most cases, such feeders are *commensals*—that is, they benefit from, but do not hinder, sapsucker activity—rather than significant competitors. Some twenty-two families of insects feed at sap wells, including wood gnats, *Aulacigaster* flies, flesh flies, muscid flies, blow flies, and pomace or fruit flies. Such butterflies as mourning cloaks and Compton tortoise shells, nocturnal moths, ants, bumblebees, and wasps all come to sap wells. Among the thirty-five bird species that feed on sap or insects at sap wells, ruby-throated hummingbirds are the most frequent and may almost totally depend on fresh sap wells in early spring; sap well trees, especially near water, are good places to look for hummingbird nests. One researcher found that the hummingbird-sapsucker association extends beyond sap wells. Away from the sap well area, hummingbirds nonaggressively "buzzed" sapsuckers, apparently associating them with a food source. Mammal sap well feeders include red squirrels, porcupines, and bats.

Probably the sapsucker's foremost nest predators are raccoons. Trees containing many excavations may weaken with repeated use and heartrot. Unless the trunk walls of the nest cavity remain solid, a raccoon can chew through them to reach the nest. Squirrels are potential predators, but sapsuckers closely monitor their movements, readily attacking if the animal approaches a nest cavity.

Focus. Much controversy existed in past years about the amount of tree mortality caused by sapsuckers. Foresters once declared them outright enemies, but subsequent research has revealed that the birds kill relatively few trees by their girdling sap wells, often preferring fungus-infected or defective trees. Certainly they kill *some* trees; these are often extensively drilled birches. One researcher estimated that a sapsucker pair may account for the death of one or two trees per year. But weighed against the abundance of destructive insects they consume, especially during caterpillar irruptions, sapsuckers more than pay their dues.

WOODPECKER FAMILY (Picidae)

Downy and Hairy Woodpeckers
(*Picoides pubescens* and *P. villosus*)

These two common black-and-white woodpeckers are similar in plumage but differ in size; downies, our smallest woodpeckers, are about six inches long, hairies about nine inches. Both display small regional variations in plumage pattern. The only North American woodpeckers with white backs, they have white-spotted black wings, black tails edged with white, and black-and-white heads. Males have a small red patch on the back of the head. Bill size is the best field mark: Hairies have disproportionately longer, stouter bills. Both species utter a sharp, emphatic "peek!" note. Downies also utter a descending "whinny" of notes; the hairy's loud rattle resembles that of a belted kingfisher.

Close relatives. Three-toed woodpeckers (*P. tridactylus*) and black-backed woodpeckers (*P. arcticus*) are boreal forest species. Southwestern species include the ladder-backed woodpecker (*P. scalaris*), Nuttall's woodpecker (*P. nuttallii*), and Strickland's woodpecker (*P. stricklandi*). White-headed woodpeckers (*P. albolarvatus*) occupy western montane forests. The red-cockaded woodpecker (*P. borealis*), an endangered species, inhabits southeastern pinelands.

Behaviors. Like most woodpeckers, downies and hairies are most typically seen on tree trunks as they forage or drum. A downy climbs a tree in jerky, fidgety movements; hairies hitch their way up in short leaps. Downies rarely excavate far into wood for food;

hairies pound deeply. Watch for sexual differences in feeding behaviors. Downies *partition* the feeding site, with males foraging in the upper parts of a tree, females in the middle canopy. With hairies, the difference lies in feeding method: Males tend to excavate deep into the wood for insects; the more opportunistic females glean the trunk surface. These behavioral differences, suggests one researcher, enable the woodpeckers "to exploit the resources of a particular piece of woodland more effectively." Some seasonal variation in feeding sites also occurs. When foraging for nestlings, downies often start at the base of a tree, work rapidly upward, then drop to another tree base; hairies often forage on the ground. Downies are present year-round, though summer birds are not necessarily the same ones present in winter. Some seasonal shifts and southward movements occur, probably depending on local food supply, but neither bird is a true migrant. Both species range across North America.

Spring. Territories and pair bonds of these monogamous species are usually already formed by early spring. Signs of breeding activity include courtship rituals: drumming by both sexes on separate drumming posts and bill waving. Frequent triangle encounters occur when a third bird of either sex intrudes on a pair, resulting in much chasing and aggressive displaying. In April, nest cavity excavation averages sixteen days for downies, twenty for hairies. Female downies and male hairies select the sites. As with all woodpeckers, nestlings are loud, incessant beepers until about two weeks old, so nest holes are fairly easy to locate.

EGGS AND YOUNG: four or five; eggs white. INCUBATION: by both sexes; twelve to fifteen days. FEEDING OF YOUNG: by both sexes; insects. FLEDGING: about three weeks for downies, four for hairies.

Summer. After fledging, the young are fed outside the nest, remaining in the vicinity for several weeks before dispersing. Parent birds usually raise only one brood. The adult birds undergo their annual molt from midsummer to early fall, hairies earlier than downies. The downies' new white plumage shows a yellowish tint that soon wears off. Some juveniles of both sexes display red crown patches, lost when they acquire their first adult plumage in late summer. "Juvenile woodpeckers usually have a geeky air," noted one observer, "a slight clumsiness that sets them apart."

Fall. Food supply probably determines the extent of seasonal movements in these birds. In downies, females tend to travel more often than males; in hairies, the first-year birds seem to move more frequently. Hairies seem generally more sedentary than downies, but except for northernmost populations, the majority of both species remains on the breeding ranges through winter. Pairs are now split, each bird excavating one or more roosting cavities for itself. Though instances of food caching occur, downies and hairies store far fewer items than red-headed and red-bellied woodpeckers.

Winter. One or two downies often mingle with mixed feeding flocks of black-capped chickadees, tufted titmice, white-breasted nuthatches, brown creepers, and kinglets. Such interspecies mingling, suggests one researcher, enables downies to rely on the flock for vigilance, thus increasing their foraging efficiency.

Hairy woodpeckers commence territorial activities—mainly drumming—in December and January; downies begin a bit later. Over a period of weeks, previously mated pairs resume courtship displays and reestablish the home range—anywhere from five to thirty-five acres—and later, within this area, the territory in a radius of forty to one hundred feet from the selected nest site. As in most woodpecker pairs, home ranges and territories tend to remain the same year after year. The birds actively defend their territories from other woodpeckers, but home ranges, which contain favorite drumming posts, often overlap with those of other pairs.

Ecology. Although the woodland habitats of these species often overlap, each has its preferences. Hairies favor mature woodlands and extensive forest areas, but downies more often frequent woodland edges, openings, and residential areas.

Mature aspen trees infected with *Phellinus* heartrot fungus are the choice nest cavity sites for both species; hairies favor live

Downy woodpeckers excavate circular holes for nest cavities, usually in dead trees. Their cavities may later be recycled by other hole-nesting birds, squirrels, or mice.

aspens, and downies prefer dead stubs or branches, often excavating near their tops or beneath an exposed limb. Typically the cavity entrance of the hairy is larger in diameter, by about an inch, than that of the downy and is somewhat elongated, whereas that of the downy is perfectly circular. Both species excavate new cavities each year; downies often return to the same tree, but hairies usually select a different one. Dutch elm disease, which has ravaged American elm trees throughout their range, has benefited both woodpeckers by providing dead standing trees and ample insect food within them.

Primarily insect eaters, downies and hairies often feed in upper dead branches, but downies focus on gleaning spiders, aphids, scale insects, ants, and caterpillars from bark crevices. Hairies seek wood-boring grubs and other larvae; tapping on the wood apparently tells them where to excavate. Downy tongues are relatively short, but the hairy's tongue is long and barb tipped. As the season advances, both birds also consume wild fruits; they relish poison-ivy berries, sometimes caching them in bark crevices. Both also feed at sapsucker drill holes; sometimes they drill for sap and cambium themselves, creating wider, larger holes than sapsuckers. Downies are foremost fall and winter predators of the fruit fly larvae (*Eurosta soladiginis,* called goldenrod gall flies) that create the familiar ball-shaped galls on goldenrod stems. Groves of white birch trees are also favored feeding sites of downies in winter. They often seek defective trees infested with a dormant scale insect (*Xylocculus betulae*) that, in summer, feeds on sap just beneath the outer bark. Downies peck around the bark containing the insect, then open the hinged

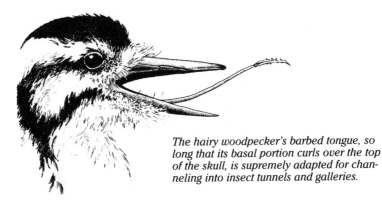

The hairy woodpecker's barbed tongue, so long that its basal portion curls over the top of the skull, is supremely adapted for channeling into insect tunnels and galleries.

fragment to expose the insect. Inspect birch trunks for these tiny trapdoors, sure signs of downy feeding.

Tree cavities are always at a premium for hole-nesting birds and denning mammals, many of which cannot excavate cavities themselves. The size of the entrance hole often determines which competitors may occupy it. Downy competitors include nuthatches, house sparrows, flying squirrels, and deer mice. Hairies contend mainly with European starlings, especially if the nest tree borders an open area; the starlings almost always win such contests. Flying and red squirrels also vie for new cavities but are usually driven off. Yellow-bellied sapsuckers sometimes compete with hairies for a nest tree, as do red-headed woodpeckers. The somewhat differing habitat preferences of downies and hairies tend to reduce nest site competition between them.

Food competition among woodpecker species appears minimal. The species focus their foraging activities in separate *niches,* using different parts of the habitat, or they use different feeding techniques.

Some of the competitors for tree cavities may, at times, become woodpecker predators. Probably the foremost predator is the European starling, which may destroy woodpecker eggs or young by poking its head into a cavity, even if the entrance hole is too small to admit its body. Raccoons can chew and claw into cavities excavated in dead, weak wood, and gray squirrels sometimes enlarge entrance

Hairy woodpecker head markings demonstrate individual variations in these and downy woodpeckers. Probably no two birds show exactly the same pattern.

holes by gnawing to gain entrance. The worst habitat enemies of all woodpecker species are salvage-harvesting foresters and landowners who like to clean out the dead standing trees from their woodlots, thus depriving the birds of nest sites and food.

Focus. Note the back-of-the head patterns of black, white, and—in males—red. "I have never found two with the same pattern," reports one eminent woodpecker researcher. These head variations, almost as individual as fingerprints, enable an observer to identify one bird from another, an invaluable aid to research.

Hairy woodpeckers, usually younger ones, often peck habitually on human-made structures—house walls, roofs, eaves, window frames, utility poles, even trash cans and boats. The louder the resonance, the better the object or material serves as a territorial drumming post. Such drumming can be highly destructive, and once the birds become habituated to such a site, they are not easily driven away. One researcher believes that this behavior begins as a displacement activity, an outlet for energy aroused by crowding or other stress situations. As the habit continues, the pecking may turn to serious food searching and excavation, and the damage multiplies.

Downy and hairy woodpeckers were stupidly misnamed, and the errors remain condoned by a wink of science. Downies have no more underlying down feathers than many other birds, and hairies have no hair. Both birds were saddled with these inappropriate names by a few early observers of questionable visual acuity who stated that both species looked somewhat hairy. Ornithologists, for some reason, often prefer to maintain long-accepted misnomers than to correct them.

WOODPECKER FAMILY (Picidae)

Northern Flicker (*Colaptes auratus*)

This conspicuous, jay-size woodpecker (twelve to fourteen inches) is brown backed and speckled on the breast. It has a narrow black bib, black tail, and red patch at the nape of the neck. Males display a black facial smear, or mustache. A prominent white rump patch is visible when the bird flies; this mark plus the bird's deeply undulating flight are distinctive field characters. Its "wicka-wicka" and "klee-yer!" calls also identify it. Three North American subspecies vary in plumage details; our common northeastern flicker, with golden yellow underwings and tail, is sometimes called the yellow-shafted flicker (*C. a. auratus*).

Close relatives. In the western United States, the gilded flicker (*C. chrysoides*), once considered a subspecies, is now classified as a species. Where their ranges overlap, the red-shafted and yellow-shafted subspecies hybridize, producing intermediate forms. Some five other *Colaptes* species range into South America.

Behaviors. Their size, abundance, and conspicuous behaviors make northern flickers the most easily observed woodpeckers. The way they soar *up* to a perch when landing plus their loud call notes and variety of squeals and other sounds also call them to our attention.

Flickers spend much more time on the ground than other woodpeckers. On the ground, however, they are awkward walkers and scarcely move, usually feeding, sunning, or preening from a stationary position. Flickers are migrants, though small numbers often remain over winter in the north. Their breeding range extends throughout east-central North America, from upper Canada to the Gulf.

Spring. Migrant flickers move north during March nights in large, loose flocks. Males usually precede females by a few days. If both birds of a pair have survived from the year before, they rejoin on their previous territory, which the male reestablishes by drumming, calling, and displays. Commonly heard now is his "wicka-wicka-wicka" call (which "really *quickens* what was dead," observed Thoreau), accompanied by much head bobbing. Resonant drumming, sometimes described as like a drumroll or miniature pneumatic drill, is done by both sexes, often alternated with loud "klee-yer!" calls around the nest tree. By the time egg laying begins in May, the defended territory has usually shrunk from a half acre or more to the nest site vicinity.

EGGS AND YOUNG: five to eight; eggs white. INCUBATION: by both sexes (males at night); two weeks or less. FEEDING OF YOUNG: by both sexes; insects (males feed regurgitant). FLEDGING: about four weeks.

Summer. After fledging, the juveniles, both sexes of which show black cheek marks like adult males, remain in family groups and continue to be fed for several weeks. As with many woodpeckers, the parent birds often revive courtship displays for a brief period following fledging. This is the period when flickers seem to be everywhere. A behavior known as *anting* (described under **Ecology**), seen in many birds, is especially conspicuous in flickers and often noticeable at this season. By late summer, the juveniles have dispersed, pairs have split, and adult birds are undergoing their annual molt.

Fall. Juveniles now acquire their first adult plumage. Small, premigratory flocks assemble, may briefly revive some courtship displays, then join other flicker flocks as migration begins. Flying at night, most of the northern population travels no farther south than the Gulf states, though some fly to Cuba.

Winter. Winter range coincides with the permanent range of southern resident flickers, from the middle tier of states southward. Little social interaction occurs among the birds until late winter, when flocks begin to gather for northward migration.

Ecology. The flicker's ability to reside in a variety of habitats helps explain its success as North America's most abundant woodpecker. Open woodlands, forest edges, orchards, roadsides, parks, and suburban areas are typical habitats, which the birds favor over dense, mature forests.

More than any other woodpecker, flickers tend to reuse their previous nest cavities, though they also excavate new ones, often in a previously used tree. Their slightly curved bills make flickers weak excavators; a pair may start and abandon several holes before selecting a final site, often below fifteen feet in a well-decayed tree or in the dead top of a broken-off trunk. A female will occasionally lay an egg in the nest of another cavity-nesting bird, including red-headed and pileated woodpeckers, tree swallows, eastern bluebirds, and house sparrows.

Northern flickers often return to nest in cavities they have previously used. A frequent site, as shown here, is the collar of a decayed-away branch stub.

At least half of the flicker's diet consists of insects. No other North American bird consumes as many ants. Flickers spend much of their time at ant mounds, licking into the tunnels with their extremely long, sticky tongues. The sticky substance, strongly alkaline, probably counteracts the formic acid ants contain. The birds also consume ground beetles and grasshoppers. In fall and winter, wild fruits become the staple, including berries of poison-ivy and Virginia creeper, dogwood and sumac fruits, cherries, and various nuts and grains.

As with all woodpeckers, strong competition exists for nest sites. Dead trees are also sought by red-headed and other woodpeckers. Flicker nest holes, whether occupied or vacant, attract eastern screech-owls, American kestrels, great crested flycatchers, European starlings, and red, gray, and flying squirrels. Soft, decayed wood, which flickers prefer, makes their excavated cavities highly vulnerable to predation by raccoons, which often claw open weak-walled nest cavities and consume eggs or nestlings.

Researchers disagree about the functions of *anting* behavior, in which the bird picks up ants and rubs them vigorously on its plumage. The traditional view is that the ants' formic acid acts as an insecticide or fungicide against feather and skin parasites. Anting often occurs during periods of high humidity, lending weight to the fungicidal theory. But other investigators find no correlation between anting and parasite or fungus presence; they speculate that anting, like sunning, is simply a comfort activity, stimulating the skin, especially during the summer molt. A recent theory suggests that anting forces the insects to expel their formic acid, thus making them more palatable to consume. Observed in more than two hundred bird species (mostly passerine) worldwide, anting needs many more detailed observations.

Focus. Flickers bear numerous vernacular names, including yellowhammer, goldenwing, pigeon woodpecker, and hairy wicket. The word *flicker,* according to one source, is an old English term for "one who strikes."

About one-third of all northeastern flickers show some degree of past genetic mixing with the western subspecies, the red-shafted flicker. Traces of red or orange in wings or tail are believed to be common indicators of such lineage.

WOODPECKER FAMILY (Picidae)

Pileated Woodpecker (*Dryocopus pileatus*)

This spectacular crow-size woodpecker is North America's largest. Its bright red crest, white neck line, all-black body, and white underwings edged with black identify it. Males also show a red mustache;

females have a black forehead. Its ringing, flickerlike call is louder and more irregular than that of the flicker, and its loud drumming fades out at the end.

Close relatives. The lineated woodpecker (*D. lineatus*) of Central America and the West Indies closely resembles the pileated. The black woodpecker (*D. martius*) is a similar Eurasian species. Pileateds also resemble the larger, probably extinct ivory-billed woodpecker (*Campephilus principalis*), last seen in 1986 in Cuba.

Behaviors. Seeing this big, shy woodpecker of the deep woods is always an uncommon treat. In areas where they are present, I have often attracted one by drumming loudly on a dead tree with a piece of wood. The bird's territory, often defended year-round, may extend to a mile or more, so these woodpeckers are much more thinly distributed than others. Also unlike the others, a mated pair stays together throughout the year, roosting in separate tree cavities at night but foraging in each other's vicinity during the day. Pileated range spans the continent; the birds are nonmigratory but may wander widely in fall and winter. Populations, most numerous in the southeastern United States, where they have adapted to urban woodland habitats, are increasing in the North as forests regenerate and mature.

Spring. Territorial and courtship behaviors peak in early spring. Often a bonded pair is challenged by a single intruder of either sex, one that has probably lost its mate. Conflict ensues between birds of the same sex, with chasing, pecking, and threat displays. In the nest vicinity, these loud, conspicuous birds become stealthy and silent. Photographic evidence reveals that if the nest tree collapses, a female pileated can transport her eggs to a new site.

EGGS AND YOUNG: about four; eggs white. INCUBATION: by both sexes (male at night); about fifteen days. FEEDING OF YOUNG: by both sexes; regurgitated insects. FLEDGING: about four weeks.

Summer, Fall. Juveniles remain with the parents for most of the summer, following them around and being fed. In late summer, as the annual plumage molt begins, juveniles disperse from the parental territory. The birds drum infrequently now and apparently do not excavate roost holes in the fall, as do hairy and downy woodpeckers.

Winter. Adult birds remain on their territories if sufficient food is available; if not, they may shift locales. As winter advances, first-year birds begin to establish their own territories. Single males drum frequently in late winter, advertising for a female.

Ecology. The presence of pileated woodpeckers is a reliable indicator of old-growth forest, at least eighty to one hundred years old. Vital components of pileated habitat include standing dead trees and rotting trunks and logs. These birds prefer large tracts of dense-canopied beech-maple woodlands, but they also inhabit lowland and mixed conifer-hardwood forests. Feeding habitats often include northern white cedar swamps and stands of aspen.

Pileateds excavate their own nest cavities, favoring large, often barkless tree trunks about fifty feet high. Cavities may extend a foot or two in depth, and the entrance hole is about four inches in diameter. The nest cavity, often facing east or south, is rounder than the characteristic oblong excavations made for feeding. Pileateds especially favor large, dead beech trees for nesting; roost cavities, in contrast, are often excavated in living trees. Previously used nesting cavities may also be used. Later users may include wood ducks, European starlings, and squirrels.

The primary year-round food consists of black carpenter ants (*Camponotus*). These ants bore into the heartwood of diseased or fungus-infected trees, creating long, vertical galleries in the dead wood. By some keen sense, a pileated woodpecker can detect ant activity—as well as winter-dormant clusters—deep inside an apparently healthy tree. Chips and splinters fly as the bird hammers and chisels directly to the heartwood. Then it extends its agile, horny-barbed tongue along the ant passages. Pileateds often demolish large parts of well-rotted trees, seeking ants and wood-boring beetle larvae. Signs of pileated presence include vertically oblong excavations in dead tree trunks plus piles of rotten wood chips at tree bases.

In the fall, pileateds consume wild fruits, especially those of wild grapes, dogwoods, sumacs, poison-ivy, and Virginia creeper.

Unlike many woodpeckers, pileateds apparently cache few if any food items for later consumption.

Competitors are mainly other cavity nesters: other pileateds, European starlings, and gray squirrels, among others.

Raccoons are probably the foremost nest predators. Black rat snakes may also climb into the cavities and devour eggs or young.

Focus. A few birds and mammals represent most vividly the spirit of wild places, and the pileated woodpecker is one of them. Yet in areas of the southeastern United States, where pileateds frequent urban habitats such as parks, these birds have come to be considered pests, mainly because they often damage telephone poles. Our pioneer ancestors called these birds logcocks and Lord God woodpeckers, among other colorful

Deep, oblong excavations and piles of wood chips on the ground indicate the work of the pileated woodpecker, which seeks ants and beetle larvae in soft-rotted timber.

epithets. American natives valued the pileated's flaming red crest for ornate calumet pipes.

Pronounce *pileated* as "pile" or "pill"—either way, I have found, will be wrong in whatever field group one happens to join and will be quickly corrected!

Anyone familiar with northern forest habitats during the past few decades will have noticed an apparent increase of pileateds. Only now, a century after the last great American forests fell to axes and ravaging fires—events that all but wiped out pileated populations in the North—are signs of pileated recovery becoming apparent as many regenerated forests mature. Pileateds will always be relatively uncommon, even in optimal habitats, because of their expansive territorial needs, but their reappearance is welcome confirmation that this grand bird's habitats can, in time, be restored. Today, however, pileateds face another habitat threat in the form of widespread forest fragmentation.

3

Black-billed and Yellow-billed Cuckoos (*Coccyzus erythropthalmus* and *C. americanus*)

Cuckoo family (Coccyzidae), order Cuculiformes. Our two native northeastern cuckoos, alike in form and size (eleven to thirteen inches), have brown back plumage, long tails, white underparts, and slightly down-curved bills. Identify black-billed cuckoos by their mostly dark tails, narrow red eye rings, and black bills. Yellow-billed cuckoos have rusty red wings, large white spots on the undertail, and a yellow lower mandible. Sexes look alike in both species, and both utter throaty notes. Black-bills usually utter a series of "cucucu" notes on one pitch; yellow-bills voice a prolonged run of rapid notes ending with several slower "kowlps." Both species sometimes sound much alike, however, so their calls are not always reliable identity markers.

Close relatives. About one hundred thirty species of this family exist worldwide. The mangrove cuckoo (*C. minor*) resides in the swamps of southern Florida south to Brazil. Other southern U.S. and tropical relatives are the anis (*Crotophaga* spp.) and the greater roadrunner (*Geococcyx californianus*), which lives in southwestern deserts. The European cuckoo (*Cuculus canorus*), on whose calls the

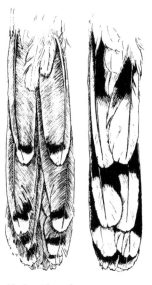

Undersides of cuckoo tails help identify the species: Black-billed cuckoo tail feathers (left) are white tipped; the yellow-bill's tail (right) shows large white spots.

traditional cuckoo clock sounds are based, parasitizes the nests of other Eurasian birds with its eggs.

Behaviors. Both species are reclusive and often perch silently in dense shade for long periods. Despite their large size and distinctive markings, their presence most often becomes known when a male's loud call notes are voiced at irregular intervals from a tangle of brush. Both species also sing in flight, and they often sing at night as well as in daytime. An old name for cuckoos was rain crow, from their supposed habit of becoming most vocal just before a shower. Cuckoos often feed on or near the ground.

Black-bill distribution extends farther north than that of yellow-bills, but the breeding ranges of both species coincide from southern Canada to the central United States. Both species are migrants.

Spring. Both species arrive on their breeding ranges in late April to mid-May but often don't begin nesting until several weeks later. There is a wide variation in nesting dates from year to year. Apparently many individual cuckoos, if not entire populations, wander extensively during this postmigratory phase, movements possibly keyed to the timing and cyclic abundance of insect food sources. Because of this floating population, there may be many or few cuckoos in a particular area from year to year as the birds gravitate toward areas of high food density.

Cuckoos are probably monogamous, though little is known about their territoriality and pair bonding. Courtship feeding occurs, and both sexes probably build the nest. Unlike most birds, cuckoos often leave eggshell remnants in the nest instead of carrying them away. Nestlings appear ugly and reptilian to humans, having black skin with quill-like bristles and performing hissing threat displays. At about six days of age, they comb off the horny feather sheaths of their sprouting plumage, and their feathers soon fluff out. When disturbed, the fledged young of black-bills often freeze into a motionless, straight-up posture similar to that of American bitterns. Yellow-bills often nest twice in a season; most black-bills nest only once in their northern range. Birds of one species often lay an egg or two in nests of the other, occasionally in those of other birds as well.

EGGS AND YOUNG: black-bills, two or three; yellow-bills, three or four; eggs greenish blue. INCUBATION: by both sexes; about ten days. FEEDING OF YOUNG: by both sexes; regurgitated caterpillars. FLEDGING: seven to nine days.

Summer. Because of the delayed breeding cycle often noted in these birds, nesting sometimes extends into late summer. After the nestlings fledge, cuckoos fall silent. Adult cuckoos begin molting by July, and molting may continue into fall.

Fall. Juveniles molt into their first winter plumage in late summer and fall, retaining only their wing primaries and tail feathers through winter. Cuckoos migrate south at night through September into October.

Winter. Cuckoos spend the winter in northern and central South America; none remain in North America. Black-bills winter mainly in Colombia, Ecuador, and northern Peru; yellow-bill populations extend to Venezuela and south to Brazil, Uruguay, and Argentina. Juveniles acquire their first adult plumage during winter, and adults may also undergo a partial prenuptial molt.

Ecology. Although typical habitats of the two species differ to some extent, broad overlaps occur where their ranges coincide. Both favor shrubby edge habitats; black-bills tend to prefer drier thickets, and yellow-bills often inhabit wetter, shadier locales, but both species can and do reside in either type.

In wetter areas, shrub willow and dogwood thickets are frequent nesting sites; upland sites include overgrown orchards, blackberry and hawthorn thickets, small pines, and red cedar. Yellow-bills seem to favor wild grape tangles. Cuckoos generally place their nests two to eight feet high. Nests are usually unkempt, flimsy platforms of sticks and twigs lined with small amounts of softer plant materials; in upland sites, these frequently consist of fern, especially bracken, pieces. Black-bills often use fuzzy catkins of willow and other trees for lining. Black-bill nests tend to be somewhat sturdier and better lined than yellow-bill nests.

Both cuckoos are primarily insect eaters, consuming huge

quantities of caterpillars, cicadas, grasshoppers, tree crickets, and other grass and foliage arthropods. They also devour tree frogs. In summer and fall, their diets extend to such fruits as elderberries, mulberries, and wild grapes.

Many birds eat caterpillars, but many avoid the hairy and spiny species. Cuckoos specialize in these kinds, however, and since some of them—such as the gypsy moth and forest and eastern tent caterpillars—irrupt in cyclic superabundance, cuckoos provide some degree of biological control. Major irruptions of forest tent caterpillars occur every ten to sixteen years; such outbreaks often attract local concentrations of cuckoos, whose delayed nesting cycles may coincide with times and places of greatest caterpillar abundance. Cuckoos do not digest caterpillar hairs; the hairs form felted masses in the cuckoo's stomach, whereupon the bird sheds its entire stomach lining and grows a new one. How often this occurs during a season remains unknown.

The few other bird species that consume hairy caterpillars offer little competition for food, since during caterpillar-irruptive years these larvae are so abundant. The degree to which the two cuckoos compete with each other for breeding territories remains unknown but appears negligible. Brood parasitism—laying eggs in the nests of other birds—may indicate space competition with other edge-nesting species. Both cuckoo species are known to parasitize each other, and they occasionally deposit eggs in nests of American robins, gray catbirds, cedar waxwings, northern cardinals, and chipping sparrows, among others. Research indicates that caterpillar

Cuckoos relish caterpillars, among them several destructive foliage pests. These include gypsy moths (top left), forest tent caterpillars (right), and cankerworms (bottom).

abundance may trigger cuckoo egg laying, and if this occurs before their own nests are completed, the females may make emergency deposits in nests of other birds.

Cuckoo predators include hawks, owls, and mammals, such as foxes and raccoons, that prey on many bird species. Blue jays are probably the foremost egg and nestling predators.

Focus. Cuckoos provide excellent examples of *countershading*—dark on top and white beneath—a pattern exhibited by many birds. Countershading tends to obscure a bird's outline, reflecting most light from below, where light is dimmest.

Cuckoos present interesting problems for habitat ecologists. Nobody has yet distinguished any clear-cut lines that invariably separate the two cuckoos within their range of overlap. It is rare in nature for two such closely related species with the same food preferences to occupy virtually the same habitats, as often occurs with cuckoos. Yet the two species seldom, if ever, hybridize. So why do they remain separate species? Clearly these birds hold secrets that few researchers have begun to analyze.

Because of the birds' often cyclical abundance, reflecting the likewise cyclical caterpillar irruptions, cuckoo population size is hard to determine. Cuckoos probably are much more numerous now than in presettlement times because of the vast increase in edge habitats, plus land and forestry practices that encourage widespread caterpillar irruptions.

4

Chimney Swift (*Chaetura pelagica*)

Swift family (Apodidae), order Apodiformes. These five-inch-long, blackish, swallowlike birds, usually seen flying in flocks, look stubby at both ends, their long wings held in a stiffly bowed crescent as they glide. Both sexes look alike. Their flight, unlike the longer, more graceful glides of swallows, often appears batlike, with flickering wingstrokes and erratic twists and turns. They are highly gregarious at most times of year, and their chittering babble of notes as they wheel overhead is distinctive.

Close relatives. Almost eighty swift species exist worldwide. In North America, Vaux's swift (*C. vauxi*) is a similar western species. Other western U.S. swifts include the black swift (*Cypseloides niger*) and the white-throated swift (*Aeronautes saxatalis*).

Behaviors. Swifts, often called the most aerial of birds, probably spend more of their lives aloft than any except a few seabirds. They fly and feed on the wing all day, except when nesting, and

Head profiles of three unrelated aerial insect predators (l–r): chimney swift, barn swallow, and whip-poor-will (heads not drawn to scale). The first two are daytime feeders, the last a nocturnal flier.

roost at night inside tall chimneys or steeples in much of their breeding range. Only the rock pigeon has adapted so completely as chimney swifts to man-made structures for roosting and reproduction.

A characteristic display occurs when one or both of a pair flying in tandem snap the wings into a V posture and glide for five or ten seconds. Near the nest, a common defensive reaction is wing snapping, clapping the elevated wings sharply together several times. Chimney swifts are monogamous. They apparently mate for life and are migratory.

Chimney swift breeding range spans eastern North America from southern Canada to the Gulf.

Spring. During northward migration, groups of twenty or thirty birds fly by day. These flocks may coalesce into hundreds of birds when seeking the roosting shelter of large factory chimneys at night. Their rate of progress, dependent on weather, cannot proceed faster than seasonal food abundance—that is, the hatching of aerial insects. Arriving by early to mid-May on their northern breeding range, pairs tend to return to the same site each year, often reusing their old nests. Despite the sociability of swifts during migrations, actual nesting is only loosely colonial. Ordinarily no more than two or three pairs may nest closely together, and often only a single pair occupies a nesting locale. Building and reinforcement of nests continue concurrently with egg laying and incubation. Often a nonbreeding adult, usually a male, becomes a third parent permitted to feed and brood nestlings. Occasionally even two extraparental helpers are observed. Whether these are yearling offspring from the same parents or simply unmated singles remains unknown. After the young leave the nest, they clamber around in the vicinity, clinging to vertical surfaces with their long, sharp claws. Swifts suffer their greatest mortality at this time; many fledglings wander too far or become isolated from the feeding brood and starve. At night the entire family group roosts on the vertical wall, an overlapped, batlike mass of bodies and feathers. Most swift pairs raise only one brood.

EGGS AND YOUNG: four or five; eggs white. INCUBATION: by both sexes; about nineteen days. FEEDING OF YOUNG: by both sexes plus one or more nest helpers; regurgitated insects at first, then insect-saliva pellets. FLEDGING: two to three weeks.

Summer. Nesting continues into July, but as juveniles leave the nest sites, premigratory flocks begin to assemble and wander, roosting communally at night. A spectacular sight during the summer and migratory seasons is a flock's arrival at a steeple or chimney roosting locale. Portions of the flock circle clockwise, other portions counterclockwise above the structure; then birds begin to peel off, dropping into it. The spiral cloud of descending birds resembles a tornado funnel. For a large flock, the entire process may last half an hour. Morning departure is quicker and more irregular. After nesting, swifts undergo a complete progressive molt. By late summer, most chimney swifts have begun migration.

Fall. Chimney swifts move southward in huge migratory flocks during daytime through September. Weather sharply affects their rate of travel; during rainy weather, they do not fly but remain in roosts.

Winter. For most of the year, chimney swifts inhabit the Neotropical rain forest. They winter in a restricted area of the upper Amazon basin of Peru, northern Chile, and northwestern Brazil. Since few chimneys or other man-made structures exist in these locales, the birds revert to ancestral roosting habits, using large tree hollows and caverns. Their aerial feeding habits remain the same. In late winter, the birds undergo another molt, either complete or partial. By March, they are again flocking for the long journey northward.

Ecology. Urban and farm structures provide chimney swifts with facsimiles of dark caves. But swifts also reside outside cities, so their dependence on humanity is far from absolute. Their original habitats were probably woodlands, as their winter habitats still are. For today's relatively small rural populations, mature forests containing large dead trees with ample hollows and cavities provide both roosting and nesting sites. Swifts frequently feed above ponds, lakes, and streams, where flying insects are often abundant.

Darkness and shelter are the prime nest site requirements, provided by the inside vertical walls of chimneys, silos, deep wells, air shafts, caverns, or hollow trees. Chimney swifts have been known to use tree cavities excavated by pileated woodpeckers. When building their nests, the birds seize dead twigs at tips of branches with both feet as they fly, then transfer them to the bill and carry them to the nest site. The swift's nest has been described as "a basket of sticks and saliva." The nest, a shelflike half saucer or hammock, is glued together and to the wall surface by a salivalike mouth secretion that hardens as it dries. Short, stiff tail feathers brace the bird as it clings to the wall, attaching its sticks one at a time.

The chimney swift's hammock of sticks adheres to a vertical wall by means of the bird's gluelike saliva, which hardens to a durable, latex-like substance.

On clear days, swifts tend to fly and feed much higher than on overcast days. One study revealed that insects less than five millimeters long (mainly flies, homopterans such as leafhoppers, flying ants, mayflies, and stoneflies) were preferred for feeding young birds. Larger prey fed to the young as they age include bark beetles, long-horned beetles, and leaf bugs. Swifts seem to avoid moths, grasshoppers, and bumblebees.

Tree-nesting swifts face cavity competition from birds and mammals such as screech-owls, woodpeckers, European starlings, raccoons, and squirrels. Food competitors may include other bird species of its *guild*—that is, a group of species that exploits a common food resource in a similar way—in this case, the guild of day-

When not flying or incubating eggs, chimney swifts are usually clinging to the walls of their nest vicinity. The strong, spiny tail, shown here, functions as a third foot to brace the bird's body.

time aerial insect feeders, such as common nighthawks and swallows.

Chimney-nesting swifts usually remain safe from most predators. Sharp-shinned hawks may nab a swift in flight, but the swift's speed and agility make this a rare occurrence. The swift's main enemy, as well as benefactor, is human; hot fumes and smothering soot in chimneys may kill thousands of birds at a time. Sometimes nests come loose from their vertical walls and fall. High mortality also results from lengthy spring rainstorms and cold spells that clear the air of insects, thus starving the birds.

Focus. The name *swift* refers to the fast flight of all Apodidae. (The fastest North American bird, estimated to attain two hundred miles per hour, is the white-throated swift.) The small feet of swifts are unusual among birds: All four toes face forward and bear hooked claws, adaptations for clinging to vertical surfaces, their only perching ability. Banding evidence indicates that the chimney swift's average life span is about four years, though occasional swifts survive a decade or longer.

Bird's nest soup, made from the nests of several Old World swifts (*Collocalia* spp.), has long been a gourmet item in parts of Asia. The birds' hardened saliva, relatively tasteless, is the chief ingredient, to which vegetables and flavorings are added. The saliva itself is regarded as an aphrodisiac by many Chinese.

Closer look. Fischer, R. B. *The Breeding Biology of the Chimney Swift.* Albany: New York Museum Bulletin No. 368, 1958.

5

Ruby-throated Hummingbird
(*Archilochus colubris*)

Hummingbird family (Trochilidae), order Trochiliformes. Measuring only slightly more than three inches and weighing only one-tenth of an ounce—less than a penny—the ruby-throated hummingbird, the smallest bird of northeastern North America, can hardly be mistaken, except, perhaps, for a large moth. Its buzzing flight and needlelike bill are obvious identity marks. The male has a bright red throat, iridescent green back, and forked tail; the female, slightly larger, has a green back but lacks the red throat and has a blunt, white-spotted tail. Juveniles of both sexes resemble the female in coloration. Ruby-throats voice no song, only a variety of squeaks, twitters, and grating notes.

Close relatives. Some sixteen other hummingbird species reside mainly in the western United States. The black-chinned hummingbird (*A. alexandri*) and rufous hummingbird (*Selasphorus rufus*) are the most common of these. All of the more than three hundred hummingbird species reside in the Western Hemisphere, most in the Neotropics. Most are vividly colored.

Behaviors. Ruby-throats are most often seen hovering, their wings beating fifty-five times per second, or darting in quick zigzag patterns. They can fly in any direction—forward, back, or straight up and down. Forward wingbeats number seventy-five or more per second, producing a wing roar similar to that of a hawk moth or bumblebee. Measured in ratio to body weight, however, hummingbird wingbeats are slower than those of most birds. Hummingbirds require vast amounts of energy to keep those wings buzzing. The

The male ruby-throated hummingbird's needlelike bill is adapted for probing into flower nectaries. This tiny bird's role in the evolution of certain flowers demonstrates that size is no measure of ecological importance.

hummingbird's metabolic rate is extremely high, more than six hundred heartbeats per minute, and it must feed almost constantly during the day. Most feeding occurs as it hovers and probes in front of a nectar source, but it also perches at frequent intervals. Hummingbirds feed not by sucking but by licking three times per second. The grooved, forked tongue fills with nectar, which is pumped by capillary action along the tongue, then swallowed. At night, hummingbird temperature drops, metabolism slows, and the bird enters a state of torpor; without this adaptation, it would starve overnight. Highly aggressive, especially toward other hummingbirds but also toward other birds and even large insects, hummingbirds are extremely territorial and spend much of their nonfeeding time chasing, threatening, and displaying.

Ruby-throats are migratory. Their breeding range spans the eastern United States from lower Canada to the Gulf.

Spring. The sexes migrate north separately, beginning in late March and early April. Hummingbirds usually migrate singly during daytime hours. Males arrive on the breeding range in early May, a week or so before females. Males and females, in fact, do just about everything separately except mate—and researchers still haven't discovered how hummingbirds subdue their innate hostilities long enough to do that. Spring migration precedes the flowering of most hummingbird food plants, necessitating the use of other food sources. Each male establishes a small territory of about a quarter acre, which usually contains a nectar food source and a perch overlook or two. As the season advances, these territories may shift boundaries to coincide with the flowering of new nectar sources.

There is a fine line, if any, between threat and courtship displays. Most spectacular, perhaps, is the male's pendulum flight, in which he swings back and forth in a buzzing, U-shaped arc that rises from three to forty feet on either side. I have sometimes elicited this display in front of my face by wearing red, a color that always attracts these birds. Two other displays are a horizontal back-and-forth motion and a straight up-and-down flight performed by two hummingbirds facing each other. Most mating occurs in June. A female entering a male's territory is threatened and chased, probably leading the male off his territory, where copulation (some observers suggest rape) occurs on the ground. The mates then go their own ways—the male to continue defending his feeding territory and mating promiscuously with other wandering females, the female to establish her own nesting territory and build a nest or reuse a previous one. After fledging, young birds remain in the nest vicinity for several days, gradually learning to feed themselves.

EGGS AND YOUNG: two; eggs white, pea-size, oval. INCUBATION: by female; about two weeks. FEEDING OF YOUNG: by female; regurgitated nectar, small insects. FLEDGING: two to three weeks.

Summer. Nesting continues in July and sometimes into August with second broods. Occasionally a female may tend two successive, closely spaced nests at the same time, feeding young in the first and incubating the second. But feeding is the main summer activity. The females, though defensive of feeding territories, seem generally less so than males and often bring the fledglings to food sources. Fall migration begins in late summer, males departing two weeks or more before females and juveniles.

Fall. Flying singly and in daytime, often quite low over land and water, ruby-throats migrate to southern Florida, Louisiana, and

Texas. Most move on to Mexico and as far south as western Panama, crossing the Gulf of Mexico nonstop.

Winter. Ruby-throats continue to feed territorially on nectar in their winter habitats. Now occurs their annual molt, when juvenile males acquire their red throats.

Ecology. In their breeding range, male and female ruby-throats often select different habitats. Males favor woodland edges, hedgerows, orchards, and flower gardens. Mated females seek out dense woodland cover, often near a stream, for nesting. Open woodlands and edge thickets are the main habitats in hummingbird winter range.

The nest site, often a downward-slanting twig or small branch some ten to twenty feet high, is frequently leaf-sheltered from above. The female collects bud scales and saddles them to the branch's upper side with spider silk, then adds lichen fragments on the exterior and lines the interior with plant down, which may include fuzz from the underside of sycamore leaves or down from willow flowers. The result is a soft, flexible cup resembling a lichened knot on the branch. Nesting trees vary, but rough-barked species coated with the foliose lichen *Parmelia* seem to be favored.

A hummingbird nest is so small and well camouflaged that the downy cushion coated with gray-green lichens often resembles a branch swelling.

Researchers once thought that hummingbird spring migration was timed to coincide with the opening of favored nectar flowers. This may be true for their southern breeding range but is not so in the North, where the birds may arrive weeks before most flowering occurs. Then observers discovered that a *commensal* feeding relationship—one in which one species benefits and neither suffers—exists between ruby-throats and yellow-bellied sapsuckers, whose northern range encompasses ruby-throat breeding range. Some researchers speculate that the limits of ruby-throat northern range may actually have more to do with sapsucker range than with nectar flower distribution. The sapsuckers drill rows of small holes, or sap wells, mainly in birches but also in other trees. The exuding sap feeds not only the sapsuckers but also the hummingbirds. Sap wells, oozing sucrose and amino acids chemically similar to floral nectar, provide a reliable food source for hummingbirds until seasonal flowering occurs. The birds also feed on the numerous small insects attracted to the sap wells.

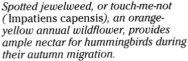

*Spotted jewelweed, or touch-me-not (*Impatiens capensis*), an orange-yellow annual wildflower, provides ample nectar for hummingbirds during their autumn migration.*

Some remarkable relationships have coevolved between hummingbirds and their food flowers, which are usually tubular, odorless, nodding down, and brightly colored. Ruby-throats forage upon more than thirty nectar-producing species, plus numerous garden flowers; at least nineteen of these are *ornithophilous*—adapted for pollination by birds. Pollen is deposited on the base of the bill and carried to another flower as the bird forages. Since hummingbirds are attracted to bright red, orange, and yellow colors, hummingbird pollination has probably influenced the evolution of colors and structure in these flowers. Examples include cardinal-flower, wild columbine, Oswego-tea or beebalm, and Indian paintbrush. Wild or mountain honeysuckle, red buckeye, fire pink, and trumpet creeper are also foraged. The white, heavy nectar-producing flowers of black locust and horse-chestnut feed many hummingbirds, as do jewelweeds, the last especially during fall migration.

Some western hummingbird species, and probably others, transport not only pollen but tiny flower mites (*Rhinoseius epoecus*) to and from Indian paintbrush flowers. The mites ride in the bird's nostrils, moving down its bill into the flower as it hovers to feed.

The ruby-throat's chief food competitors are probably other ruby-throats. Not uncommonly, while one hummingbird is aggressively chasing another, a third hummingbird will sneak in on the food source. Large nectar-feeding insects, such as bumblebees and wasps, may discourage hummingbird feeding at times, but insect competition is probably insignificant.

Hummingbirds occasionally fall victim to bizarre circumstances. They become enmeshed in spiderwebs and are sometimes captured by leaping leopard frogs and bass, even by insects such as mantids and large dragonflies. American kestrels, merlins, and great crested flycatchers occasionally seize a hummingbird. Natural predation, however, is probably negligible. A recent hazard on farms is red insulators on electric fences; if the attracted hummingbird perches near one and its tail brushes a tall weed, the resulting ground circuit electrocutes the bird. Far more hazardous than these occurrences, however, are the bird's semiannual thousand-mile migration flights.

Focus. Wildlife folklore has long held that hummingbirds hitch rides on migrating geese in spring and fall. Aside from the fact that northern geese arrive earlier and depart later than hummingbirds, there is no evidence that this occurs. The tale probably stemmed mainly from incredulity that this tiny bird can wing so far on its own power.

But genuine superlatives abound. The hummingbird family is the largest family of nonpasserine, or nonperching, birds, has the relatively largest breast muscles of all birds, carries the fewest feathers (less than a thousand in ruby-throats), and has one of the proportionately largest bird brains, at 4 percent of body weight. Mobile shoulder joints enable hummingbird wings to twist in flight, generating lift in both forward and backward strokes.

In recent years, a minor industry has grown from public interest in attracting hummingbirds to suburban yards and gardens; advertisers display many styles of hummingbird feeders plus colorful plantings for hummingbird gardens. Probably such activities have helped compensate for natural habitat loss through urbanization and wetland food-plant depletion. Present ruby-throat populations seem relatively stable.

Closer looks. Johnsgard, P. A. *The Hummingbirds of North America.* Washington, DC: Smithsonian Institution, 1983.

Skutch, A. F. *The Life of the Hummingbird.* New York: Crown, 1973.

Stokes, D. and L. *The Hummingbird Book: The Easy Guide to Attracting, Identifying and Enjoying Hummingbirds.* Boston: Little, Brown, 1989.

6

TYPICAL OWL FAMILY (Strigidae), order Strigiformes

Owls and hawks are collectively called *raptors* because of their grasping talons. Three major owl adaptations—in vision, hearing, and flight—characterize the success of these birds as avian predators.

Frontal eye placement gives owls binocular vision. At night, their pupils dilate hugely, each eye independently; in daylight, the pupils contract in size, though day vision remains acute. Numerous light-receptor rod cells in the retina can detect any glimmer, and a chemical known as visual purple, contained in all bird and mammal eyes, further amplifies and resolves the image. The reflective *tapetum lucidum,* essentially a mirror that increases light intensity in the eye, gives the yellow iris of many owls a reddish eye shine when caught in headlights at night. Owls lack color vision; their world consists of gray and white shades. Since their eyes are fixed like headlights, owls must rotate their heads to see in different directions. Most owls can rotate their heads three-quarters of a turn, and they often bob, sway, and yo-yo their heads when triangulating their gaze on an object.

The owl's hearing apparatus enables some owl species to pinpoint sound sources even in total darkness. Oblong ear slits beneath the skull feathers are lopsided, the right one slightly higher than the left, enabling precise triangulation. Also aiding sound pickup is the facial disk, the concave mask of short, stiff feathers that widely circles the eyes in most owls. This parabolic reflector probably enhances and channels sound into the ears. Despite the owl's hearing acuity, however, its range of hearing is not wide; it has deaf spots and cannot hear sounds below about seventy cycles per second. Ear tufts, or horns, occur only in nocturnal, forest-dwelling owls. Ear tufts have no hearing function and probably aid in camouflage when the owl is perched.

Having seen or heard its prey, an owl must approach it stealthily. Modifications for dampening sound in flight can be seen on owl wing feathers. Leading edges of the outer primaries have a fringe with comblike projections, trailing edges are soft and elongated, and the feather surface shows a velvetlike pile. This soundproofing reduces air turbulence over the wing as the bird flies. Calling in an owl at night can be an eerie experience; the bird approaches phantomlike, unheard—suddenly it is just there.

Owls often snap their bills in a series of audible clicks when disturbed or alarmed. Owl sign on the ground beneath perches is fairly distinctive (see Hawk Family). Regurgitated pellets have characteristic features, and feeding debris—feathers and carcass fragments—often lie beneath roosting trees; splashes of "whitewash" occur beneath nesting trees, where owlets have voided over the nest rim.

Owls have carried a heavy symbolic load through history. Probably because most owls are birds of night, they have been considered omens of death and doom back to ancient Egypt and Rome. It

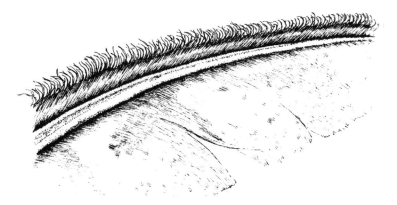

A wing primary feather of an owl shows adaptations for stealthy flight. The leading, or front, edge (top) is softly fringed; a plush matting covers the wide trailing edge (bottom).

was even believed to be worse luck to see an owl in daytime. To imitate an owl's hoot in some cultures is believed to risk bewitchment. In Wales, hearing an owl's hoot informed you that somewhere at that instant a maid was losing her virginity. The "wise old" owl's reputation of intelligence, patience, and all-seeing awareness contrasts with the actualities of its relatively small brain, slowness to learn, and fiercely predatory instincts.

More than one hundred twenty typical owl species range worldwide; ten breed in eastern North America. Well-known species not included as separate accounts here include the snowy owl (*Nyctea scandiaca*) and barred owl (*Strix varia*), among others. The common barn-owl (*Tyto alba*) occupies a separate family (Tytonidae).

Closer look. Craighead, J. J., and F. C., Jr. *Hawks, Owls and Wildlife.* New York: Dover, 1969.

TYPICAL OWL FAMILY (Strigidae)

Eastern Screech-Owl (*Otus asio*)

This small (seven- to ten-inch-long) woodland owl shows conspicuous ear tufts resembling erect horns over its yellow eyes. Sexes look alike except that females are somewhat larger. Plumage coloration occurs in one of two phases, or *morphs*: reddish brown or gray, permanent for each bird. Gray morphs are most numerous in this owl's northern range, red morphs more common in its southern range, but both morphs readily interbreed. Two commonly heard calls are a tremulous, descending whinny and a whistling trill or bounce call. (The screech is seldom heard). Males usually voice lower-toned call notes.

Close relatives. Similar species include the western screech-owl (*O. kennicottii*), whiskered screech-owl (*O. trichopsis*), and flammulated owl (*O. flammeolus*), all residing in the western United States; and the scops-owl (*O. scops*), a Eurasian resident.

Behavior. These are probably the most common owls of eastern North America, more abundant than most of us realize. One most often detects them by hearing their calls during the evening and night. In the daytime they roost in tree cavities or huddle on branches close to the trunk, resembling bark-colored stubs of the branch itself. They become active after sunset, often hunting prey and feeding throughout the night. On launching from a perch, they drop, then fly straight and low to the ground, rising abruptly to another perch. This low-flying habit results in many collisions with vehicles along highways. Nonmigratory and sedentary, a pair often resides in the same area year-round if food sources remain sufficient. Feeding areas typically cover about fifteen to one hundred acres. Screech-owls are monogamous and apparently mate for life.

Spring. Screech-owls are cavity nesters. The cavity vicinity—a tree, nest box, or wall crevice—is the only territory they defend, though aggressive encounters with other screech-owls occasionally occur outside the territory. A pair often reuses the same cavity, or finds another in the same vicinity, each year. In late winter and early

spring, both sexes begin to voice the monotonic trill call, signal that a cavity home exists. Courtship activities include male bowing, blinking, and bringing food to the perched female, and the pair may reciprocally preen and duet. After the owlets hatch, both parents become busy hunters, making many back-and-forth trips each night, bringing prey from a usual distance of several hundred feet or less. When fledging occurs, parental attention centers on the first owlet to leave the cavity, still unable to fly. Its ignored siblings soon scramble to leave too, and feeding is resumed outside the cavity, where

A recently fledged screech-owlet, still unable to fly, snaps its bill and spreads its wings in a threat display. Note the strong raptorial feet.

the owlets often huddle together on a branch. This is the stage when parent owls, especially the female, become vigorously defensive, attacking any intruders, including humans, with needle-sharp talons. As they gain strength and flight feathers, the owlets begin following the parents as they hunt, gradually learning to feed themselves. Screech-owls raise only one brood per year.

EGGS AND YOUNG: four or five; eggs white, round. INCUBATION: by female, which is fed by male; about one month. FEEDING OF YOUNG: by both sexes; large insects, small mammal prey. FLEDG-ING: about three weeks.

Summer, Fall. Owlets continue to be fed by the parents at intervals, but by late summer they begin to disperse in all directions. They usually settle in home ranges less than a mile from their original nest cavity. Territorial disputes often occur, and the screech-owl's whinny call is most often heard at these seasons. The annual feather molt, beginning in July or August, continues into late fall. Until leaves drop, a screech-owl pair usually roosts on branches or in vine tangles outside the nest cavity.

Winter. Pairs now roost during the day in tree cavities. Winter mortality, from predation, starvation, or flying into cars or windows, takes a heavy toll, especially of juvenile owls. As food becomes scarcer, screech-owls often range widely to seek prey. Studies indicate that gray morphs may be better adapted than the red for withstanding extreme cold. By late winter, courtship activities become increasingly apparent as pairs prepare to mate.

Ecology. In rural areas, screech-owls favor open woodland and deciduous woodlots, often near water. They tend to avoid dense or dry forest habitats. Screech-owls have also adapted to the plant mosaic of older suburban areas that contain large trees or groves. Parks, cemeteries, and residential areas often provide more plentiful food than rural woodland and have become frequent nesting habitats. Screech-owls tend to avoid conifer groves for both nesting and roosting.

Screech-owls do not excavate their own tree cavities. They use natural hollows or holes previously excavated by northern flickers and other woodpeckers. They bring no nesting materials, but prey remnants and owl pellets often accumulate to form a deep litter. A screech-owl peering from its cavity makes the cavity hole disappear, as the owl's plumage blends with the pattern of tree bark.

A curious owl-snake association occurs in the south-central and southwestern United States, where screech-owls capture Texas blind snakes (*Leptotyphlops dulcis*) as live prey. These small, worm-like snakes often escape from the owls inside the nest cavity and thrive there, feeding on nest debris and probably on larval insect parasites. Owlets in these nests seem to grow faster and survive in greater numbers than those in nests without the resident snakes.

Screech-owls are exclusively carnivorous, capturing any prey they can seize and carry with bill or talons (rats are the largest mammals they can carry). During warmer seasons, their diet mainly consists of large insects, including moths, June beetles, katydids, cicadas, and crickets, many captured from around lights at night. They also raid songbird nests for adult and nestling birds; wade in the shallows for frogs, crayfish, and minnows; and consume earthworms on wet pavements. Mammal prey includes many mice and shrews. Much of their fall and winter diet consists of small birds such as sparrows and juncos, as well as rock pigeons and mourning doves. Screech-owls often decapitate their vertebrate prey when they capture it.

Woodpeckers, European starlings, and squirrels are probably the screech-owl's main competitors for cavity sites. Since a screech-owl pair sometimes roosts apart in separate cavities, a high screech-owl population may increase territorial conflicts among the owls.

Screech-owls often become the prey of other nocturnal predators. Great horned owls capture many. Raccoons, opossums, and squirrels rob the nest cavities of eggs and owlets. Day-roosting owls outside their cavities are often discovered and mobbed by American crows, blue jays, and smaller birds, driving them to flight and thus exposing them to daytime raptors, mainly hawks.

Focus. The average adult screech-owl lives two or three years, some much longer. Screech-owl abundance, though probably much greater today than in presettlement North America, is declining. Urbanization, loss of hedgerows and fields conducive to mice, and the forester's compulsion to "clean up" woodlots by eliminating dead trees have tended to drive out screech-owls. Where tree cavities are sparse, a nest box placed in the right habitat may attract a pair.

Birders have made increasing use of taped screech-owl calls in the field, not only for owling at night but also for year-round daytime censusing of songbirds, since the calls excite mobbing behavior in many species. These tapes should generally not be used during the breeding season, as the calls may evoke unnecessary disruption and territorial disturbances.

Closer look. Gehlbach, F. R. *The Eastern Screech Owl: Life History, Ecology, and Behavior in the Suburbs and Countryside.* College Station, TX: Texas A&M University Press, 1994.

TYPICAL OWL FAMILY (Strigidae)

Great Horned Owl (*Bubo virginianus*)

This brown woodland owl can be recognized by its large size (eighteen to twenty-five inches), erect ear tufts, yellow eyes, white throat bib, and horizontal barring on breast and belly. Sexes look alike except that females are larger. Identify this owl on the wing by its four-foot wingspread, large head, and neckless appearance. When flying, a great horned owl typically glides from its roost, courses low, then abruptly rises at a steep angle to land on its perch. More often heard than seen despite their large size, these are true "hoot owls," voicing several mellow "hoo" notes in rhythmic succession. The male usually utters four or five notes, the female six to eight. Much controversy exists over whether male or female notes are lower pitched; there are owl experts who firmly opine each way. Often a pair duets back and forth. The notes, though resonant, sound curiously muffled, resembling a low-pitched foghorn that nevertheless carries over great distances. Other sounds—hisses, bill snapping, and a medley of barks, squeals, grunts, and shrieks—are occasioned by territorial or aggressive encounters.

Close relatives. The eagle owl (*B. bubo*) of Europe is even larger than the great horned. In North America, only the great gray owl (*Strix nebulosa*) of boreal forests and sometimes the snowy owl (*Nyctea scandiaca*) are larger.

Behavior. A great horned owl specializes in surprise, not pursuit. Like most owls, it is a nocturnal still-hunter; it waits for sight or sound of prey on the ground, then drops in a swift, silent dive. It slams its prey feetfirst, its fisted talons locking into the victim's

Note the relative sizes of a great horned owl (left) and an eastern screech-owl (right). Ear tufts and facial disks characterize both species.

body. It carries prey, however, in its bill. Except for larger prey, which it tears apart, most of its captures are swallowed whole, head end first after it has been decapitated. If prey is abundant, the owl sometimes eats only the skull contents, leaving the rest of the carcass. Bird prey is often plucked. Great horned owls periodically regurgitate undigested fur, feathers, and bones in pellets two to four inches long. Pellets form in the stomach about eight hours after feeding and are usually ejected before the owl launches forth at night, about one per day. "Each pellet is a mystery," wrote zoologist Bernd Heinrich, "and behind it is the drama of a predator lurking in the night."

Great horned owls often shift their roost locations. An exception may be feeding roosts—particular stumps, branches, or old nests where they regularly bring their prey, often littering the ground beneath with prey remnants. Some researchers believe that this owl's night vision is only slightly better than that of humans and that it does most of its hunting in late evening and predawn hours and on moonlit nights.

Its distribution spans both North and South America. Great horned owls are nonmigratory throughout most of their range, often residing in the same vicinity year-round.

Spring. In many localities, great horned owls are completing incubation by mid-March. Human intrusion at this stage may result in viciously aggressive attacks by the parent owls, whose talons can inflict serious damage. The male often brings huge quantities of prey items to the nest, sometimes overloading it. Owlet fledglings often tumble to the ground, then clamber up leaning trees to perch and await feeding. Parent owls continue to feed owlets in the nest vicinity for three or more months. Such long dependency on the parents, rare in birds, accounts for the winter breeding of this species. Parent owls are mostly nonvocal during nesting.

EGGS AND YOUNG: two or three; eggs dull white. INCUBATION: mainly by female, also male at intervals; about one month. FEEDING OF YOUNG: by both sexes; small mammals, birds. FLEDGING: six to eight weeks.

Summer. Many great horned owls abandon their territories and squalling owlets in summer and wander for several weeks. Pairs may remain together or drift apart. For juveniles, this is a prolonged learning period; they make clumsy mock attacks on various objects and just about anything moving. During hot weather, these essentially cold-climate birds, covered to their toes in thick plumage, suffer obvious discomfort. They become mostly inactive, drooping their wings, like other birds, and pumping their throat muscles to aid breathing because they cannot expand the chest cavity. The annual molt begins in midsummer, lasting until late fall. Juveniles of the previous year now gain their first complete adult plumage.

Fall. Juvenile owls disperse at this season, seldom more than twenty miles or so, where they begin to establish their own territories. Adult owls return from wandering to their breeding territories. Males, especially, begin to hoot in evening and predawn hours, and an old or future nest may also be selected and defended at this time. Size of the home range depends on food resources; two or three square miles is probably a typical size, within which the owls occupy nesting and roosting territories that may shift at intervals before nesting begins.

Winter. Courtship activity, beginning about January, consists of much hooting, bowing, fluffing, bill snapping and rubbing, and ritual feeding. Incubation has begun by mid-February in many areas. Snowfall often covers the female as she sits on the nest.

These owls typically begin breeding in their second year; older mated pairs often breed only every other year or two. Prey abundance may determine whether a pair nests in any given year. In this owl's northern range, a cyclic drop in snowshoe hare populations, occurring about once per decade, brings winter influxes of owls south into the northern United States, sometimes in large numbers.

Ecology. Home ranges of great horned owls are typified by a mixture of large woodlots, either deciduous or coniferous, with adjacent fields and smaller tree groves. Often this owl will roost in a distinctive tree of a grove or woodlot—the tallest or shortest pine, for example, or a lone hemlock or white pine in a stand of other trees. Winter roosting sites are often evergreens with high grapevine tangles or dense foliage.

Great horned owls are prime nest recyclers and do not build nests of their own. They often select the previous nest of a red-tailed hawk. They also use old nests of great blue herons, bald eagles, ospreys, American crows, and common ravens, as well as leaf nests of fox squirrels, which they flatten and scoop out. Occasionally these owls nest atop a tall, dead tree stub or inside a tree cavity. Their nests often have a skunky odor, as do the birds themselves.

Much has been made of great horned owl association with the red-tailed hawk, the latter a daytime raptor nesting in the same upland woods habitats favored by this owl. Each species is sometimes closely tolerated by the other, and the presence of one may indicate *possible* residence by the other. Yet the mutual occurrence of these predators as day-night counterparts is, in my experience, hardly consistent enough to call it an equation. Since red-tailed hawks tend to reuse their own previous nests, a hawk pair building a nest from scratch may indicate that the earlier-nesting owls have taken over the hawk pair's previous, and often nearby, nest.

Exclusively meat eaters, great horned owls are opportunistic hunters. Rabbits are the preferred staple, but frequent mammal prey also includes flying squirrels and other rodents, domestic cats, opossums, and skunks. Porcupines are also occasional—if danger-ous—prey. Bird prey, often captured on nests or roosts, includes ducks, geese, grouse, pheasants, American crows, a variety of song-birds, and occasionally poultry. Screech-owls are sometimes cap-tured as they hunt. Great horned owls also capture snakes, amphibians, and insects.

Since most of its prey consists of nocturnal creatures, this owl's chief food competitors are other night hunters, including other owl species, foxes, coyotes, raccoons, skunks, and opossums. Its early breeding gives it a competitive edge over the later-breeding hawks and American crows, whose previous nests it often adopts.

Aside from human gunners and occasional large hawks that attack roosting owls, the great horned owl has few predators, although American crows are known to kill owlets in the nest if the parent owls are absent. The great horned owl attracts numerous bird mobbers and harassers, however. American crows and blue jays express noisy antipathy to all raptors. Songbirds, too, hearing the excitement, often join this raucous ganging, which never approaches the owl *too* closely. The owl, lethargic in daytime, usu-ally ignores the yelling until its tormentors tire and drift away. (One of the best ways to locate roosting raptors is to listen for these loud mob actions).

Focus. Young owls suffer the highest annual mortality of the great horned population; about half of them succumb, mainly from starvation. Many, when they disperse, fail to find prey-rich habi-tats. Great horned owls may live thirteen or fourteen years, sel-dom longer.

Great horned owls can sometimes be attracted by other owl calls and by distress squeaks, simulated by rapidly kissing the back of the hand. Look for roosting great horned owls in the middle part of a tree's crown, especially close to the trunk.

Closer looks. Austing, G. R., and J. B. Holt, Jr. *The World of the Great Horned Owl.* Philadelphia: Lippincott, 1966.

Heinrich, B. *One Man's Owl.* Princeton, NJ: Princeton University Press, 1987.

7

Whip-poor-will (*Caprimulgus vociferus*)

Goatsucker family (Caprimulgidae), order Strigiformes. Recognize the whip-poor-will by its dark, mottled-brown color, white throat band and tail patches (buffy in females), rounded tail, and rounded, owllike wings. Almost ten inches long, it bears numerous bristles at the base of its tiny, flaplike bill, which opens to a wide-mouthed gape. The whip-poor-will's repetitive chant—"whip-poor-*weel*," with heavy accent on the last syllable—whistles from the deep woods for periods of a few minutes to much longer.

Close relatives. The chuck-will's-widow (*C. carolinensis*) resides in the southeastern United States, while the buff-collared nightjar (*C. ridgwayi*) inhabits the arid Southwest. Three *Caprimulgus* species (called nightjars) are European residents. North American family members include the common nighthawk (*Chordeiles minor*) and the common poor-will (*Phalaenoptilus nuttallii*). Almost seventy species range worldwide.

Behaviors. The whip-poor-will lives "on the borderland of invisibility," wrote ornithologist Winsor Tyler. Seldom seen in daytime unless one happens to flush it from underfoot, this nocturnal, ground-nesting bird is more often heard, a breathy voice of spring and summer nights. It frequents several regular singing stations on its territory, covering the circuit of these perches each night. During daytime, the bird roosts on a low perch or on the ground. When perched, it usually sits lengthwise on tree limbs, aiding its camouflage coloring. Its flight is agile and batlike; sometimes it tilts almost vertically when changing direction. Primarily an insect eater, it feeds at night, flying open mouthed, and also forages from

The whip-poor-will lies well camouflaged in its nesting habitat. Its barely visible bill surrounded by rictal bristles and its large gape form an aerial scoop for insects as it courses batlike at night.

bark and on the ground. Its red eye shine, seen in a beam of light, indicates its night-adapted vision. Like owls, whip-poor-wills possess numerous rod cells and a mirrorlike tapetum lucidum in the eye. When cold, overcast, or moonless nights hinder them from feeding, whip-poor-wills, like other goatsuckers, enter a state of torpor, temporarily slowing their metabolic rate, thereby reducing energy needs.

Whip-poor-wills are seasonally monogamous migrators. Their breeding range spans the eastern United States from southern Canada and extends south to Honduras.

Spring. Whip-poor-wills begin their spring migration in late March; moving at night, most arrive on their northern breeding range by mid-May. Males often sing at areas en route and begin their nocturnal territorial singing, which peaks at dusk and near dawn, soon after arrival. Females rarely, if ever, sing. Twilight courtship performances on the ground consist of bobbing, hovering, circling, and tail flashing, but few people ever see these behaviors. Little information exists on territory size. A nesting whip-poor-will often remains invisible until practically stepped on, when it flits away like a big, silent moth.

EGGS AND YOUNG: two; eggs white, gray- and brown-spotted. INCUBATION: by both sexes; about twenty days. FEEDING OF YOUNG: by both sexes; regurgitated insects. FLEDGING: about twenty days.

Summer. Male whip-poor-wills may continue territorial singing as nesting and brooding continue through July or early August. Most pairs raise only a single brood, but if the female renests, the male takes over care of the first brood. The parent leads fledglings from the nest—they walk as awkwardly "as a man in a bag," said naturalist John Burroughs—and continues to feed them on the ground. If disturbed at this stage, the parent birds exhibit a piteous distraction display. Anecdotal observations record that they may also carry and relocate eggs or nestlings on occasion. Whip-poor-will reproduction seems to correspond with the lunar cycle; males sing longer on moonlit nights, and hatching is apparently synchronous with the waxing moon, when parent birds are visually best able to hunt insects. The next waxing lunar cycle enables the fledglings to become totally independent. This subtle, complex timing of breeding events remains poorly understood, but researchers believe that natural selection has favored such synchronicity.

As summer advances, whip-poor-wills fall silent for several weeks, a period that coincides with their annual molt. Often they resume nonterritorial vocalizing just before migration in late summer.

Fall. Southward migration is well advanced by mid-September. The birds desert the northern and central parts of the continent and may settle for the winter along the Gulf Coast and Florida peninsula. Most, however, fly to Central America as far south as western Panama, where they arrive in November and December.

Winter. On their winter range, whip-poor-wills feed at night in wooded marsh hummocks and coastal lowlands. They rarely vocalize except occasionally just before spring migration.

Ecology. For breeding habitat, whip-poor-wills favor fairly dry upland deciduous or mixed woodlands of intermediate shade. Degree of openness seems a more critical factor than plant composition. Since most feeding is done in open spaces adjacent to woodland, such openings are also vital elements of the habitat.

Whip-poor-wills usually nest beneath an overhanging shrub or log in a sun-flecked spot containing sparse undergrowth. They build no actual nest. The matted dead leaves holding the eggs gradually form a slight depression as incubation proceeds.

Much of the diet consists of night-flying moths, especially the larger sphinxes, silkmoths, and noctuids. Mosquitoes and flying beetles are also frequently captured. In areas where pesticide use has severely reduced moth populations, whip-poor-wills have declined.

Food competitors include other night-feeding insectivores such as bats and eastern screech-owls. Declines in insect abundance increase such competition, in which whip-poor-wills probably come out last, since they rely exclusively upon vision for food capture, whereas bats and owls use other senses for tracking prey.

Any ground-nesting bird is vulnerable to foraging predators, such as opossums, skunks, raccoons, and squirrels. The whip-poor-will's camouflage is its best defense against predation. Other birds occasionally mob roosting whip-poor-wills, possibly mistaking them for owls (birder mobs have also made this mistake).

Focus. The whip-poor-will's name is onomatopoeic—imitative of its call. Native Americans named many birds by this means; the Cherokee called the whip-poor-will "wa-gu-li," the Malecite tribe "hwip-o-lis." To Henry Thoreau, its call "is the voice with which the woods and moonlight woo me." The family name goatsucker reputedly originated from an old husbands' tale that these large-gaped birds draw milk from goats; the story has long been discredited, but modern ornithologists choose to maintain the name.

Until the early 1800s, observers regularly identified the whip-poor-will and its close relative the common nighthawk as the same species. Thus the earliest records of its presence are unreliable. Northern populations have declined in the past thirty years, but whip-poor-will range has expanded in the southeastern states. Habitat changes probably account for most of these shifts.

8

PIGEON AND DOVE FAMILY (Columbidae), order Columbiformes

Doves and *pigeons* are interchangeable terms for all birds in this family. These birds are characterized by small heads, plump bodies, partially iridescent plumage in many species, and gregarious behavior. Unlike most birds, they drink by sucking. They regurgitate a crop secretion known as pigeon's milk for feeding their young.

Head profiles of the rock pigeon (top) and mourning dove (bottom) show the cere, the soft covering over the nostrils and base of the upper mandible. Its precise function remains unknown.

Pigeons and doves do not have functional oil, or *uropygial,* glands for maintaining their plumage. Instead, they grow *powder down,* a modified type of feather, throughout their plumage. These inconspicuous feathers disintegrate at their tips into a fine, talclike, waterproofing powder that the bird distributes over itself by preening. All family members have loosely attached feathers, perhaps an escape adaptation for eluding capture by raptors or other predators. Almost three hundred pigeon and dove species exist worldwide, most inhabiting tropical regions. An additional

North American species, the passenger pigeon (*Ectopistes migratorius*), is now extinct.

Rock Pigeon (*Columba livia*)

Also known as the rock dove, this is the common or domestic pigeon, noted for its ubiquitous presence in urban and rural areas alike. Plumage colors vary, as any glance at a flock reveals; the birds may be gray, brownish, mostly black or white, or any combination thereof. Typical coloration is gray or slate blue with a whitish patch above the tail and reddish feet. Iridescent feathers often color the neck and upper breast. The birds utter various cooing and gurgling sounds, all of them given in social, usually sexual, contexts. The only visible differences between sexes are behavioral. Rock pigeons reside on every continent except Antarctica.

Close relatives. Nearest North American relatives include the band-tailed pigeon (*C. fasciata*) and red-billed pigeon (*C. flavirostris*), both southwestern U.S. residents, and the white-crowned pigeon (*C. leucocephala*), which inhabits the Florida Keys. The stock dove (*C. oenas*) and wood pigeon (*C. palumbus*) are common European species.

Behaviors. Anybody who has sat for five minutes in a park where pigeons converge for handouts or to scavenge food already knows something about their behaviors. These birds *walk* in a rather stately manner (often pigeon-toed) rather than hop or run. Their thrusting head movements when they walk are also characteristic. These movements may be an innate balancing act to compensate for the bird's small head and consequently skewed center of gravity. Another common behavior is wing clapping in flight, most often done by male birds, perhaps signaling a readiness to mate.

Rock pigeons feed mainly on the ground. Gregarious in every aspect of their life history, they feed, fly, roost, and nest together. Individual birds may shift between flocks, but the flock itself remains the dominant social structure. In a flock, the birds fly close together; this flock pull instinct is probably a protective adaptation that distracts a hawk predator from focusing on a single bird. In a turning or wheeling flock, each bird is geometrically repositioned.

Rock pigeons are generally nonmigratory, though some far-northern populations apparently shift southward in winter.

Spring, Summer, Fall. In contrast to most North American birds, rock pigeon breeding activities are not seasonally based, although northernmost populations seldom nest during winter months. Nesting in many areas is continual; a female may nest up to nine times per year. Stylized courtship behaviors are easily observable; in any large flock, one may see various phases of the breeding cycle occurring simultaneously. A male inflates his neck feathers, bows, and turns in front of a female or chases her on the ground and in the air. Courtship has reached the ultimate stage when a pair *bills*—the female places her bill inside the male's, and the birds bob their heads rhythmically in this posture. Rock pigeons are monogamous; the pair bond is apparently lifelong. Five months after hatching, the young are sexually mature and ready to mate.

Even though pairs often nest in close proximity, they vigorously defend their nests. The nesting territory, writes one researcher, "is remarkably compressible or expandable according to circumstances." Where more than one pair occupy a single ledge or beam, the birds defend only the immediate area around their nests. Renesting pigeons usually build new nests near the previous site.

In late summer, rock pigeons undergo their molt, an annual "change of clothes" signified in the city by pigeon feathers everywhere.

EGGS AND YOUNG: two; eggs white. INCUBATION: by both sexes; about seventeen days. FEEDING OF YOUNG: by both sexes; pigeon's milk for first few days, then seeds. FLEDGING: about three weeks.

Winter. Even in areas where rock pigeons reproduce year-round, the frequency and success of winter nesting lag because of harsh weather and decreased access to food. Sheltering and feeding are the main pigeon activities during this season.

Ecology. The rock pigeon's foremost associate is humankind, a coexistence dating from the Neolithic period. The farmer is its friend, the city dweller its closer friend. Pigeons seldom exist apart from people.

Safe nesting shelter is a foremost necessity for pigeons. The nest locale is usually a partially enclosed or semisheltered flat surface on a building or bridge. Window ledges, cornices, bridge beams, and barn rafters are common sites. The male collects short sticks or pieces of straw, selecting them for their stiffness, and brings them to the female, which arranges them beneath her. The final structure is a shallow, flimsy platform.

The abundance of city pigeons directly reflects the feeding attention lavished upon them. For many people, bird feeding consists entirely of feeding pigeons in the park. Without such handouts, huge city flocks could not exist, for these birds invariably breed to the limit of their food supply. Rock pigeons are mainly seed eaters, preferring vetches and cultivated grains, but they have learned to consume popcorn, peanuts, french fries, bread, meats—just about any fast food item—and they scavenge sidewalks, streets, and parks for garbage debris. Rural flocks are mainly grain scavengers. Insects, snails, and other invertebrates are sometimes taken, especially for nestlings graduating from a pigeon's milk diet. Rock pigeons rarely eat green vegetation.

Scavenger competitors include American crows, house sparrows, and squirrels, among others. In some places, pigeons may compete with barn swallows, eastern phoebes, and American robins for ledge nesting sites.

The rock pigeon's foremost natural predator is the peregrine falcon, which shares similar habitats to ancestral rock pigeons. A few American cities have released pairs of these cliff-dwelling raptors in the canyons of tall city buildings, hoping to control rock pigeon populations. The results so far remain unspectacular. American crows sometimes raid pigeon nests and devour the eggs. In most cities with pigeon problems, however, people's ample provision of food items swamps all efforts to curb rock pigeon populations by biological controls.

Rock pigeons carry numerous parasites. The birds' gregarious habits permit rapid transmission throughout a flock, sometimes leading to disease epidemics. Probably 80 percent of all pigeons are infected with trichomoniasis, caused by the internal protozoan *Trichomonas columbae*. Ornithosis, also called psittacosis or parrot fever, results from primary infection by *Chlamydomonas,* a green alga that resembles bacteria. Although it is seldom fatal to mature rock pigeons, this disease is highly contagious to humans, who may experience flulike symptoms. Pigeons also transmit the fungus *Cryptococcus neoformans,* which in humans may cause the often fatal cryptococcal meningitis. Many human cases of these diseases are air-transmitted during cleanups of pigeon droppings from roost sites; wearing of face masks is advised while performing such tasks.

Focus. Native populations of rock pigeons exist today in only a few scattered locales, mainly in remote coastal mountains of northern Europe and the Balkans. In such places, the birds nest on cliff ledges and in caves. Several European dove species, including the rock pigeon, figured in the early flood myths of various civilizations. The dove's early symbolic connection with love, sex, procreation, and the goddess Venus probably resulted from observations of the birds' conspicuous courtship and nesting behaviors. Doves later came to represent various aspects of divine love in Christianity. As a popular icon of peace, the bird regularly appears in editorial cartoons.

Opinion is divided on whether most of today's rock pigeon populations are feral (that is, descended and escaped from domestic flocks) or, like house sparrows, simply opportunistic, having successfully adapted to human-created environments. Both possibilities exist, and for U.S. populations, at least, the distinction between them remains unclear. The spread of some fourteen worldwide subspecies plus numerous strains developed by pigeon husbandry and dovecote cultures have thoroughly mixed the genes of this species. Variations in plumage color alone indicate the genetic mixtures present in any flock. Researchers point out genetic behavioral differences between wild rock pigeons and our common city pigeons; many even fear that the native populations of Europe have become endangered by genetic leakage from feral pigeons.

Our North American rock pigeon populations stem from dovecote pigeons domesticated by artificial selection. These were introduced into Britain by the Romans (c. A.D. 100) and brought to this continent by French and British colonists in the early 1600s. They became so common that nobody bothered to study them, an appalling neglect of scientific opportunity. We would know far more than we do about the pigeon's history in North America if naturalists and ornithologists had not, until the 1970s, regarded them as a trash species. Today, even if pigeons remain uncharismatic to birders, numerous cadres of experts who raise, train, study, and value them feel otherwise.

Throughout human history, pigeons have provided blessing and curse, both in abundance. They are important food (squab) and pernicious pests. They are readily bred and trained for fancy show racing and homing activities. For science, they provide easy subjects for experimental and behavioral research. As pests, their overpopulations befoul public structures. Cleanup involves much labor, cost, and potential health hazards.

Medieval monasteries throughout Europe raised pigeons for meat. Dovecote architecture became a specialty, and pigeon fancy, the term used for the breeding and care of flocks, grew into an avocation of the very rich. Today the aviculture of some two hundred breeds and many varieties of rock pigeons—bred for color, plumage patterns, flight, speed, and meat—parallels the development of rose and iris culture. Numerous organizations and journals explore every complex nuance of pigeon fancy.

The homing ability of rock pigeons—actually their nest-site tenacity, which drives them to return to their dovecotes, sometimes from hundreds of miles—was put to extensive use during World War I. Trained carrier pigeons delivered messages, often from the front lines at night, back to support units. Pigeon use continued during World War II and the Korean War, usually in situations where telecommunications became impractical or dangerous.

Some thirty-two pigeons have received medals citing them for "brave service."

How pigeons are able to home on their dovecotes from long distances has puzzled researchers for many decades. Visual cues are apparently of minor importance. The birds seem to orient themselves by innate sun and magnetic compasses, but compass direction is only part of the complex. One discovery is that rock pigeons are sensitive to infrasound ranges far below the capacity of human ears, down to .05 hertz, twelve octaves below middle C. But the whole story of how pigeons navigate remains elusive. The secrets still held by this lowly draper of our statues may give even "The Thinker" pause.

Closer looks. Abs, M., ed. *Physiology and Behavior of the Pigeon.* New York: Academic Press, 1983.

Kligerman, J. *A Fancy for Pigeons.* New York: Hawthorn, 1978.

PIGEON AND DOVE FAMILY (Columbidae)

Mourning Dove (*Zenaida macroura*)

Our most abundant native dove is a foot-long brown bird with a pointed, white-edged tail and a black spot behind each eye. Male birds show a rose-tinted breast and grayish cap, while females are duller brown on breast and head. The distinctive cooing notes are one of the most familiar bird sounds of spring.

Close relatives. The white-winged dove (*Z. asiatica*) has a southwestern U.S. range; the zenaida dove (*Z. aurita*), a West Indies species, occasionally appears in Florida. Other family members include the common ground dove (*Columbina passerina*), the Inca dove (*C. inca*), and the rock pigeon (*Columba livia*).

Behaviors. Be reminded when you observe mourning doves of their extinct North American relative, the passenger pigeon (*Ectopistes migratorius*), which they resemble in general form; passenger pigeons were larger, with reddish breasts. Mourning doves are tree nesters and ground feeders. Except when nesting, they are gregarious, often feeding and roosting in flocks. They walk and drink like rock pigeons. In flight, their wings make characteristic whistling sounds, especially when the birds are alarmed or displaying, though they can also fly silently. Overhead, a mourning dove can sometimes resemble a sharp-shinned hawk or American kestrel, but the dove's pointed tail is the giveaway.

Mourning doves are the only native North American birds to breed in every state—they have even been introduced to Hawaii. Most doves migrate south in the fall, but increasing numbers remain on their northern range over winter.

Spring. The plaintive cooing notes that give this bird its name are usually uttered by an unattached male advertising for a mate, though females and mated males occasionally voice this call, too. Males often use favorite perches for calling, but the perch-coo does not signify territoriality (beyond the perch itself), since the birds may range and call over a large area. Migrants arrive back at their birth or previous nesting locales in late winter or early spring; from then through summer, courtship and nesting activities are continual. Males bow and coo in front of females and perform a flap-glide flight, ending in a long, spiraling glide. The short coo, a briefer version of the perch-coo uttered by either sex, often signals selection of a nest site. Three-bird chases occur when an unmated male pursues the female of a mated pair. Perch-cooing ceases when a pair bond is formed.

Territoriality begins with nest building. The territory may radially extend fifty or more yards from the nest but often shrinks in size as incubation proceeds. Males select the nest site and collect sticks from the ground, bringing them to the female; sometimes he stands on her back as if supervising her arrangement of sticks. More than two eggs in a nest usually indicates *brood parasitism,* or dump nesting—an invading female dove has added one or two eggs to those already present. A parent bird, if frightened off the nest after the eggs hatch, may launch into a distraction display, fluttering on the ground. Mourning doves are monogamous throughout the nesting year; sometimes the pair bond lasts over several nesting seasons.

EGGS AND YOUNG: two; eggs white. INCUBATION: by female at night, male during the day; about two weeks. FEEDING OF YOUNG: by both sexes; pigeon's milk and regurgitated seeds, insects. FLEDGING: about two weeks.

Summer. Fledglings may roost in the nest tree and follow the parents about for ten or twelve days. Juvenile doves can be recognized by their shorter tails, the scaled appearance of wing and breast feathers, and lack of head spots. Adult females may begin renesting several days after their first offspring fledge, often while the male is still feeding them away from the nest. In their northern range, mourning doves average two or three matings per season, an average nesting cycle requiring about thirty-two days. A small percentage of doves are still nesting in September and October. Young doves often gather in all-juvenile flocks that feed, roost, and wander together. As nesting ceases, adult pairs also form flocks that often merge.

Fall. From September to November, mourning doves molt into a drabber winter plumage. Migration timing and sequence appear related to age and sex—a system called *differential migration*—though some mixing does occur. Juvenile flocks begin staging on electric wires and other perches and start moving south in late August and September; adult female flocks and finally male flocks follow. The young birds also move farthest south, some to Panama and Costa Rica. Most doves, however, winter in the southeastern United States and Mexico. Doves migrate leisurely, both day and night at fairly low altitude in flocks of fifty birds or less. Banding records indicate that movements of nineteen to thirty-four miles per day are average and that the Wabash River valley in Indiana marks the boundary between southeast- and southwest-migrating doves.

Winter. Many if not most resident doves of the southern United States remain in place and do not migrate farther south. Mourning dove winter range lies south of the thirty-ninth parallel. But small population segments, consisting mainly of males, remain in their northern breeding range, probably held by a reliable food supply such as waste or stored grains and yard feeders. Harsh winter weather takes a lethal toll on them each year; not uncommonly one sees frozen toes and feet on north-wintering doves. Wintering flocks in the South tend to mingle sexes, and dominance hierarchies, or peck orders, govern social relations within the flocks. Whether another plumage molt occurs before spring migration or spring breeding plumage results from wear of the winter plumage, as in several passerine bird species, remains uncertain.

Ecology. Mourning doves range over a broad spectrum of habitats. The basic environs are woodland edges, but agricultural land practices and suburban yards have expanded mourning dove options. Landscaped areas, hedgerows, and parks with a mix of trees and open areas attract these birds. Because of such habitat expansion, probably many more mourning doves exist today in eastern North America than in presettlement times. This trend of expansion in both breeding and winter ranges has continued over the past century.

The nest, hardly a construction marvel, is a loose, flat platform, mostly unlined. Often it is so flimsy that the eggs can be seen from beneath. It is placed in a tree fork or, more often, on a horizontal branch up to forty feet high, occasionally even on the ground. The birds favor conifers, especially spruce, as well as hawthorn thickets. Though surprisingly strong for their frail appearance, branch nests often blow down in storms. Mourning doves build about 40 percent of

Mourning dove nests are flimsy platforms of sticks, often placed in conifers or thickets. Contrary to most parent bird behavior, mourning doves do not remove nestling feces.

their nests atop their own previous nests or on vacated nests of other birds, especially those of blue jays, American robins, and common grackles. Occasionally doves nest semicolonially, with several pairs building in the same tree.

In most areas, mourning dove diet consists almost entirely of seeds foraged from the ground and plant stalks. Most preferred are cereal grains and other grass family seeds, such as canary grasses, corn, common oat, wheat, millets, foxtail grasses, and panicums. Seed sources also include buckwheats, common ragweed, pokeweed, knotweeds, sunflowers, and white pine, all highly nutritive. Animal food is insignificant, most frequently snails taken during the nesting season for their calcium content. Sand and gravel grit are essential for dove digestion, and the birds also ingest salt, often along winter-salted roads.

There is little evidence of any large-scale food competition. Blackbird and house sparrow flocks scavenge grainfields where mourning doves feed; one study, however, indicated that blackbirds favor cracked corn damaged or scattered by harvesting or livestock, whereas doves consume mainly whole-kernel corn. Food competition probably becomes severe at times for north-wintering doves.

High on the list of mourning dove predators are domestic cats and dogs (though their ranking compared with hawk and owl predation may reflect observer bias). American crows sometimes consume the eggs. If the mourning dove's most important habitat benefactors are humans, so also are we their major predators. Mourning doves are classed as gamebirds in thirty-seven states, and fall hunting seasons harvest about fifty million doves annually—more than all other migratory wildfowl combined. Southeastern states account for more than half of this harvest.

Focus. Prehistoric native peoples consumed mourning doves as food; the birds figured prominently in Native American folklore and mythology, and various tribes still have dove clans. It was probably a migrating mourning dove blown off-course that greeted Columbus before his West Indies landfall in 1492. Early American explorers and naturalists named the bird turtledove, identifying it with its Eurasian relative of that name (*Streptopelia turtur*). English naturalist Mark Catesby first distinguished the differences for science in 1731. Nineteenth-century market hunters largely ignored mourning doves, since the larger, more trusting passenger pigeons were far easier to kill in quantity. In a few states, such as Michigan, which officially classifies doves as songbirds, the issue of declaring them a legal gamebird is highly controversial. Hunters generally favor it; birders and naturalists generally fight it. From a purely biological view, little evidence exists that hunting seasons severely affect mourning dove populations. Why one would consider them worthwhile shooting is another matter.

Banding studies indicate that about 75 percent of mourning doves live less than a year, mainly because of predation and weather factors, though life spans of twelve years and longer have been recorded.

Closer look. Baskett, T. S., M. W. Sayre, R. E. Tomlinson, and R. E. Mirarchi, eds. *Ecology and Management of the Mourning Dove.* Harrisburg, PA: Stackpole Books, 1993.

9

American Woodcock (*Scolopax minor*)

Sandpiper family (Scolopacidae), order Ciconiiformes. This ground bird can be identified by its brownish dead-leaf color, chunky form, extremely long bill, short rounded wings, and transversely barred crown. Its wings whistle in flight. Females weigh slightly more than males and have slightly longer bills (about two and one-half inches or more).

Close relatives. Nearest kin include the entire snipe subfamily of shorebirds. The Eurasian woodcock (*S. rusticola*) is similar in appearance, as are three other *Scolopax* species. Related North American snipes include the common snipe (*Gallinago gallinago*) and short-billed and long-billed dowitchers (*Limnodromus griseus, L. scolopaceus*). Other family members include the yellowlegs, sandpipers, curlews, godwits, and phalaropes—almost forty North American species of more than eighty worldwide.

Behaviors. The American woodcock and upland sandpiper are the two best-known North American dry-land shorebirds. Although woodcocks may inhabit wet thickets, they often reside far from water. Woodcocks feed on earthworms by plunging their long bills two inches or more into the ground. The birds are *crepuscular*—most active during twilight hours—but also feed after dark. I have seen them grouped around large puddles at night, sometimes in pouring rain, quite unalarmed by car headlights. Except for occasional social feeding, however, woodcocks are usually solitary and do not flock even during migrations. Like many shorebirds, they bob their bodies up and down, especially when feeding or alarmed. When flushed, a woodcock often bursts straight up from cover, then flies a short, zigzag route before settling back to the ground.

Woodcocks breed throughout the eastern United States from southern Canada to the Gulf states.

Spring. One of the earliest birds to arrive in spring, often even in late winter, the male woodcock begins performing his spectacular courtship flights during stopovers on his journey north. Once he arrives in his breeding territory, to which he returns each year, he continues his dawn and dusk courtship flights into May or even summer. A male's flight-display territory may consist of only a few hundred square feet or several acres defended from other male woodcocks. Apparently territories shift frequently during the breeding season.

Courtship flights usually begin at a light measurement of 0.05 to 2 footcandles, about forty-five minutes before sunrise and a half hour after sunset. The flights are difficult to see in twilight, but the birds' distinctive sounds are unmistakable, hence the nickname little brown ghost. The male spirally ascends to two hundred feet or higher, producing a trilling or tremolo sound that rises in pitch and tempo. This sound emanates from vibrations of each wing's three outer primary feathers, which are narrow and sickle shaped. At the apex of flight, these sounds cease. Then, as the bird drops in a zigzag, falling-leaf descent, he *vocalizes* his ventriloquial kissing song, in groups of five or six notes: "chip-CHIP-chip-chipchip." The entire flight lasts forty to sixty seconds. Back on the ground, often near the spot from which he arose, he repeats a rasping note, "beezp," similar to that of the common nighthawk. (I have often carried on lengthy "beezp"

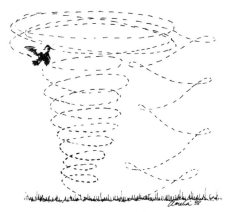

The male woodcock's twilight courtship flight rises in a spiral, then quickly descends in a coasting, zigzag pattern. (Courtesy of Kalamazoo Nature Center.)

Vibrations of the woodcock's three outer primary feathers, smaller and narrower than the others, produce the whistling sounds heard during the male's courtship flight.

conversations with grounded woodcocks.) A minute or so later, he again launches skyward.

A male woodcock may make ten or twenty such flights in the course of a morning or evening session. Series of courtship flights last about forty to fifty minutes and are performed at irregular intervals throughout moonlit nights. Males defend their launching pad territories, chasing away other males. These flights, which Aldo Leopold called sky dances, attract female woodcocks, which silently approach the promiscuous male's territory. Mating occurs on the ground, and no pair bond is formed.

Females begin nesting in April and May, often within several hundred yards of a male's territory. The nest, a slight, usually unconcealed ground depression, may or may not be lined with pine needles, sometimes rimmed with twigs. An incubating female may sit tight on her nest, even permitting herself to be stroked by hand.

Woodcock eggs hatch by distinctive lengthwise splitting and infolding. After the chicks dry off, the female leads them into the woods, where she probably feeds them earthworms for their first few days. The group travels by foot almost constantly, ranging far from the nest site. If disturbed by intrusion during this period, the female exhibits impressive distraction displays. Chicks grow rapidly, and survival rates are usually high. Some reputable observers have reported seeing a flying female carry a chick by clasping it between her legs or toes. Others suggest that the tucked-in tail of a flushing female may create the illusion of something being carried. Perhaps this is also a distraction display, as has been observed in the Eurasian woodcock.

EGGS AND YOUNG: usually four; eggs tan, brown spotted. INCUBA-TION: by female; about three weeks. FEEDING OF YOUNG: probably during their first few days, by female; earthworms. FLEDGING: Young can fly in two weeks.

Summer. Broods may remain together for several weeks, roaming and foraging over several miles, often moving to areas of denser vegetation than where nesting occurred. Soon, however, the groups split up and each bird goes its separate way. Woodcocks can be difficult to find at this season; they often seek daytime molting cover, dense thickets in swampy areas or near water. At night, however, they often emerge into fields and openings to feed. Most male display flights that occur now are probably juveniles trying their wings. From June through October, woodcocks gradually replace their plumage, the adult birds' only complete molt of the year.

Fall. "Woodcock seem almost as reluctant to leave their northern haunts in the fall as they are eager to reach them in the spring," wrote one observer. Severe weather provides the foremost push to their fall migration. Through October into November, they solitarily move southward at night, often in short hops. Sitting by a campfire on cold October nights, I have often heard the whistle of woodcock wings, seemingly at almost ground level, as they singly pass southward. Many woodcocks collide with electric wires and buildings during migrations. Storms and cold snaps also claim many victims.

Winter. Most American woodcocks spend the winter in Louisiana and adjacent Gulf Coast states. Migrants join the permanent resident woodcocks of these areas for the duration of the season. A few woodcocks, however, may remain in the North over winter, usually residing along ice-free streams where food is most accessible.

Ecology. Woodcock habitats vary considerably throughout the bird's seasonal ranges. Typical nesting and foraging cover consists of early plant-successional stages, chiefly mixed hardwoods and conifers. The most consistently occurring plants in areas of high woodcock populations are aspens and alders, each forming a distinct cover type (alder thickets often become favorite summer and fall refuges). One study found beaked hazel a frequent shrub component. More important than the type of vegetation, however, is its density, ranging from light to medium for nesting cover to much thicker growth for the rest of the year. Male territories consist of wooded edges and groves, where the bird rests during daytime, and grassy openings or clearings with scattered shrubs, which constitute the singing ground where courtship flights occur. Optimal feeding habitats include patches of bare, moist soil. Certain forest types such as beech-maple do not produce soils conducive to earthworms, and thus are often sparsely populated by woodcocks. On their winter ranges, woodcocks usually inhabit dense thickets and swamps by day, emerging at night to feed in fields, in pastures, and along streams.

In all seasons, the woodcock's main food—up to 90 percent—is earthworms. Round poke holes can be seen in soft ground or around puddles where the birds have probed. A woodcock may eat its own weight in earthworms in one night. *Aporrectodea tuberculata* and *Dendrobaena octaedra,* the most common earthworm species

Woodcocks feed mainly on earthworms in all seasons. High placement of the eye provides a zone of binocular vision behind the head. (Courtesy of Kalamazoo Nature Center.)

consumed, usually occur in light or sandy loam soils. Yet one study found that *darker* soil color is the bird's most important visual cue for selecting a probing site, and that blacker, more humic loams usually contain more earthworms per square foot than lighter, sandier soils. Beetle grubs and other insect larvae, mainly flies, are also consumed. About 10 percent of the total diet consists of seeds, mainly of grasses and sedges, but also blackberries and alder seeds in summer and fall.

Woodcock competitors are few. Wildlife management programs aimed at improving white-tailed deer and ruffed grouse habitats benefit woodcocks, too, since prime edge habitats for all three species coincide.

Hawk, owl, and mammal ground predators capture woodcocks on occasion. The chief predators are probably feral and domestic cats, which destroy many nesting woodcocks. Black rat snakes also consume eggs and chicks.

Focus. Woodcock head anatomy is an evolutionary wonder. Various organs are shifted from the positions they occupy in most vertebrate heads. The brain, for example, lies almost upside down, while the high-set eye placement gives woodcocks more binocular vision above and behind than in front. The ears, instead of opening behind the eyes, are located between eyes and bill; hearing centered in this position may aid the bird's quest for earthworms. The woodcock's long bill is a sensory plunging device that contains nerve endings in its tip end. The flexible upper-mandible tip resembles a forceps and can grasp earthworms deep in the soil. Some observers speculate that the bird's bobbing or rocking motions may cause soil vibrations and consequent earthworm movements that the bird hears or sees.

Often called timberdoodle by hunters, the woodcock has become a popular gamebird throughout most of its range, although in my opinion the morsel of dark breast meat tastes quite gamy. Native Americans apparently seldom hunted the bird. Although market hunting depleted woodcock numbers during the nineteenth century, human land practices have indirectly benefited the woodcock. Regrowth of former agricultural land, providing new forest and edge habitats, has probably expanded woodcock range and abundance far beyond the bird's presettlement populations. Despite this fact, woodcocks have declined by some 40 percent in eastern states since 1966, a worrisome statistic that is currently receiving much attention from game regulators.

Closer look. Sheldon, W. G. *The Book of the American Woodcock.* Amherst: University of Massachusetts, 1967.

10

HAWK FAMILY (Accipitridae), order Ciconiiformes

Hawks are hunter-predators, their diet consisting exclusively of meat and animal matter. They number more than two hundred species worldwide; some seventeen are eastern North American residents. Subfamilies include the kites, bird hawks (accipiters), harriers, buzzard hawks (buteos), and eagles. Together with owls, ospreys, caracaras, and falcons, these birds are collectively called *raptors,* so named from their strong, taloned, *raptorial* feet, adapted to seize prey. The foot is a locking mechanism; its grasp cannot be released by will. The weight of the prey keeps the talons locked; only pushing against the solid surface of ground or nest can release the tension and cause the bird to let go. If the hawk seizes an animal too heavy for it to carry, it may become the prisoner of its prey until it can shove its load against something solid.

The hawk's eye, its supreme hunting organ, is two or three times more acute than human twenty-twenty vision. Each eye functions like a telescope, with a long focal length between lens and retina, whose receptors produce a sharp, fine-grained image. Vision is both monocular and binocular, the latter covering about fifty degrees of the visual field. Raptor eyes occupy as much head space as the brain.

Most hawks soar in flight. In many hawk species, females are larger than males. Hawk and owl sign look somewhat similar. Hawk excreta, or whitewash, is ejected away from the nest, occurring in streaks or spots; owls eject whitewash puddles directly beneath habitual perches. Regurgitated hawk pellets, about two inches long

Raptor pellets are regurgitated masses of fur and bones. Hawk pellets (top) contain eroded bone fragments buried in a spongy mass; owl pellets (bottom) show intact bones on the pellet surface.

or smaller, are spongy soft and contain corroded bone fragments buried in the mass. The thumb-size pellets of owls, on the other hand, are tightly compact masses showing many small, well-preserved animal bones on the pellet surface.

Closer Looks. Craighead, J. J., and F. C., Jr. *Hawks, Owls and Wildlife.* New York: Dover, 1969.

Dunne, P. *The Wind Masters: The Lives of North American Birds of Prey.* Boston: Houghton Mifflin, 1995.

Dunne, P., D. Sibley, and C. Sutton. *Hawks in Flight.* Boston: Houghton Miflin, 1988.

HAWK FAMILY (Accipitridae)

Sharp-shinned Hawk (*Accipiter striatus*)

Short rounded wings, a long square-cornered tail, and several quick wingbeats alternating with short glides characterize the sharp-shinned hawk in flight. The sharpie is about pigeon size, ten to fourteen inches long, and females are larger than males. Adult birds have a dark bluish gray back and rust-colored, horizontal barring on the underparts. Immatures are brown backed and brown streaked. Not vocal at most times, the birds often utter a series of shrill cackling notes when alarmed near the nest.

Close relatives. Other North American bird hawks, so called because their prey is chiefly birds, are the Cooper's hawk (*A. cooperii*) and northern goshawk (*A. gentilis*). Some thirty-eight other accipiters range worldwide.

Behaviors. The sharp-shinned is our smallest accipiter, but female sharpies and male Cooper's hawks often appear to overlap in size, making positive field identification difficult—in fact, one of birding's toughest challenges.

The sharp-shinned hunts mainly by ambush from inconspicuous woodland perches or by low, gliding flights amid trees and thickets. Unlike the larger buteo hawks, it can quickly maneuver, abruptly turning or dropping when it spots prey. It may suddenly snatch a warbler from its perch or chase a bird into dense brush at top speed. During bird-banding operations, I have watched sharpies dive into mist nets after captured blue jays, often tearing through the net with the force of their attacks. Their deft reflexes "seem not just to mirror the escape tactics of prey," wrote hawk biologist Pete Dunne, "but to anticipate them." Observers also cite instances of play attack, when a sharpie suddenly scatters a group of finches for the apparent sport of it. Even toward birds larger than itself, it sometimes feints an attack. Sharpies also soar high, usually in the morning and extensively during migrations.

Spring. In April, most sharp-shinneds move north from their winter range as far as the tree line in Canada, traveling singly and in small or large flocks. They sometimes accompany other accipiters or buteos, such as broad-winged hawks. On the breeding range, which spans most of the continent, aerial courtship displays occur near the future nest site, which is often located in a previous nesting vicinity. Within a home range of two or three miles, a pair occupies a territory of several acres. Usually the birds build a new nest each spring.

EGGS AND YOUNG: four or five; eggs white, splotched with brown. INCUBATION: by female, which is fed by male; about a month. FEEDING OF YOUNG: by both sexes; bits of meat. FLEDGING: almost a month.

Summer. Family groups remain together, often in the nest vicinity, for most of the summer as the juveniles gradually learn hunting skills. By late summer, most have dispersed from their family groups. The prolonged annual feather molt extends into fall. Yearling birds gain full adult plumage during their third summer. Juveniles and yearlings often begin migrating in mid-August.

Fall. Migration numbers peak in mid-September. This movement usually coincides with warbler and sparrow migrations, and sharpies capture many of these smaller migrants. The hawks often travel in large numbers, both by active flight and by riding thermal updrafts.

Winter. Some sharp-shinneds travel as far south as Central America, males and juveniles apparently migrating farthest south. Many winter in the southern and central midwestern United States, however, and some wintering sharpies typically remain in the lower Great Lakes and New England areas. These and Cooper's hawks are the predators that frequently haunt suburban yard feeders, sometimes crashing into picture windows while chasing a junco or sparrow.

Ecology. Open woods, edges, and openings in dense forests are the sharpie's favored habitats.

For nesting, the sharpie often selects a tree near the outer edge of a small, dense conifer grove, building a twig nest close to the trunk. Nest height averages about thirty feet. Occasionally sharpies adopt and refurbish old crow or squirrel nests.

About 96 percent of the sharpie's diet consists of birds, almost any species smaller than itself. Probably it captures more adult passerines—finches, warblers, and other perching birds—than anything else, but it also takes nestlings, rock pigeons, and young chickens in poultry yards (so-called chicken hawks, however, are usually Cooper's hawks). The sharpie's diet also includes mice, young rabbits, frogs, and large insects. A common feature of this hawk's near-nest vicinity is a butcher's block or plucking post—a stump, fence post, or other perch where the bird habitually brings its prey, tears it apart, and feeds. Feathers or other remnants on the ground may indicate a butcher's block perch and nearby nest. Often, however, the birds leave little refuse at such sites. Probably sharpies find their easiest, most abundant prey during migration seasons as they trail or accompany passerine flocks.

The foremost food competitors are probably other bird hawks, depending upon habitat and weather conditions. Accipiters seldom share the same woodland acreage with other accipiters, however, so sharpies largely avoid competitive encounters. In areas where sharp-shinned and Cooper's hawks do coexist, the latter apparently forage lower in the tree canopy.

Sharp-shinned predators are mainly larger raptors, including Cooper's hawks, northern harriers, red-tailed hawks, and peregrine falcons.

Focus. This bird's common name results from its pencil-thin legs, or *tarsi,* a helpful field mark when the bird is perched in good light. But even veteran observers find it difficult to distinguish sharpies from Cooper's hawks in the field; the sharp-shinned's squarish tail, contrasted to the Cooper's less squarish tail, is often an unreliable mark. In flight, the sharpie's head barely extends in front of the wings, while the Cooper's head extends quite visibly. The key visible difference between the two is size, plain to see and measure in the hand but hard to judge through binoculars; any birder who says otherwise is leading you astray. As one raptor expert states, "One should not be too proud to list a bird as an 'unidentified *Accipiter*' or even 'unidentified hawk or falcon.'"

Along with Cooper's hawks, sharp-shinneds sometimes evoke the wrath of poultry farmers, gamebird hunters, and even some bird lovers who still believe that hawk attacks on yard feeders are heinous crimes of nature. It's true that any bird hawk can get into the habit of raiding a chicken yard or yard feeder. Hawks are opportunistic predators, and as

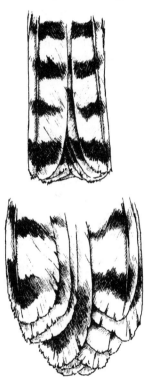

The sharp-shinned hawk tail (top) often appears more square cornered than the rounder-shaped Cooper's hawk tail (bottom). Tail shape in this species is not always a reliable field mark, however.

such they cull the weak and unwary. Yet they usually avoid human environs unless hunger drives them to bold actions.

Gunners once shot sharpies by the hundreds during fall migrations. Widespread use of DDT caused a dramatic decline of sharp-shinneds in the early 1970s, but populations are now recovering in many areas. Eastern seaboard censuses, however, show massive declines of this species in recent years, which some observers attribute to concurrent declines in passerine bird prey. Sharpie eggs, once regarded as the handsomest of all hawk eggs, were prized by egg collectors for their rich brown markings. Egg collecting has been legally banned since 1918.

Closer look. Kaufman, K. *A Field Guide to Advanced Birding.* Boston: Houghton Mifflin, 1990.

HAWK FAMILY (Accipitridae)

Red-tailed Hawk (*Buteo jamaicensis*)

In flight, this large hawk with a four-foot wingspread displays the typical buteo shape: chunky body, broad wings, and broad, rounded tail. Typical redtail adults have brown backs and copper red tails; viewed from beneath, their white chests and brown-streaked bellies are distinctive. Plumage variations are common, however, ranging from almost all black to nearly white. Viewed overhead, the most reliable field mark is the dark *patagial bar* on the fore edge of the wing. Immatures have gray, banded tails. Females are slightly larger than males. Listen for the redtail's raspy squeal, which some have likened to the sound of steam escaping from a valve.

Close relatives. Other buteo hawks of eastern North America are the red-shouldered hawk (*B. lineatus*), broad-winged hawk (*B. platypterus*), and rough-legged hawk (*B. lagopus*). Western U.S. species include the Swainson's hawk (*B. swainsoni*) and ferruginous hawk (*B. regalis*). The buzzard (*B. buteo*) is a Eurasian resident. Some twenty other species exist worldwide.

Behaviors. This is our most common and widespread buteo, or buzzard hawk, a soaring predator whose distribution spans the continent. Redtails are mainly still-hunters, often perching for long periods on telephone poles or electric towers as they scan the countryside. A large hawk perched in a roadside tree is usually a redtail. But it also hover-hunts; in a strong wind, sometimes it hangs motionless in place (kiting). Often it quarters back and forth over a field in low flight. It also hunts while soaring; when it spots prey, it may plunge, or stoop, into a steep, fast dive.

A red-tailed hawk pair scans its foraging habitat for signs of mammal activity. White chests, visible when they perch, identify these large hawks from a distance.

Redtails are only partially migratory, withdrawing south in the fall from the northernmost parts of their range. Their breeding range spans the continent south to Panama.

Spring. The redtail's spectacular courtship flights, begun in winter, continue through early spring and at intervals thereafter. Pairs usually mate for life. Breeding territories average more than a square mile in size but are often larger. Yearling birds occasionally nest, but most first-time breeders are at least three years old. Often a pair reoccupies one of several previous nests in March or April, adding fresh material, or builds a new nest nearby. Until their eggs hatch, redtails are extremely sensitive to disturbance and may quickly abandon the nest at slight provocation. Incubation begins with the laying of the first egg, and thus eggs hatch at successive intervals. An older nestling sometimes kills a younger sibling. By late spring, the surviving young become conspicuous by their noisy calling and rambunctious movements in the nest vicinity.

EGGS AND YOUNG: two or three; eggs white, brown spotted. INCU-BATION: by both sexes; four or five weeks. FEEDING OF YOUNG: by both sexes; meat fragments. FLEDGING: six or seven weeks.

Summer. Juveniles often continue to roost in the nest vicinity, even returning at times to use the nest as a feeding platform. They soon begin to develop strong flight, learning to hunt by trial and error; those that can't consistently find and kill prey soon starve to death. By midsummer, they may still linger near their parents or disperse in any direction. The adult annual molt begins after fledglings depart the nest, proceeding gradually and with great variation in timing, sequence, and duration. Older birds sometimes show evidence of molting throughout the year.

Fall. Immatures attain their full adult plumage (including their red tails) by autumn of their second year. Northern populations may remain on their breeding range or migrate slightly southward, depending on the amount of snow cover. Southern redtails usually remain on their summer territories. Young redtails tend to move earlier and farther than adult birds, sometimes as far south as Panama. The birds migrate singly or in small groups, soaring on thermals.

Winter. Redtail nests in deciduous trees become most visible in winter, when both hawks and foliage are gone. Spotting the nests provides advance notice of where the birds are likely to nest again, either on the same nest or nearby. Since many old nests are taken over by other raptors in winter or early spring, they're always worth checking out.

Influxes of fall-migrating redtails on the winter range sometimes result in territorial conflicts with year-round redtail residents. The newcomers may be forced into marginal feeding territories, which they seem less inclined to defend than resident birds on permanent territories.

Migrants begin moving northward in late winter and early spring. Courtship behaviors may become conspicuous in late February through March. The pair soars together, circling, spiraling, recrossing each other's flight paths. The male sometimes dives toward the female, and the two briefly interlock feet. Many of these aerial maneuvers resemble the birds' territorial displays. The pair also perches closely together, preening and feeding each other.

Ecology. Redtails favor forest edges or woodlots surrounded by open fields and pastures.

Nests are usually placed high in tall trees that give the hawks an outlook on the countryside. Frequent nesting sites include crotches of oaks, American beech, American elm, and (especially in the hawks' northern range) white pine. Redtail nests are large— repeatedly used ones may measure three or more feet high and four feet across. Like many hawks, redtails often add green sprigs of white pine, northern white cedar, hemlock, or other leafy twigs to their nests. Presence of fresh greenery reveals an active nest. Theories suggest that this habit helps camouflage the nest, aids nest sanitation, or helps inhibit the growth of insect parasites. Nest lining includes long grasses, bark strips from red cedar and wild grape, pine needles, and corn husks. Redtails may recycle old squirrel or crow nests as foundations for their own.

"To list the feeding menu of redtails in summer," writes one hawk researcher, "would be to name almost every living creature within their domain, from the larger insects to half-grown woodchucks." The preferred prey of the redtail—some 90 percent of the diet where abundant—is rodents, especially meadow voles and ground squirrels. Red squirrels, cottontail rabbits, moles, bats, and shrews are also commonly taken, as are crayfish, toads, garter snakes, and carrion. Among bird prey, red-winged blackbirds and ring-necked pheasants are frequent victims.

Although the breeding ranges of other buteo hawks concur with the redtail's, habitat preferences reduce competition between these species. A raptor associate in some areas is the great horned owl, sometimes called the redtail's nighttime counterpart. This large owl favors similar food and habitats and often nests close to redtails, probably because it often adopts old redtail nests.

Redtails have no significant predators except humans, but blue jays and American crows often mob and harass perched hawks. Eastern kingbirds fearlessly chase and strike hawks, as they do most large birds. Insect parasites are often numerous in redtail nests. Most redtail nestlings suffer from myiasis, a nonfatal disease caused by bloodsucking fly larvae. Bird lice (Mallophaga) may damage flight feathers to an extent that flying ability is affected.

Focus. The oldest leg-banded red-tailed hawk on record lived twenty-three years, probably far longer than the average. Redtails make easy targets for gunners and are still illegally shot by dimwits who believe in overpopulating the countryside with mice and rabbits. Formerly legal bounty hunting all but wiped out redtails in many northeastern states. Now protected, their populations are thriving and increasing throughout their range. Redtails seem more tolerant of human activities than most other hawks. Their habitat preferences coincide with agricultural land use, and public enlightenment about predator ecology is on their side.

Closer look. Austing, G. R. *The World of the Red-tailed Hawk.* Philadelphia: Lippincott, 1964.

11

Turkey Vulture (*Cathartes aura*)

New World vulture family (Ciconiidae), order Ciconiiformes. Both sexes of these large birds are brownish black with small, red, featherless heads and silvery underwings. The shallow-V (*dihedral*) posture of their five- to six-foot wingspread and their rocking, tilting flight as they soar are also characteristic.

Close relatives. Other North American species include the black vulture (*Coragyps atratus*) and the California condor (*Gymnogyps californianus*). Three other species reside in South America.

Behaviors. Vulture flight requires daytime updrafts of warm air, known as *thermals,* on which the birds, seldom flapping their wings, ride. As they circle and coast from one updraft to another, they sink at a rate slower than the warm air rises. Thermals usually begin rising at midmorning, and that's when vultures go aloft. You'll see few vultures in the air on a cold, cloudy day without strong thermals.

Not a pretty profile, the turkey vulture's red head is bare of feathers, an adaptation for carcass feeding. This carrion scavenger performs vital ecological functions.

Turkey vultures settle in the evening to roost in habitual sites such as these power-line towers. Communal vulture roosts may serve as prey information centers for the birds.

The ratio of low body weight to area of their broad, planklike wings gives turkey vultures their tippy flight; primary feathers at the wing tips extend like fingers, providing deeply slotted air flow that reduces turbulence and lowers stalling speed.

Except when nesting, turkey vultures are social birds, often soaring at different levels in groups of three, four, or many more. These spiraling formations are called *kettles*. Turkey vultures also feed together on large animal carcasses. They are most gregarious at night, when hundreds may roost together, often in tall electric towers or large trees. These communal roosts occur year-round, and the birds' fidelity to the same roosting sites may last for years. Before leaving roosts in the morning, vultures often stand with wings outspread in the sun, raising their lowered nighttime temperatures. On the ground, turkey vultures are awkward and graceless. They hop, shuffle, and sidle as if crippled, sometimes uttering hisses and raucous grunts. They often defecate on their legs, which gives the legs a whitened appearance and may help regulate their temperature on hot days.

Turkey vultures are migratory in North America. Their breeding range spans the Western Hemisphere from southern Canada to Cape Horn.

Spring. Turkey vultures move into their northern breeding areas from early March through May. From Panama they travel by day, covering more than three thousand miles to the upper Midwest in about ten days without feeding. Often while traveling, they ride up over advancing storm fronts, sometimes up to four miles high. Courtship behaviors include follow flight, in which a female leads a male in a series of soaring maneuvers. Breeding territory probably extends only around the nest vicinity. Turkey vulture home range, however—the aerial distance it covers in hunting for carcasses— probably extends many miles. One study arrived at a figure of about eleven thousand acres.

Regurgitation of carrion makes the nest a putrid-smelling site. When threatened near the nest, turkey vultures often vomit; the stench may have the same defensive function as a skunk's spray. If that doesn't work, the birds may collapse and play dead. Vulture pairs, which probably mate for life, often return to the same nest sites year after year.

EGGS AND YOUNG: two; eggs white with brown spots and blotches. INCUBATION: by both sexes; five or six weeks. FEEDING OF YOUNG: by both sexes; regurgitated carrion. FLEDGING: about six weeks.

Summer. Juvenile vultures have brownish, smooth heads instead of red, wrinkled ones, and their beaks are dark tipped in contrast to the adult's uniformly ivory-colored one. The juveniles join adult birds at communal roosts, which may serve as information centers; that is, birds may follow roost mates to known carcass sites. Often the birds settle into roosts about an hour before sunset. The annual feather molt of adult birds proceeds gradually through summer into fall.

Fall. Turkey vultures begin their withdrawal from northern areas in September and October, often grouping into large, soaring kettles that circle steadily southward. Probably even southern U.S. turkey vultures shift southward as northern vultures supplant them. Wintering turkey vultures reside north to the Ohio River; isolated vultures may remain farther north, especially during mild winters. But much of the North American population passes south through Mexico and Central America. Peak flights in early November over Panama City have numbered almost two hundred thousand birds per day.

Winter. Winter activities consist solely of hunting carrion and feeding. In the Neotropical rain forest, turkey vultures cruise low above the dense tree canopy. Their northward movements begin in late winter. During this migration, they appear at certain locations with great regularity, seldom varying by more than a day or so each year.

Ecology. Nesting and feeding habitats differ. The birds favor isolated nest sites—dark recesses in caves, rocky cliffs, hollow logs, tree snags, or brush piles; on the ground in dense thickets; or in abandoned barns or other buildings. Foraging habitats, except in the rain forest, are open lands and fields where carrion may be easily located.

Turkey vultures use no nesting materials. The nest itself is merely a bare surface of gravel, rotted wood debris, or old flooring.

Debate raged for years among scientists over whether vultures locate carrion primarily by sight or by smell. Probably they use both senses. Vultures cannot detect a carcass by smell until it is about twelve hours old, and they prefer fresher carcasses over badly rotted ones. Above a certain height, it seems unlikely that their smell apparatus, good as it is, can detect food. In the rain forest, where they must cruise low, they apparently locate carcasses exclusively by smell. Their keen vision, equaling that of hawks, enables vultures to spot carcasses from high altitudes and also to watch the movements of other soaring vultures or ground scavengers that may find food.

A favorite food is dead snakes. Often a vulture's first item of choice is the eyes of a carcass. When feeding on dead skunks, they leave only bones and scent glands (great horned owls are not so fastidious). Occasionally they also feed on vegetable matter such as rotting pumpkins. One study found that turkey vultures fed on carcasses mainly during midday hours; during later afternoon, when thermal updrafts were strongest, they soared at high altitudes, possibly searching for the next day's meal. A few records exist of turkey vultures' attacking small or weak living prey, but these cases are rare. After feeding, the birds regurgitate pellets containing fur, bones, and other indigestible materials.

Especially in the rain forest, vultures must compete with mammal and insect scavengers in finding carcasses quickly. In North America, American crows, common ravens, and many mammals, including foxes, coyotes, and raccoons, vigorously compete with turkey vultures, especially at large carcasses.

No regular predators exist, though eggs and young may sometimes be taken by ground mammals such as skunks or raccoons that may brave the foul "barf barrier."

Focus. Turkey buzzard is a popular name for this vulture, though the true buzzard (*Buteo buteo*) is not a vulture at all but a European hawk. The turkey designation refers to the bird's red, turkeylike head (a few American colonial hunters, thinking they had shot turkeys, reported a "most disagreeable flavor"). The word *vulture* derives from a Latin word meaning to pluck or tear.

New World vultures were long classified as raptors closely related to hawks, ospreys, and falcons. Recently, however, bird taxonomists officially certified what vulture researchers had long known—that the birds are "nothing but short-legged storks," as one eminent ornithologist stated. Vulture feet, unlike those of raptors, are not adapted for grasping; the talons are weakly hooked, and the foot cannot fist.

The vulture's image in our culture is one of grim death, symbolizing the charnel house; it is the sinister, patient awaiter of a victim's certain demise. Even many famous bird lovers have found it difficult to accept this "winged ghoul" in the same class of creatures as robins and bluebirds.

Today, however, we know that vultures perform vital environmental services. Not only do they scavenge dead animals, helping recycle their bodily constituents, but they also are sanitarians in another sense: Their corrosive digestive system kills several deadly disease organisms, including *Salmonella* and bacteria that produce hog cholera, anthrax, and botulinum toxins. Other vulture adaptations include their bald heads, which shed gore, allowing them to probe deeply into carcasses; their razor-sharp, hooked beaks, efficient as butchers' shears; and their rough, raspy tongues.

Turkey vulture populations have shifted remarkably at various times and places. Since about 1920, the birds have expanded their range considerably, and they continue to do so. Probably the abundance of road-killed carcasses and increasing white-tailed deer populations account for much of this expansion. In some areas they have become aircraft hazards. The U.S. Air Force blamed them for the loss of ten military planes from 1989 to 1994 and began mapping their seasonal densities. Highest concentrations—up to forty vultures per ten square miles—were found in skies over Florida and Texas.

The northward movement of turkey vultures in March has put one small town on the tourist map. Hinckley, Ohio, located south of Cleveland, celebrates a Buzzard Sunday festival every year on the first Sunday after March 15, the date when townsfolk claim the vultures show up. The vultures usually are there by that date, but most years they probably first appear days or weeks earlier, when the chamber of commerce isn't looking.

Closer look. Wilbur, S. R. T., and J. A. Jackson, eds. *Vulture Biology and Management.* Berkeley: University of California Press, 1983.

12

TYRANT FLYCATCHER FAMILY (Tyrannidae), order Passeriformes

Flycatchers introduce the order of perching birds, or *passerines.* Passerines include about 60 percent of all bird species—some fifty-seven hundred. All birds in the remainder of the book are passerines, thus the order name will henceforth be omitted from species headings. Passerine birds show a distinctive *anisodactyl* foot, in which three toes point forward and one backward, all joining the foot at the same level—a foot adapted for perching rather than clinging (as in swifts and woodpeckers), grasping (as in raptors), or scratching (as in gamebirds). The passerine foot relates to many behavioral characteristics, enabling these birds to specialize in certain ecological slots, or *niches,* that might otherwise remain unexploited by birds. Except for flycatchers, most passerines are classified as songbirds, or *oscines.* Flycatchers, though many sing by any conventional definition, possess fewer syrinx, or voice, muscles than true songbirds and are therefore labeled *suboscines.*

North American flycatchers show somewhat flattened bills bearing *rictal bristles,* or whiskers, at the base. Strong ligaments connecting upper and lower jaws snap the bill shut, as if spring loaded, on a flying insect. Flycatchers use a sit-and-wait strategy, launching forth in brief, looping flights from a perch to capture insects.

Despite the name, flies actually rank fairly low in most flycatcher diets; hymenopterans (ants, bees, and wasps), moths, and beetles are more frequent food items. Flycatchers provide important biological controls on insect populations, and sizes of various flycatcher species correlate with the sizes of the flying insects they seek. The ecological pattern in eastern deciduous forests, one well-known study concluded, seems to be a ratio of one large flycatcher (the great crested) to one small flycatcher (wood-pewee or a forest *Empidonax*) in any given woodland. Other studies point to a pattern of large, medium, and small flycatcher species coexisting. Food size differences apparently reduce competition between great crested flycatchers and the smaller woodland flycatchers.

Northeastern tyrant flycatchers omitted from the following accounts include the olive-sided flycatcher (*Contopus borealis*), the yellow-bellied flycatcher (*Empidonax flaviventris*), and the eastern kingbird (*Tyrannis tyrannis*). More than three hundred sixty tyrant flycatcher species, thirty-two of which breed in North America, reside in the Western Hemisphere. Most occupy numerous habitats in South America, where some 10 percent of all birds belong to this family. All North American flycatchers are night-traveling migrants.

TYRANT FLYCATCHER FAMILY (Tyrannidae)

Eastern Wood-Pewee (*Contopus virens*)

This sparrow-size woodland flycatcher, more easily identified by sound than by sight, is a drab, olive-gray bird. It bears strong similarities to eastern phoebes and *Empidonax* flycatchers. Its size, habitat, two narrow white wing bars, and lack of an eye ring are useful visual field marks. Most distinctive are its plaintive, slurring "pee-a-wee" and "pee-ur" whistles, often uttered at regular intervals over long periods. Sexes look alike.

Close relatives. The olive-sided flycatcher (*C. borealis*), a far northern species, is the wood-pewee's closest eastern relative. In the West is found the western wood-pewee (*C. sordidulus*) and in the Southwest the greater pewee (*C. pertinax*).

Behaviors. Wood-pewees seem sedate, often perching at long intervals in one spot. Residing in the forest subcanopy, they sally out occasionally to capture a flying insect, then return to the perch. In one study, wood-pewees fed at a mean height of thirty-five feet. In many areas of their breeding range, which spans the eastern United

States from southern Canada to the Gulf, these are the most abundant flycatchers.

Spring. Wood-pewees are among the latest spring arrivals, appearing on their breeding range after tree foliage has fully emerged—about mid-May in the North. Males precede females by a few days and begin singing immediately. Rise early to hear the wood-pewee's dawn song; unlike its typical daytime song, which contains long pauses between phrases, the early song is a continuous soliloquy, lasting for a half hour or longer. Males establish woodland territories of two to six acres; courtship chases through the trees may originate as male defensive behavior, since both sexes look alike. Pairing occurs with little ceremony, and nesting seldom begins before late May. These birds are probably seasonally monogamous. Some females may return to the same branch to build where they have previously nested.

EGGS AND YOUNG: usually three; eggs white, wreathed with brown splotches. INCUBATION: by female; about twelve days. FEEDING OF YOUNG: by both sexes; insects. FLEDGING: about fifteen days.

Summer. Wood-pewee nesting in the North usually peaks in early summer, but late nesters may still be feeding young into July or August. Unlike most passerines, which cease regular singing as summer progresses, wood-pewee males continue vocalizing and are often the only regular songsters to be heard as migration time approaches. Juveniles, showing lighter, more distinctive wing bars than the adults, follow their parents for much of the summer. The annual molt begins in late summer, extending into fall.

Fall. Most wood-pewees have left their northernmost range by the end of September, but their migratory progress, as in spring, is leisurely. They arrive on their winter range in October to early November.

Winter. Wood-pewee winter range extends from Panama to Bolivia, occupying Pacific and Amazon rain forests. Most arrive in rainy-season October, coinciding with peak insect populations. The birds remain solitary in a variety of wooded and edge habitats. Individuals of both sexes sing and defend their own feeding territories. In some areas, wood-pewees replace a resident ecological counterpart, the vermilion flycatcher (*Pyrocephalus rubinus*), which migrates southward to breed before wood-pewees arrive.

Ecology. Wood-pewees strongly favor deciduous forests with open or broken canopies, usually near an opening or edge area. But their adaptability to diverse wooded habitats—deciduous and mixed, mature and open, plus forest edges—probably accounts for this flycatcher's abundance. Residential areas, parks, and orchards are also common wood-pewee habitats. Wood-pewees most often perch and sing on high, shady branches just beneath the tree crown. On its winter range in the rain forest, the bird frequents the cecropia canopy and young stands of fig along rivers and forest openings.

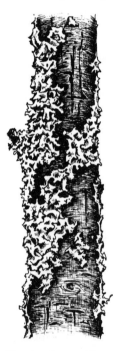

The wood-pewee's small, shallow nest is a marvel of camouflage almost impossible to detect from beneath; it resembles a knot or fungus growth, much like a large version of the ruby-throated hummingbird's nest. The cup typically straddles a horizontal fork of a dead, often lichen-encrusted limb well out from the trunk some twenty or thirty feet high, although nests also may be found on apple tree limbs in overgrown orchards. Grasses, plant fibers, and hairs are attached with spider silk, and the nest is sheathed with lichens on the outside.

Tree trunks provide abundant lichen sources for nest building by the wood-pewee and a few other species. Often these birds nest in trees that show much lichen growth, which helps camouflage the nests.

Wood-pewees feed almost entirely on insects, mainly flies, small wasps, beetles, and moths. They also glean caterpillars, beetles, ants, and other insects from leaves, twigs, and spiderwebs. In summer and fall, they consume berries, including elderberries, blackberries, and dogwood and pokeweed fruits, but fruits make up only a small percentage of their total diet.

Although Acadian and least flycatchers also inhabit woodlands and might seem likely food competitors, each flycatcher species exhibits somewhat different habitat preferences regarding the degree of canopy shading and density of undergrowth.

Blue jays are probably the wood-pewee's foremost nest predators, consuming both eggs and young. Brown-headed cowbirds occasionally lay one or more eggs in the nests, but wood-pewees are relatively infrequent victims of cowbird parasitism.

Focus. The name peewee is onomatopoeic, deriving from the bird's song rather than its size (many flycatchers are smaller). The wood-pewee's slurred whistle somewhat resembles the long-drawn, high-pitched call of the broad-winged hawk.

TYRANT FLYCATCHER FAMILY (Tyrannidae)

Acadian, Willow, and Least Flycatchers (*Empidonax virescens, E. traillii,* and *E. minimus*)

Looking much alike, the empids are virtually impossible to distinguish from one another by sight. They are best identified by their varying habitats and songs, which are sharply accented or sneezy "exclamations." Each species measures slightly over five inches long; is grayish with tinges of olive, brown, or yellow; and has eye rings and two whitish wing bars. Sexes look alike.

Close relatives. Of the eleven North American empids, five are northeastern U.S. summer residents: the three discussed here, plus the yellow-bellied flycatcher (*E. flaviventris*), which inhabits northern bogs and conifer forests; and the alder flycatcher (*E. alnorum*), which favors swamps and wetland thickets. Western U.S. empids include the Hammond's flycatcher (*E. hammondii*), dusky flycatcher (*E. oberholseri*), gray flycatcher (*E. wrightii*), buff-breasted flycatcher (*E. fulvifrons*), Pacific-slope flycatcher (*E. difficilis*), and cordilleran flycatcher (*E. occidentalis*).

Behaviors. Trust no expert who purports to identify all empids by sight alone, even in the hand. "Their specific characters are so subtle," warns ornithologist Kenn Kaufman, "that there is often more variation *within* a species than there is *between* any two species in the genus." One researcher suspects that to avoid hybridizing, "even the birds depend heavily on song." But except during migrations, when most empids are silent and may appear in anomalous habitats, their breeding sites and voiced expletives, taken together, are usually reliable identity markers.

Acadians, which have the most southerly breeding range, extending north to the Great Lakes and New England, look greener than the other empids and often seem lethargic and droopy winged as they perch. Their loud, explosive notes, "peet-sah!" or "hick-*up!*" are anything but lethargic, however.

Willow flycatchers, which have a central and more northern breeding range, are also relatively sedate and emit a sneezelike "*fitz*-bew!" The songs of willow and alder flycatchers, unlike those of most birds, are innate rather than learned.

Least flycatchers, grayest of the eastern empids, breed farther north than the other two. Probably the most common empid of the Northeast, the least flycatcher is hyperactive and vocal, seldom remaining long on a perch and often flicking its wings and tail. It sounds a repetitive, snapping "che-*beck!*"

Breeding ranges of all three species overlap in a relatively narrow band from New England west to the southern Great Lakes region. All empids exhibit typical fly-catching behavior when feeding, darting from a perch to snap up insects, then returning. Their breeding territories are not large, usually fractions of an acre. In some areas, loose colonies of least flycatchers sometimes include several nests per acre, each nest pugnaciously defended.

Spring. Least flycatchers usually arrive early in May on their breeding range, two or three weeks before the other two species. Acadian and willow males arrive earlier than females. All three species show courtship chasing behaviors. Acadians, at least, usually mate for life and return to the same territories each year, but all three species occasionally exhibit polygyny (one male mating with more than one monogamous female).

EGGS AND YOUNG: three or four; eggs white in least flycatchers, buff in willow, brown spotted in Acadian and willow. INCUBATION: by females; about two weeks. FEEDING OF YOUNG: by both sexes; insects. FLEDGING: about two weeks.

Summer. Acadian flycatchers often raise a second brood in July, but willows and leasts usually renest only if the first attempt fails. As late spring breeders, leasts are still nesting in early summer; nesting of willow flycatchers extends into July or August. Adult leasts often are moving south by late July, their juveniles following in late August or early September. Willow flycatchers depart their territories in August, and Acadians before mid-September. Acadians are the only eastern empids that molt into new plumage before migration; the others often look very worn and drab by late summer.

Fall. All three species have left the continental United States by early October (leasts about a month earlier), moving southwest through Mexico. Willow and least flycatchers undergo their annual molt after their arrival on winter ranges.

Winter. Acadians concentrate mainly in eastern Colombia and eastern Ecuador, where they occupy rain-forest habitats. Here they often follow columns of army ants (*Eciton, Labidus*), capturing insects flushed by the ants.

Central and northern South America are the winter homes of willow flycatchers.

Least flycatchers mingle with yellow-bellied flycatchers in mimosa thickets and forest undergrowth in Mexico and Central America south to Panama. Willow and least flycatchers apparently undergo another partial molt in late winter before migrating north.

Ecology. Acadian flycatchers are forest-interior birds, favoring large tracts of contiguous, dense-canopied, wet or moist deciduous forests, as in floodplains and river lowlands. Less favored habitats include mesic (moderately moist) and dry woodlots and mixed hardwood-conifer forests. On their winter range, they occupy thickets and humid forest edges.

Willow flycatchers reside in shrubby edges—swamp and forest borders, roadsides, and overgrown fields—often in the same habitats as yellow warblers and American goldfinches. Though they favor more open, drier habitats than alder flycatchers, the two species sometimes coexist in shrubby wetland sites. Willow flycatcher winter habitats are mainly brushy edges and second-growth woodlands.

Least flycatchers are probably the most adaptable of the three to various habitats. They primarily reside in open deciduous and mixed woodlands, as well as orchards and parks. They especially favor young aspen stands, but they also occupy river borders and damp woods. In winter, they inhabit brushy clearings and edges.

Females of each species do all the nest building. Cup shaped and often placed in shrubs, empid nests usually show defining species characteristics.

Acadian flycatcher nests, which usually dangle materials, may resemble clumps of vegetation deposited by flood waters.

Acadians build near the end of a shaded, downward-slanting branch about thirteen feet high, often over a path, woodland pool, or other opening. The shallow, hammocklike basket looks unkempt and trashy, dangling long stems and grasses as if falling apart (the eggs occasionally do fall through). American beech trees are frequent nesting sites. Nest materials include fine plant stems and fibers, rootlets, coiled tendrils of wild grape, and adherent webbing, the source of which is the silk of geometer moth caterpillars, such as cankerworms, dangling from tree foliage.

Willow flycatcher nests, often built in the fork of a hawthorn, dogwood, or willow shrub, are placed about four feet high. The compact grassy cup commonly contains feathers in the rim as well as cottony down from milkweeds and thistles. Milkweed bark on the outside gives it a silvery resemblance to yellow warbler and American goldfinch nests, though the willow's nest often has materials dangling from the bottom.

Nests of least flycatchers, which resemble yellow warbler and American redstart nests, are typically placed about fifteen feet high adjacent to the trunk or straddling a forked limb close to the trunk. Leasts often build in spindly trees such as young aspens, but they also favor old apple trees. This bird uses bark shreds, fine stems, plant fibers, and down to craft its compact cup; often it weaves spider cocoons and bits of paper and string into the nest body.

Empids are almost exclusively insect eaters; hymenopterans (ants, bees, and wasps) constitute some 40 percent of their diet. Moths—both caterpillars and adults—also rank high as foods, as do beetles. Many insects are caught in flight, but empids also glean from leaves and twigs. In late summer and fall, they consume relatively small quantities of berries, including elderberries, blackberries, and dogwood fruits, plus seeds.

In some areas leasts share breeding habitats with Acadians, in others with American redstarts; toward the latter, leasts are strongly territorial. Although favored habitats of Acadian and least flycatchers usually differ, food competition may occur in areas of overlap. Willow and alder flycatcher habitats often overlap, and these birds defend their territories from each other, probably indicating competition for food and nest sites. On their winter ranges, as biologist Julie A. Craves points out, North Amer-

Least flycatcher nests, though resembling nests of several other species in its habitats, usually show pieces of curled bark strips on the outside.

ican flycatchers "must fit in with the numerous resident flycatchers as well as other families of birds. The lives of all these birds interlock . . . to fit together like a finely-crafted jigsaw puzzle," thus narrowing competitive interactions. Probably no major predator exists. I once watched a black rat snake climb a shrub in the vicinity of an Acadian nest. House sparrows and gray squirrels have been observed attacking least flycatcher nests. Nests of all three empids, especially those in edge areas, are vulnerable to nest parasitism by brown-headed cowbirds, and most parasitized Acadian and least nests raise only cowbird nestlings.

Focus. *Empidonax* is a Greek term meaning "king of the gnats," probably a reference to the birds' insect diet. The Acadian supposedly owes its common name—as do so many of our birds—to bad science. The first bird given this name, goes the tale, was taken in Acadia, an early name for Nova Scotia. Since this land lies far north of the Acadian's range, the empid was probably misidentified. The name was preserved, however, for the bird that later ornithologists also mislabeled as green-crested flycatcher. So one misnomer succeeded another, and the first survives.

The Acadian is an area-sensitive species, dependent on contiguous forest tracts of more than one hundred twenty acres; thus forest fragmentation is depleting its abundance. Willow flycatchers are apparently expanding their breeding range northward. I bear nostalgic affection for this flycatcher, since it was the first bird that I identified by using a field guide. Vibrating with energy and almost explosive with song, it lured me into serious bird study. The naming history of this bird is tortuous; deciding what to call it has kept two generations of bird taxonomists busy (and given the rest of us fits). As a lad, I knew the bird by its then accepted name, the alder flycatcher. Later it was renamed Traill's flycatcher (*E. traillii*). In 1973, taxonomists upgraded its two subspecies into separate species named willow and alder flycatchers, based on vocal and habitat differences (both species are now collectively designated Traill's flycatchers). Naming these nondescript little birds correctly is only one of the problems arising from their lookalike appearances.

The least flycatcher's name is accurate, since it's the smallest northeastern empid, by about a quarter inch. It was once known as the little flycatcher.

Closer look. Kaufman, K. *A Field Guide to Advanced Birding.* Boston: Houghton Mifflin, 1990.

TYRANT FLYCATCHER FAMILY (Tyrannidae)

Eastern Phoebe (*Sayornis phoebe*)

The phoebe can be recognized by its sparrow size, darker head than back, lack of eye rings or wing bars, frequent tail bobbing, and hoarse, emphatic "fi-*bree!*" song. Sexes look alike and both sing, though females less often than males. Juveniles are olive-brown with dull wing bars and yellowish breasts.

Close relatives. The three phoebe species all breed in North America. The black phoebe (*S. nigricans*) and Say's phoebe (*S. saya*) are western U.S. residents.

Behaviors. To many people, phoebes, despite their nondescript plumage, are the most familiar flycatchers of all because they frequently nest on buildings and other human-made structures. Perching conspicuously and uttering their incessant two-note song, phoebes are easily observed, especially in early spring. They are migratory, though a few may linger north over winter. Breeding range encompasses most of the eastern states extending into Canada.

Spring. One of the earliest migrants, the phoebe often arrives on its breeding range during the last days of winter or first days of spring. Males precede females by a week or two, returning to their previous breeding territories and quickly announcing their arrival by repetitive song. Flying insects, their chief food, are not yet abundant, but gnats and other tiny flies become numerous and active around water and in sheltered microhabitats during warmer daylight hours; thus the phoebe's arrival heralds the awakening of seasonal insect life. With the arrival of the female—either a previous mate or another female attracted by the male's song—song lessens in frequency. Males patrol the territory, which usually encompasses

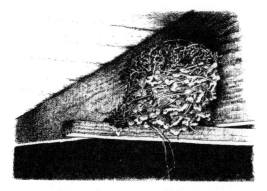

Phoebes often build their cushiony moss nests atop vacated mud nests of barn swallows. Mites frequently infest phoebe nests, sometimes killing the nestlings.

several acres, sometimes with wing-fluttering flight displays, but since phoebe territories usually are well dispersed, conflicts seldom occur. Females build the nests, sometimes only adding materials to a nest of the previous year or renovating a barn swallow's old nest. Sometimes she builds several nests, in whole or in part, before selecting one. Often after finishing a nest, a female abandons it for up to three weeks before she returns to lay eggs. Ground foraging by parent birds, instead of insect catching on the wing, signals that they are feeding nestlings.

Fledglings remain in the nest vicinity for about three weeks. Only a few days after the first brood fledges (early June), the female is ready to renest, often in the same renovated site; the male may resume morning singing while also feeding the first fledglings.

EGGS AND YOUNG: four or five; eggs white. INCUBATION: by female; about sixteen days. FEEDING OF YOUNG: by both sexes; regurgitated insects for first few days. FLEDGING: about eighteen days.

Summer. Second broods have usually fledged by early July, but juveniles of both broods remain on or near the parental territory until late summer. Phoebes fall silent after breeding, uttering only occasional notes. In August and September, the annual feather molt occurs.

Fall. Pairs have now split, juveniles have dispersed, and the birds become solitary until next spring. Having arrived early, phoebes also stay late, commonly into November, and drift south slowly.

Winter. Most phoebes spend winter in the Gulf states south to eastern Mexico; occasional birds remain north to the Great Lakes and Long Island. Many of the latter, plus northward migrators caught in late-season blizzards, do not survive. The migrants are moving north again by late winter.

Ecology. Open woodlands, wet woods, and wooded streambanks are favored natural habitats, but this species has, to a large extent, adapted to human environs—farmyards, roadways, and suburbs. Bridges, abandoned houses, old barns, outhouses, and structures overgrown by weeds and thickets provide ideal nest sites. Ponds or streams, where phoebes often feed on the wing, are important habitat components.

A flat or vertical surface with at least minimal overhead shelter is the phoebe's main requirement for a nest site. Before human settlement, it found these sites in rocky ravines, cliff niches, and tree blowdowns. Today the most commonly used sites include girders, trestles, road culverts, rafters, windowsills, well shafts, and ledges.

Two kinds of nests exist, depending on the site. *Statant* nests (nests built on flat surfaces) are the most common. Phoebes also build *adherent* nests, semicircular nests attached to vertical walls. Adherent nests are often mud-plastered against a surface projection such as the mud tubes of mud-dauber wasps. To begin building, the female tosses mud from her bill against the vertical surface. Nests, whether statant or adherent, are built of mud, grasses, and weeds; lined with soft plant materials and hairs; and commonly covered with mosses, a distinctive feature. Moss species used include *Funaria, Hypnum, Mnium,* and *Polytrichum.*

Winter and early-spring diets, before flying insects become abundant, consist of seeds, wild berries, and occasionally small fish and frogs. Insects and spiders, however, form 90 percent of the annual diet. As with most northern flycatchers, hymenopterans (wasps, bees, and ants) are the most frequently consumed insects; dragonflies, beetles, grasshoppers, and adult tent moths also rank high.

Phoebe nesting associates may include rock pigeons, chimney swifts, barn swallows, and American robins; other phoebes, however, are not tolerated. Thanks to the abundance of human constructions, phoebe nesting sites are also abundant, and little competition exists with other species that favor similar sites. Food competitors may include swallows and perhaps some of the *Empidonax* flycatchers, but again competition seems negligible. For early-spring migrants and north-wintering phoebes, however, food resources can be sparse, and many fruit and seed foragers may compete for nourishment at these times.

Raptors and raccoons are probably the foremost predators; house wrens are also known to kill phoebe nestlings. White-footed mice sometimes prey on the eggs. Fowl mites (*Ornithonyssus*) often infest phoebe (especially second-brood) nests, and nestlings can be literally eaten alive. I have seen old nests containing desiccated phoebe nestlings, the final result of severe mite infestation. Some researchers believe that phoebes might easily raise third broods but for mite affliction.

Another frequent nest parasite is the brown-headed cowbird, which in some areas may lay eggs in 25 percent of all phoebe nests. Often the phoebe builds over a cowbird egg, burying it along with her own eggs at times. Phoebe nests built on bridge girders seem less often parasitized than those in other sites.

Focus. Novice birders often mistake the clear "*fee*-bee" call of black-capped chickadees for phoebes, whose notes are hoarser, more emphatic. Like songs of some other flycatchers, the phoebe's is innate, not learned.

Eastern phoebes are associated with a notable first in the history of American birding. In his Pennsylvania home, a young John James Audubon tied silver-colored threads on the legs of several phoebe nestlings in 1803. Two of the banded birds showed up the next spring, and the technique of bird banding—an invaluable research tool—was born.

TYRANT FLYCATCHER FAMILY (Tyrannidae)

Great Crested Flycatcher (*Myiarchus crinitus*)

This largest northeastern woodland flycatcher can be identified by its eight- or nine-inch size, yellow belly, gray breast, reddish-brown tail and wing feathers, and loud, emphatic "wheep!" and rolling "prrr-eet!" calls. The bushy crest becomes visible only when an agitated bird erects it. Sexes look alike.

Close relatives. Brown-crested flycatchers (*M. tyrannulus*), ash-throated flycatchers (*M. cinerascens*), and dusky-capped flycatchers (*M. tuberculifer*) are all southwestern U.S. species. Most of the twenty-two *Myiarchus* species reside in South America and the West Indies.

Behaviors. Active and noisy, great crested flycatchers always make themselves vocally known in spring; visually, though their plumage is distinctive, they are hardly spectacular. They pursue flying insects in swift, erratic forays from a perch, sometimes hovering on beating wings. In the treetops, where they most typically perch and yell, they also hop from limb to limb like blue jays with motionless wings and spread tail. Their boisterous clamor voices their extremely defensive territorial behaviors toward other birds and squirrels that venture too near the nest tree, and they often chase and dive at such intruders.

Their breeding range spans the eastern and central United States from southern Canada to the Gulf.

Spring. Great crested flycatchers arrive on their northern breeding range in May, usually to the same territories and mates of the previous year. Males precede females by about a week. In characteristic courtship behaviors, the male chases or hovers in front of a female that is peering from the nest cavity. Nesting commonly begins in June.

The great crested flycatcher profile shows the rictal bristles characteristic of flycatchers. The crest, when erected, is bushy, not pointed as in cardinals or titmice.

EGGS AND YOUNG: usually five; eggs whitish, marked with brown streaks and splotches. INCUBATION: by female; about two weeks. FEEDING OF YOUNG: by both sexes; insects. FLEDGING: two to three weeks.

Summer. Great crested flycatchers produce only one brood, which typically fledges in early summer. Juveniles remain in the parental vicinity for an indefinite period, learning to feed themselves. Adult birds fall silent after nesting is completed. The annual feather molt begins in August, extending into fall.

Fall. This species migrates later than most other flycatchers, often in mid-September. By November, most have left the continent.

Winter. Winter range extends from southern Florida and Mexico south to Cuba, Colombia, and northern Venezuela. The bird occupies open woods and rain forests in these areas. Many great crested flycatchers are migrating northward by early March.

Ecology. Great crested flycatchers favor deciduous and mixed (but rarely coniferous) woodlands of sufficient maturity to provide nest-cavity trees and high canopies for foraging. These habitats may be dense or open, mesic or wet. Forest edges, old orchards, and bottomland woods are also frequent habitats.

As the only hole-nesting flycatcher of eastern North America, this species does not excavate its own cavities. It may choose a natural cavity or hollow in a live tree or an old woodpecker hole in a dead one. Cavity height and tree species are variable. If the cavity is deep, the birds usually fill it almost to the entrance hole with bulky plant materials plus feathers, bits of fur and string, and almost always pieces of cast-off snakeskin, cellophane, or other papery items. They also use birdhouses (often purple martin boxes) and rural mailboxes at times.

Large flying insects—mainly moths, butterflies, beetles, bees, and wasps—are their main food source. The birds also forage from tree leaves and the ground, especially in early spring, taking caterpillars, grasshoppers, crickets, katydids, and true bugs. Other insects plus spiders and occasionally lizards and even hummingbirds are consumed. In late summer and fall, these flycatchers relish fruits, especially those of sassafras and Virginia creeper, as well as wild cherries, viburnum fruits, common spicebush fruits, wild grapes, and common elderberries.

They may face competition for nesting cavities from woodpeckers, especially red-bellied woodpeckers and northern flickers, which do not always excavate new holes each year, as well as from squirrels. Once a cavity is claimed by the flycatchers, however, they defend it vigorously and usually successfully. The foremost cavity usurpers are probably European starlings, whose abundance may preempt most cavity sites in some areas. Food competition from other flycatchers is probably negligible. In any given habitat, various flycatcher species probably select flying insect food by size, thus reducing direct competition.

Squirrels and tree-climbing snakes probably destroy eggs and young on occasion. Past observers theorized that pieces of shed snakeskin in the nest serve as a scarecrow element to frighten off possible predators. Most modern researchers discount that theory, since pieces of onion skin, plastic wrap, or shiny foil are used about as often. Brown-headed cowbirds seldom parasitize cavity nests.

Focus. The regrowth of former timberlands in the northeastern United States has resulted in population expansion of this species. Decrease of Neotropical forests, on the other hand, makes it, along with many other North American migrants, vulnerable to loss of winter habitats. For now, the great crested flycatcher appears to be thriving throughout most of its breeding range. Wise landowners, recognizing the direct bearing of breeding habitat on the presence of this and other insect consumers, take care to preserve standing cavity trees in their woodlots.

13

Red-eyed Vireo (*Vireo olivaceus*)

Vireo family (Vireonidae). With this family we enter the suborder Passeri, the oscines, or true songbirds, comprising some seventy bird families in which singing (though an arbitrary definition) is most highly developed. As ornithologist Gary Ritchison writes, "Singing by male passerines clearly has more kinds of functions than simply territorial advertising and mate attraction. However, discovering such functions requires detailed studies of song use throughout an entire breeding cycle because even subtle changes in singing behavior may convey information." All of the remaining accounts in this book are of songbirds.

This largest (six-inch-long), most common northern vireo can be identified by its olive-gray upper parts, gray cap, black-bordered white eye stripe, and—in close view—red eyes. It voices its robin-like song in short, abrupt phrases—"Who is it? You know it. Is that

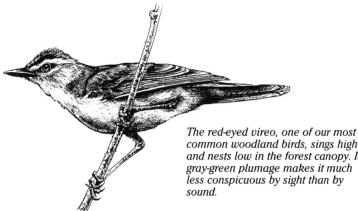

The red-eyed vireo, one of our most common woodland birds, sings high and nests low in the forest canopy. Its gray-green plumage makes it much less conspicuous by sight than by sound.

you? Who sees it?"—often repeating for an hour or longer without a break. Vireo bills are slightly arched and hooked at the tip. Sexes look alike.

Close relatives. Five other northeastern vireos include the white-eyed vireo (*V. griseus*), yellow-throated vireo (*V. flavifrons*), solitary vireo (*V. solitarius*), warbling vireo (*V. gilvus*), and Philadelphia vireo (*V. philadelphicus*). Several others inhabit the western and southern states. The more than forty total species are exclusively New World residents; many of the smaller Neotropical species are called greenlets.

Behaviors. This vireo is often the most abundant bird in northeastern mature deciduous forests. Nicknamed the preacher because of its monotonous song (the namer, wrote naturalist Bradford Torrey, "could have had no very exalted opinion of the clergy"), the male voices some forty song phrases, rarely repeated in succession. The bird's greenish plumage, closely resembling that of the Tennessee warbler, blends well with the leaves of the high canopy. There it forages and sings, often perched on an outer branch. I have spent many frustrated minutes of my life looking directly at this songster, I felt certain, without seeing it. Red-eyeds also voice notes quite unlike their song—a nasal whining *"chway"* or "peevish snarl," as variously described.

Red-eyed vireo breeding range spans almost the entire continent from mid-Canada south except for the southwestern states. These birds are migrators.

Spring. Males precede females on the breeding range by a few days, establishing territories one or two acres in size by song, noise, and much aggressive chasing. In vertical space, vireo territory has been described as a cylinder extending from the forest canopy down to the lowest shrubs. Probably most adult vireos return to their previous territories; they are at least seasonally monogamous. Females, when they arrive, rarely sing and tend to forage in the lower canopy. Males, by contrast, sing and feed in the upper tree zones. Courtship behaviors include a distinctive, trance-like swaying of the perched male in front of a female. Nesting seldom begins before June; females do the work, both of site selection and of building, while their mates proclaim from the treetops. This incessant male song, which continues all through nesting, apparently forms a vital stimulus to female incubation—she becomes restless and agitated when he ceases for any length of time.

EGGS AND YOUNG: usually four; eggs white, sparsely brown spotted. INCUBATION: by female; about two weeks. FEEDING OF YOUNG: by both sexes; insects, land snails, spiders. FLEDGING: about ten days.

Summer. Red-eyeds usually raise only one brood in the North, but often two in their southern breeding range. Territorial bounds lapse after the young birds fledge. The parents continue to feed them for several weeks as family groups roam. Males may resume singing briefly in late summer, just before migration.

Fall. Molting into new plumage occurs more or less concurrently with southward migration in September. Vireos migrate at night. The entire population departs the continental United States, passing singly or in small flocks through Central America.

Winter. "And where is that young family now," wondered Thoreau in February, "while their cradle is filled with ice?" The red-eyed's winter range is in the Amazon rain forests, including much of northern South America, where it joins and may compete with a year-round resident subspecies (*V. o. chivi*). Here the birds, now seldom vocal, often feed in flocks.

Ecology. During the breeding season, red-eyed vireos are *the* characteristic tree-canopy birds of the eastern deciduous forest. They thrive best in contiguous forest stands containing moderate to dense understory shrubs or small trees. On the winter range, they inhabit tropical evergreen forest.

Red-eyeds often place their tree nests near a trail, road, or opening in the woods. Vireo nests are distinctive, durable pieces of architecture—pensile cups suspended by their rims from two small, forking, horizontal branches. In contrast to the bird's elusive visibility in the treetops, nests are often easy to spot; many are placed less than ten feet high. Grasses, weed filaments, bark strips, bits of paper (sometimes from wasp nests), and rootlets form the main construction. Spider silk and lichens are often worked into the exterior. After the birds vacate, white-footed mice sometimes adopt the nests, piling them with soft plant materials.

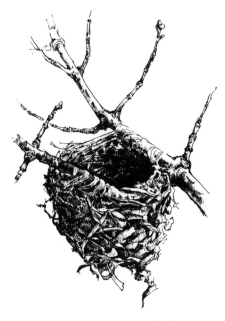

In their breeding range, red-eyeds are foliage gleaners. They consume leaf insects, mainly caterpillars, almost exclusively. Much of this diet consists of irruptive foliage eaters, including gypsy moths, eastern and forest tent caterpillars, and fall web-worms. In summer, they vary their insect fare with blackberries, elderberries, and fruits of dogwoods, sassafras, cherries,

Vireo nests are strong, suspended cups, often lasting long after the birds have vacated. Easy to find, especially after leaves drop in the fall, the nest frequently hangs from head-high branches or lower.

and others. Slow, methodical foragers, they eat few dry seeds, though an important food during fall migration through southern states is the oily, beanlike seed of the southern magnolia. In their winter range, red-eyeds are primarily fruit eaters.

Competitors consist mainly of other foliage-gleaning vireo species. In the red-eyed's northern breeding range, Philadelphia vireos show similar foraging strategies and diets, and each species defends its territories from the other. Yellow-throated vireos also forage in the canopy, but whereas red-eyeds hover and glean, yellow-throateds often stalk insects along branches. They also favor habitats with less shrub understory than red-eyeds select.

Accipiter hawks sometimes capture vireos, and chipmunks and red squirrels are known nest predators. The birds also react aggressively to blue jays. But probably the red-eyed's foremost enemy is the brown-headed cowbird, which parasitizes 40 to 70 percent of its nests (see illustration, Brown-headed Cowbird). Vireos frequently incubate a full nest of cowbird eggs and none of their own. Occasionally they may bury a cowbird egg in the nest. The indirect cause of this parasitism is probably forest fragmentation by humans. Pesticide campaigns against irruptive moth species also result in vireo nest failures.

Focus. Many ornithologists believe that this vireo was once North America's most abundant forest bird (presumably discounting the now-extinct passenger pigeon). Cowbird parasitism and the red-eyed's sensitivity to loss of contiguous forest habitats, including Amazon rain forests, have resulted in a general, long-term pattern of decline, as is true of many songbirds. Yet despite such threats, this vireo continues to hold its own in many areas. An important indicator of forest well-being, the red-eyed is a key species to watch for early-warning signs of environmental distress.

The word *vireo* is said to be Latin for "greenfinch." I prefer, however, to think that the trisyllable simply derives from a phrase of the bird's own language.

14

CROW AND JAY FAMILY (Corvidae)

Testing the definition of songbird are the corvids, which include our largest passerine birds. Raucous songs and calls; strong, heavy bills; various dark or bright plumages; and omnivorous feeding habits mark this group. Many corvids forage by a jaw muscle movement called *gaping,* and many cache food items for later consumption. Corvids often harass—and are harassed by—other bird species. About one hundred species, including magpies *(Pica)* and nutcrackers *(Nucifraga),* exist worldwide.

Closer look. Angell, T. *Ravens, Crows, Magpies, and Jays.* Seattle: University of Washington Press, 1978.

CROW AND JAY FAMILY (Corvidae)

Blue Jay *(Cyanocitta cristata)*

Its foot-long size; blue crest, back, and tail; black "necklace"; gregarious behaviors; and harsh "jay" calls easily identify this common corvid. Actually, it produces a whole repertoire of sounds, including imitations of other birds. Sexes look alike, but summer jays in worn plumage sometimes appear more gray than blue.

Close relatives. Steller's jay *(C. stelleri)* is the blue jay's western counterpart, often hybridizing with it where their ranges meet. The gray jay *(Perisoreus canadensis)* of northern forests is the only other northeastern jay. Three scrub-jay species *(Aphelocoma)* inhabit Florida and the western states. About forty jay species exist worldwide.

The blue jay, ecologically one of our most important birds, is also one of the most common in all seasons. It loudly mobs large raptors and mimics the calls of several.

Behaviors. Flocking in blue jays is common at most times of the year. A troop of blue jays invariably announces its presence, but when blue jays pair during the breeding season, these birds seem to change personality and become silent, even secretive. Blue jays are noisiest when they spot a hawk, owl, prowling cat, squirrel, or snake, often mobbing the creature and excitedly advertising its presence (listening for blue jay caucuses is a good way of locating perched raptors). When not nesting, blue jays vocalize numerous sounds. Besides the familiar raucous alarm or attention calls, the squeaky gate call—"queedle queedle"—and a rattle that sounds like stones clicking together are commonly heard. Blue jays also imitate to perfection the "kee-yer" calls of red-shouldered hawks and, less commonly, the calls of red-tailed and broad-winged hawks. Amid all this jay cacophony, count yourself favored if you hear a much more infrequent sound—the soft, sweet, musical soliloquy of a solitary blue jay perched in dense foliage. In contrast to most birds, vocal behaviors of blue jays apparently have little to do with territorial defense or attracting mates; instead, they are most often flock related, serving as messages of contact, stimulation, and alarm. At food sources, a blue jay often gobbles as fast as it can, storing nuts and seeds in its expandable throat, later disgorging them for caching or feeding. When actually feeding, it grasps the seed or nut between its feet, pounding with unerring aim until the shell cracks open.

Northern blue jay populations migrate in large daytime flocks to and from the upper Great Lakes and Canada. The birds are year-round residents, however, throughout most of the eastern states.

Spring. Northern breeding populations move northward in April and May, often in noisy flocks of thousands. Nowhere have I seen so many blue jays massed as at Whitefish Point Bird Observatory on Lake Superior, a prominent migratory channel. Here the passage of some fifty thousand blue jays has been recorded in one spring.

Blue jay courtship, as so many of their behaviors, occurs in the flock context. Small groups of three to ten males (probably yearling birds) attach to one female, bobbing and uttering bell-like "toolool" and rattle calls. Gradually the males drop out, perhaps intimidated by displays of other males, until only a male-female pair is left. Older jays that have previously bred apparently pair earlier without joining courtship flocks. After pairing, the male often feeds the female, transferring food from bill to bill. Blue jays strongly defend their nests from intruders but seem oblivious to other jays in the vicinity except those in the same stage of the breeding cycle. Away from the nest, territorial boundaries seem ill defined in this species, though the birds usually remain within a given home range (also of indeterminate size) throughout the breeding season. Two or three pairs per hundred acres is probably an average figure. Nesting jays fall silent until the nestlings fledge but often rob and consume the contents of other species' nests at this time. Most jays probably remain monogamous only for a single breeding season.

EGGS AND YOUNG: four or five; eggs olive or buff, brown spotted. INCUBATION: by female; about seventeen days. FEEDING OF YOUNG: by both sexes; insects, other invertebrates, carrion. FLEDGING: about twenty days.

Summer. Blue jays raise only one brood in their northern range, two in the southern. Family groups remain together for one to two months, the parents continuing to feed clamorous juveniles even when full-grown. The annual feather molt occurs in late July and

August, and observers sometimes report bald blue jays when head feathers molt.

Fall. With fresh plumage, the birds appear their most immaculate blue. Family groups join in late summer and fall to form larger foraging flocks, which disperse into smaller flocks as the weather chills. Farthest north populations in Canada withdraw south in September and October, and the juveniles of northern U.S. populations also move south. None of these migrants, however, depart the continental United States.

Winter. Blue jays remain throughout winter in most of their central and southern range. Farther north—in Michigan, for example—winter jays may be either local year-round residents or wintering migrants. Winter flocks average four to six birds, which feed and roam together, though solitary jays are not uncommon. Larger flocks begin to form in late winter as courtship activities commence.

Ecology. Mature, deciduous, mixed, and pine forests are the blue jay's foremost breeding habitats. Jays also reside in open woods and savannas, small woodlots, orchards, conifer plantations, and suburban areas. This bird's adaptable use of so many habitat types accounts in large part for its abundance.

Both sexes gather nesting materials, males breaking twigs directly off trees, and several preliminary nest platforms may be started and abandoned. This mock nest building is apparently also a courtship behavior. The actual breeding nest, built mainly by the female, nears completion when mating occurs. Blue jay

Densely foliaged conifers, such as these red cedars, frequently host blue jay nests. Females may partially build several dummy nests before choosing a final site.

nests are bulky masses of sticks, bark strips, mosses, string, paper, and occasionally mud, holding a cup lined with fine rootlets. Nests are usually well camouflaged, placed ten to twenty feet high in a crotch or outer branch. The birds often build in pines and red cedars, as well as in other trees, woodland shrubs, and even garden vines and trellises.

Although it consumes many sorts of plant and animal foods, this omnivorous bird is mainly vegetarian; acorns, beechnuts, fruits, and seeds are its staples. But in spring, as it seeks protein foods, it frequently becomes a bird predator, devouring eggs or nestlings in any nest it can find; these are important food items for many, if not most, blue jays. Insect food includes ants, caterpillars, grasshoppers, and beetles. Frogs, mice, and carrion are also occasionally consumed. Fall foods, besides nuts, include corn and blackberries. Jays occasionally raid ripening fruit crops in berry and tree orchards. They have also been observed eating sand and paint flakes from buildings, presumably for digestive and mineral needs.

Blue jay food habits are ecologically important in at least two ways. In spring, the birds are major consumers of hairy caterpillars, which include gypsy and tent moths, two of the most common irruptive pests of northeastern forests, and which most insect-eating birds won't touch. In the fall, blue jays cache many acorns and other nuts, collectively called mast, in the ground for later retrieval, sometimes transporting them a mile or more. I have even found acorns, beechnuts, and corn cached in cattail seed heads, probably also placed by blue jays. Many observers have reported watching streams of nut-laden blue jays disperse from woodlots during peak nut seasons. Forest clearings and fallow meadows are their favorite cache sites. The stored food items become important winter sources of nourishment. Since blue jays never retrieve all the nuts they bury, however, new oaks and beeches sprout. Blue jays thus become important agents of forest regeneration, especially on burnt and cut-over lands.

Competing mast feeders and cachers include many birds and mammals. Woodpeckers and squirrels are probably the blue jay's foremost nut competitors. This bird's aggressiveness probably gives it advantage over some food collectors. Also, because it feeds more omnivorously than some of its competitors, jays enjoy more food options, thereby offsetting competitive pressures. Nut production in any given year may be poor or bountiful, and a poor mast year increases competition for the crop that exists. For northern blue jays, the abundance or scarcity of mast in the autumn may determine the extent of their southward migration.

Accipiter hawks are probably the blue jay's foremost predators, especially in northern areas during jay migrations. I have watched sharp-shinned hawks attack mist-netted jays captured for banding, sometimes also entangling themselves in the nets. These hawks often accompany jay flocks like wolf predators, capturing unwary or weakened birds. Peregrine falcons also capture blue jays, and American crows raid their nests. Blue jays are rare victims of brown-headed cowbird nest parasitism.

Focus. The blue jay longevity record is sixteen years, though few reach anywhere near that age. Estimated annual adult survival rate is 55 percent.

Predation by jays where dense populations exist may affect the abundance of small, non-cavity-nesting birds, such as vireos, warblers, and sparrows. Biologist Stephen Fretwell's analysis of breeding bird census records for one area concluded that "every blue jay costs a woodland seven pairs of small, open-nesting birds, but appears to add two pairs of hole nesters," such as woodpeckers, nuthatches, chickadees, or titmice, presumably because of reduced food competition. One of the negative effects of forest fragmentation is that it gives blue jays and other predators easier access to the nests of smaller woodland birds.

Yet, in contrast to its influence as a predator, the blue jay's ecological importance as a forest regenerator—thus creating new habitats for many more species—can hardly be overestimated. Pioneering botanist William Bartram recognized almost two centuries ago that "these birds are capable, in a few years' time, to replant all the cleared land." Biogeographers believe that the rapid northward spread of oaks—almost four hundred yards per year—following the retreat of Pleistocene glaciers was primarily due to blue jay acorn dispersal. The association of blue jays and oaks, in fact, appears rather tight. Another study concluded that "the distribution of oaks in nature may mirror the collective behavioral decisions made by the community of jays as they select, disperse, cache, and retrieve nuts." Blue jays far surpass nut-burying squirrels as oak planters. Probably natural selection has "opted" for relatively small acorn size in most oaks, thus favoring dispersion by jays. As naturalist Vaughan Edmonds writes, "If the oaks had had an age-old contract with the squirrels, acorns might be as large as pecans or walnuts."

Acorns, a staple blue jay food item in fall and winter, may have evolved their relatively small size partly in response to blue jay dispersion.

If you hold a blue jay feather directly between your eyes and the sun, its blue color disappears. That's because, unlike the pigment-produced coloration of most plumage, blue in birds is a structural color, resulting from physics instead of chemistry. Minute air pockets, or *vacuoles,* that cannot absorb the blue part of the spectrum cause light reflected from any angle on the feather to scatter blue wavelengths. Light transmitted through the feather, on the other hand, is not reflected, and the feather appears dark.

CROW AND JAY FAMILY (Corvidae)

American Crow (*Corvus brachyrhyncos*)

The crow is about twenty inches long and all black. Its gregarious behaviors and loudly distinctive caws, along with other sounds and call notes, also identify it. Both sexes look alike, though adult males are usually an inch or so longer than females. Yearling crows can be distinguished from adults by their frayed, pointed tail feathers, which give the tail a squarish shape, and, close up, by the brownish cast of their plumage; adult crows, whose truncated tail feathers form a more rounded tail, show a purplish cast. In flight, crows plow through the air with distinctive, rowing wingbeats.

Close relatives. Some forty-two *Corvus* species exist worldwide, most residing in the Northern Hemisphere. North American species include the fish crow (*C. ossifragus*) of eastern seacoasts and Florida; the northwestern crow (*C. caurinus*) of British Columbia; and the common and Chihuahuan ravens (*C. corax, C. cryptoleucus*). European corvids include the jackdaw (*C. monedula*), rook (*C. frugilegus*), and carrion crow (*C. corone*).

Behaviors. "If a person knows only four birds, one of them will be the crow," wrote early ornithologist Edward Forbush. The more that one observes crows, the more one must agree with Forbush that "each crow is a character." Crows are highly social year-round; even their nesting is an extended family affair. They also display much intelligence and adaptability. A rich anecdotal literature details their cooperative behavior, their ability to distinguish subtle cues and clues, and their apparent strategies for obtaining food. (A friend who feeds crows in his yard believes that they move road-killed animals from road margins into the driving lanes, then perch and wait for passing vehicles to macerate the carcasses.)

American crows display relatively advanced social behaviors. Their abundance probably owes much to vehicle traffic that provides a steady supply of road-killed carcasses. (Courtesy of Kalamazoo Nature Center.)

Crows can be taught to mimic human words, and in the woods they sometimes imitate barred owl calls. Most of their vocabulary, however, consists of raucous "aw" and "ah" notes, together with a cacophony of bill clacking and moaning, growling, and even musical notes. Once, while sitting alone in the silent woods, I heard several soft, tentative, almost dovelike "cu-koos." Looking around, I saw a single crow eyeing me from a tree across a shallow ravine. These soft notes, I learned, are often uttered as a vocal greeting between crows in unalarmed social contexts.

One index of crow intelligence is what appears to be creative play behavior. Crows are sometimes seen repeatedly sliding down embankments or church domes, perversely yanking the tails of mammals, or provoking chases by other birds. Noisy crow mobbing of hawks and, especially, owls is a common behavior. One noted crow researcher states emphatically that crows think. Yet, as naturalist Bil Gilbert cautions, "Crows, like people, cannot be known generally. All descriptions and judgments about them are necessarily parochial, limited to what some crows, sometimes, in some places have been known to do."

In most of their continent-wide range, American crows are permanent residents. Much winter wandering occurs, however, as the birds seek food, and many northern crows are migratory. A crow's life span may reach about fifteen years; most do not begin breeding until two or more years of age.

Spring. Northern crows have arrived on their breeding range by late winter. By early spring, the birds have settled into basically two groups: small, wandering flocks of nonbreeding birds; and family flocks consisting of a previously mated pair and several nonbreeding crows, usually one to three yearlings and older offspring, which may remain with the parent birds for up to four years or longer. Such is the complex variability of crow relationships, however, that a breeding-behavior continuum exists, from a single pair nesting alone to a small group endeavor at the nest. Often a family group returns to a previous nesting tree.

The breeding pair spends much time in reciprocal preening and billing. As breeding commences, the male parent becomes more aggressive, driving away some of the hangers-on while allowing selected others to bring in nesting material. From my living room window in April, I often watch crows collecting dead twigs from tree branches and flying off with them. Another sign of incipient nesting is when the pair begins chasing hawks, common ravens, and turkey vultures that happen to fly over the nest site. The unmated helpers seem eager to exercise their own parental impulses by fetching nest materials, feeding the female on the nest, and later feeding the nestlings (male parent permissiveness increases as the season advances). Crows become silent and secretive during the nesting period. Territoriality, like almost everything else in crows, is a group function. The area defended from other family groups may extend to thirty-six acres.

EGGS AND YOUNG: four to six; eggs bluish to olive green, spotted with brown and gray. INCUBATION: by female, which is fed on the nest by male parent and nest helpers; about eighteen days. FEEDING OF YOUNG: by both parents plus nest helpers; insects, small invertebrates and vertebrates, carrion. FLEDGING: four or five weeks.

Summer. Northern crow populations raise only one brood; those in the southern breeding range often raise two. Juveniles, extremely vocal beggars, remain with the family group after fledging. As summer progresses, flocks enlarge as family groups merge and join flocks of unmated crows. Flocks roost together in trees at night and fan out over the countryside to feed in daytime. In midsummer, many observers report crow anting behavior—wallowing in anthills and inserting ants, which release formic acid, into their plumage. Since this is also the period of the annual feather molt, anting behavior may be related to skin irritation as new feathers emerge or to feather parasites.

Fall. Many, though not all, northern crow populations migrate south in September and October. Those from the midwestern Canadian provinces travel farthest—up to two thousand miles—but most eastern migrants move only a few hundred miles south at most.

Winter. Fall and winter are seasons of communal roosting, often in immense flocks. Flocks arrive from miles around in late afternoon, often roosting at sites they have used for generations. They usually fly to roosts along established flight lines, gathering in successively larger staging areas before arrival at the roost. Night roosts may hold from several hundred to millions of birds. In daytime, flocks leave the roosts at staggered intervals and move to feeding grounds that may lie twenty or more miles distant. Most of the larger winter crow roosts occur in midlatitudes between the thirtieth and fortieth parallels. But exceptions, as in all things corvid, abound. Not all crows join the large communal roosts; many remain in or near their summer territories. Crow migrants are usually moving north again in February and March.

Ecology. Crows require open areas for ground feeding and trees for nesting and roosting. Open woodlands, farmland, and forest edges are typical rural habitats. During the past century, however, many crow populations have become urbanized, scavenging from trash bins, loading docks, and shopping malls. Winter roost habitats, as Bil Gilbert points out, are quite similar botanically. Typically they consist of tall, mature trees in a small grove—an island of oaks, ashes, conifers, or others—with thicket understories of locust, box elder, vines, and briers, the whole surrounded by extensive open areas.

Crows seem to prefer nesting in tall conifers when available, usually over thirty feet, often near the top, in a crotch or near the trunk. The paired female builds most of the nest, sometimes after one or two preliminary attempts elsewhere, from materials brought mainly by the helper birds. The bulky nest basket, about two feet across, consists mainly of sticks on the outside, lined with bark fibers, moss, grasses, hair or fur, and leaves. Crows usually build new nests every year; old nests are often adopted by great horned owls.

An adult crow must consume about eleven ounces of food daily to maintain body weight. Both animal and vegetable foods—the latter predominating in winter—are consumed. Road-killed carrion supplies much of the diet in all seasons. We have crows to thank for cleaning up most of the small carcasses left in the wake of our vehicles. This steady food supply probably accounts in large part for the increase of northern crow populations in winter: Up to a half century ago, few crows wintered in northern areas. Animal prey includes a variety of insects plus frogs, salamanders, bird eggs and nestlings, and occasionally mice. The crow's fondness for corn, wheat, and oats has enraged many a farmer, but much of this diet is gleaned from fields after harvest. Crows also consume fruits, including wild cherries, mulberries, grapes, and pokeberries. Acorns are favored foods in fall and winter.

Upon locating a food source, crows often carry and bury the food items, placing them in scattered ground sites and tree crevices. Since many cached items, such as pieces of carrion, are perishable, food caching is usually short-term. Like the blue jay, a crow can carry several acorns, many corn grains, or pieces of other foods in its *antelingual pouch,* the distensible floor of the oral cavity behind the lower bill. Like raptors, crows eject pellets of indigestible materials after feeding.

Carrion competitors include common ravens and turkey vultures, both somewhat better adapted for finding and consuming carcasses than crows. Crows harass and rob these birds at food sites when they can. Because crows are omnivorous feeders, food competition likely is insignificant except, perhaps, for northern crows in winter. Probably crows are their own foremost competitors for nesting habitat. Their abundance may influence the amount of cooperative breeding (that is, with nest helpers) that occurs.

Great horned owls are major predators of American crows. These raptors raid crow nests and roosting sites at night, killing and eating both adults and nestlings. Raccoons are regular nest invaders, consuming eggs and nestlings, and goshawks also threaten. Gray squirrels, daytime intruders, are noisily driven away, and crows attack red-tailed and red-shouldered hawks during the breeding season, although they often tolerate their presence at other times. Their chief predators are humans, and roosting sites become frequent targets of recreational gunners. Federal migratory bird laws have made indiscriminate shooting and poisoning of crows illegal, but shooting is permitted under various state regulations.

Focus. Thoreau rhapsodized about the "delicious sound" of crows in winter, blessing the Lord "for wildness, for crows that will not alight within gunshot!" Capitalizing on the crow's natural wariness of people, scarecrows became stock characters of farm and rural folklore. Many Native American tribes revered the crow as a spiritual being, and crow tales abound in many of these cultures. These peoples probably saw fewer crows than we do, for the birds were far less abundant in the Northeast before agriculture created optimal habitats and abundant food for them. In Michigan, for example, they remained unknown until about 1850, when the landscape was being opened up by logging. Since then, large foraging flocks and piles of droppings beneath roost sites have given crows gigantic pest status in many quarters. Probably the biggest crow massacre occurred in 1940 near Rockford, Illinois, where state officials dynamited some three hundred thousand crows into oblivion.

Yet to view these native birds of legend solely through the biases of farmers and sanitation engineers gives us an incomplete picture of this bird. If crows can indeed think, our inviting habitats and simultaneous crow shoots must seem baffling indeed.

Closer look. Kilham, L. *The American Crow and the Common Raven.* College Station, TX: Texas A&M University, 1989.

CROW AND JAY FAMILY (Corvidae)

Common Raven (*Corvus corax*)

Measuring two feet or more in length with a four-foot wingspread, the all-black raven is the largest northern passerine bird. Its size, shaggy throat, prominent rictal bristles at the base of the bill, and rounded tail distinguish it from crows, as do its distinctive croaking and guttural notes, which carry far through the forest. Both sexes look alike, although males are somewhat larger and utter deeper, more resonant call notes. Juvenile birds show brown on wings and tail.

Close relatives. All other *Corvus* species (listed under American Crow).

Behaviors. To zoologist Bernd Heinrich, a raven is "the ultimate corvid in size, intelligence, and inaccessibility." Behavior biologist Konrad Lorenz called ravens "specialists in nonspecialization."

This splendid bird's breeding range extends worldwide in the Northern Hemisphere. Once abundant in the North American wilderness, it probably outnumbered crows. Today, because of wilderness depletion, its haunts are remote areas of forest, mountain, and tundra, though it is again ranging southward in reforested areas. Like the calls of the common loon and wolf, the raven's note is a voice of the wild places. Its repertoire of sounds probably exceeds that of any other creature except humans.

The raven's steady, plowing wingbeats much resemble crow flight, but ravens also soar hawklike at times. Also like crows, they often mob large birds and, in turn, are mobbed and harassed by smaller ones, including crows. A raven flying over an eastern kingbird territory, for example, is relentlessly chased and attacked by this aggressive flycatcher. I have often watched such attacks, noting with amusement the raven's alarmed head turning in flight as the faster-flying kingbird dives and strikes. Unlike crows, which can launch directly into flight from the ground, a raven needs several hops to become airborne. Apparent play behaviors include acrobatic flights and dives.

Ravens probably mate for life and may live for thirty years. Most begin breeding in their third or fourth year, but courtship behaviors may begin much sooner and continue year-round. In forested areas, ravens hunt food by flying low over the treetops and listening for carrion cues from other birds. But ravens are notoriously shy, not only of humans but also of stationary food on the ground, where they typically feed. "For a carcass specialist," wrote Heinrich, "a potential meal may be an injured or sleeping predator or another animal that would normally defend itself." Hence ravens may spend hours watching a carcass before approaching it. They probe and jump back repeatedly, testing its deadness. At carcass sites they are often team players: One raven will distract a competitor, such as a turkey vulture or fox, while another robs it of its morsel. Some portion of the raven population is gregarious at any season, though breeding pairs are usually solitary. Ravens are not migrators, though they often wander far in fall and winter, and some southward shift of population occurs.

Spring. By the time snow cover disappears from the north woods in late April, raven nesting is already well advanced. Also in March and April there is a northward movement of mostly unmated birds that had traveled south the previous fall. A raven's nest I watched in 1993 held mid-April nestlings, which fledged in early June. Sometimes three or more adult ravens frequent a nest site—presumably the parents plus yearlings that may help feed the young. Loose flocks, probably of yearling or older, unmated ravens, also wander extensively in spring without establishing territories.

Summer. After nestlings fledge, ravens usually remain in family groups for two or three months, often roaming far from their original territories. The annual feather molt begins in July, lasting into fall.

Fall. Some far northern ravens move south in September and October (nobody knows exactly where they go), but many remain year-round on their breeding range. Family groups split up in the fall. During fall and winter, individual ravens gather into communal nighttime roosts in trees or marshes. Such roosts may consist of up to several hundred nonrelated ravens. From these roosts, the birds may fly twenty miles or more in smaller flocks for daytime feeding. Though ravens may use a roost site for decades, roost populations remain constantly in flux, with individual birds coming and going over periods of days and weeks. As with crows, raven social groupings show wide variability.

Winter. Roosting behavior usually peaks in January, gradually decreasing as pairing begins. As pairs reestablish their bonds, often returning to previously used nests, aerial courtship displays include acrobatic wheeling, rolling, tumbling, and soaring closely together with wing tips touching. The common territorial call, a loud, resonant "quork" or "krok," is now heard, although the territory consists only of the immediate nest area. Separate pairs usually nest several miles apart. Either sex or both may build the nest, a two-week endeavor unless the pair revamps a previous nest, which many do. Egg laying may begin in late February extending into March. Only one brood is raised.

EGGS AND YOUNG: three to five; eggs greenish, marked with brown and olive patterns. INCUBATION: by female, which is fed on the nest by male; about three weeks. FEEDING OF YOUNG: by both sexes plus an occasional unmated adult; carrion, insects, other invertebrates, small vertebrates. FLEDGING: about forty days.

Ecology. Raven habitats vary extensively, probably more than any other North American bird's. The birds occupy both wet and dry environments, dense forests, bleak deserts, arctic ice and tundra, and rocky mountaintops—wherever, it seems, man is not. Unlike their crow and blue jay cousins, they do not frequent the field, edge, and urban habitats created by human settlement, though exceptions do occur. In the Northeast, their main habitats are extensive, mature forests, both mixed and coniferous. Common roosting habitats are dense pine groves.

A jumble of fallen branches littering the ground beneath a conifer may indicate a raven's nest in the tree above. Ravens' nests seem in a constant state of disrepair whether occupied or not.

Cliff ledges in the West and pine trees in the East are the most common nest sites. Nests, which may measure up to four feet across, often lie near the tops of tall pines or spruces, but sometimes younger trees are used. (One raven nest I observed had been built near the top of a red pine only forty feet high, located close to the outer edge of a dense pine plantation.) The birds break off sticks, some of them as long as three feet, from dead branches (often aspen), piling them in a thick mass. They thickly line the six-inch-deep nest with grasses, animal hair from carcasses, mosses, and other fine materials. Raven nests are notorious for their messiness, stench, and loose construction. Often the nest rim and ground area beneath it are stained white from the nestlings' defecation; incubating females drench the nest with their own excrement as well. Sticks fall from the nest, and eventually large portions of the nest end up on the ground. Raven nests can be found by looking for clutters of large sticks and branches beneath conifers. Old, vacated nests are often reused by red-tailed hawks and great horned owls; and merlins (pigeon hawks) almost exclusively adopt raven nests for their own nesting. Often, however, ravens rebuild atop their own remnants.

Ravens, which are omnivorous, are mainly scavengers and carrion feeders, cleaning up vast amounts of road-killed carcasses, the increasing abundance of which has probably enlarged raven populations. Raven researcher Bernd Heinrich discovered some complex social interactions occurring among the birds at large carcasses. Resident paired ravens always establish a feeding territory at the carcass, attacking unmated yearling or vagrant ravens that venture to feed. The excluded ravens often set up a clamorous yelling that recruits other single ravens from surrounding areas. When at least nine or so are assembled, they all descend on the carcass, safely able to ignore the defending pair. This recruitment is not altruistic sharing behavior, because no individual vagrant can benefit until a mob assembles.

Many researchers have noted feeding associations between ravens and both coyotes and wolves. The birds keep a close eye on these predators, often following them about. In turn, especially during winter, the yelling of ravens at a carcass may attract these mammals to the site. Unable to penetrate the hides of large, fresh carcasses, ravens seem aware of their dependency on the sharp teeth of these canines to make the meat available. "But food is not the full extent of their relationship," wrote ornithologist Lawrence Kilham of ravens and wolves; each "appears to be fascinated by the other." Instances of mock aggression and apparent play between them have often been observed.

Ravens also consume small creatures, including frogs, crayfish, lizards, and mice. As opportunists, they raid bird nests, often of waterfowl and seabird colonies, consuming eggs and nestlings. Their insect diet includes grasshoppers, cicadas, beetles, hymenopterans (ants, bees, and wasps), and insect scavengers on carcasses. In summer and fall they also feed on corn, blackberries, and other fruits and seeds. Like crows, ravens frequently cache pieces of carrion in the ground, and they eject castings of indigestible fur and bones. Scattered castings, some of them six inches or longer, often lie beneath nest trees.

Ravens compete vigorously with bald eagles, turkey vultures, and American crows at carrion sites. Sometimes they yank a vulture's tail to distract the scavenger, and they chase and rob crows. Large mammal predators seem remarkably tolerant of ravens at carcass sites, seldom attacking them. By making carcass innards available to ravens, coyotes and wolves probably benefit the birds at these sites as much as they compete with them.

Though various hawks and eastern kingbirds sometimes harass ravens, and blue jays, crows, and several smaller birds mob them on occasion, the raven's size and aggressiveness, especially near its nest, make predation insignificant. This bird's foremost nemesis has been forest clearing and fragmentation.

Focus. The raven, crow, and coyote, among others, are creatures invested with heavy spiritual significance. To Native Americans, their presence was never purely circumstantial and always provided omen, comment, or clue. These creatures participated in the truth-seeking visions of the young, the councils of elders, and the prophecies of shamans. They embodied tribal clans (and still do) and were simulated in ceremonial rites. In certain tribal mythologies, Raven was the all-important deity, the creator of life and bringer of light. He was also a notable trickster and rascal, full of taunts and mischief, but he was never an evil figure and never hunted or killed.

According to Hebrew folklore, ravens behaved disgracefully on Noah's ark: They were the only creatures that copulated thereon. In Norse and other mythologies, however, the raven became a sinister figure that foretold the carnage of battle and disaster. The raven standard of Viking raiders became as lethal a symbol as the swastika in a later age. Ravens croak in Shakespearean tragedies, and Poe's poem "The Raven" (though more of a literary device than a bird) adopted the worst of an ample tradition. Yet exceptions to the evil image also abounded. The six ravens that range the fortress grounds at the Tower of London are kept there to preserve England. Ravens alerted Charles II's guards against a Cromwell raid; if they ever leave, goes the tradition, disaster will befall England, so their wings are carefully clipped.

Most American settlers hated the raven (along with the wolf and coyote), believing that it was a killer of lambs and chickens, not realizing that killer and carcass feeder are not invariably the same creature. Ravens, along with bison and wolves, were mercilessly exterminated by gun and poison wherever people passed or settled. The birds had all but disappeared from their original northeastern U.S. range by 1800. Today they have begun to recover some of the country whose human inhabitants once deified them.

Closer looks. Heinrich, B. *Ravens in Winter.* New York: Summit, 1989.

Kilham, L. *The American Crow and the Common Raven.* College Station, TX: Texas A&M University, 1989.

15

Cedar Waxwing (*Bombycilla cedrorum*)

Waxwing family (Bombycillidae). Sleekly brown and crested, cedar waxwings are seven to eight inches long. They have a yellowish belly, yellow band at the tail tip, and waxy red tips on the wing secondaries. Their wheezy, high-pitched notes are distinctive. Sexes look much alike, but juveniles show brown streaking.

Close relatives. The Bohemian waxwing (*B. garrulus*), a larger version of its cousin, is a northwestern species that also resides in Eurasia. The only other species is the Japanese waxwing (*B. japonica*) of Asia.

A cedar waxwing juvenile (left) and adult (right) perch in a typical pose. These highly social birds, when thus perched, often pass berries back and forth.

Behaviors. Debonair, dapper, and elegant are adjectives frequently used to describe the color-dabbed cedar waxwing. Waxwings are gregarious and nonchalant, even almost sluggish. They sometimes resemble starlings in flight, with an undulating pattern of quick wingflaps and soars. They also make brief sallies from perches, capturing aerial insects much as flycatchers do. In flocks, their thin, sibilant notes sound almost incessantly as they feed, fly, and perch.

Breeding and winter ranges span the continent, but seasonal movements are irregular. In many northern areas, waxwings are nomadic rather than migratory, but substantial north-south migrations also occur.

Spring. Waxwings move to their breeding sites from early to late spring. Some observers suggest that spring migrations occur in double waves—one in March, and one in May or June. Traveling in large flocks, waxwings pair during migration, but they may not return to the previous year's breeding sites. They often delay territory formation and actual nesting until summer—thus, unlike many birds, females select mates on the basis of individual attraction rather than quality of territory. In the meantime, the birds split into smaller flocks of six or more. A common courtship display is the side-hop: A pair sidles alongside each other, hopping close, then away, passing a berry or cherry back and forth for up to fifteen minutes before one of the birds eats it.

Summer. Breeding territories (up to an acre in size) and nest sites are largely determined by the proximity of fruiting trees or shrubs. Territorial food sources are not defended, however, and the birds continue to feed communally. A prominent territorial feature is the male's sentinel perch, from which he watches as nesting proceeds. Nesting usually begins in mid-June, often continuing into late summer, especially when the birds raise two broods. Subtle differences in waxwing call notes are good indicators of the precise phase of nesting. Often several pairs may nest semicolonially, with nests as close as twenty-five feet. Nesting overlap is common, with nestlings fledging in the first nest while egg laying begins in a second. Pairs probably remain monogamous for the entire season. After the young achieve total independence—about twenty-five days—they join other juveniles to feed in small flocks. Mixed juvenile-adult flocks occur in late summer.

Various theories explain the delayed breeding dates of the waxwings—the latest passerine nesters, except for American goldfinches. One theory suggests that their late timing is a recently evolved response to brood parasitism of brown-headed cowbirds, which breed earlier. More likely, perhaps, is the theory that waxwing breeding coincides with seasonal fruit ripening, since berries and tree fruits constitute the main diet of nestlings.

EGGS AND YOUNG: four or five; eggs gray, brown spotted. INCUBA-TION: by female, which is fed by male; about twelve days. FEED-ING OF YOUNG: by both sexes; insects for first two days, regurgitated berries thereafter. FLEDGING: about fifteen days.

Fall. The annual feather molt occurs in late summer and early fall. Most waxwings do not gain their red secondary tips until their second-year molt, though exceptions do occur. Many, if not most, waxwings migrate south in September and October, some moving as far as Panama.

Winter. Most eastern waxwing populations winter on the coastal plain from South Carolina to Texas. Little interchange of western and eastern populations occurs; birds west of the Rockies probably form the bulk of Central American migrants. Roaming flocks, however, remain in the northern breeding range, appearing locally wherever there are food sources. Their occurrence and abundance fluctuate from year to year.

Ecology. Cedar waxwings favor edge habitats—open woodlands, thickets, hedgerows, orchards, and suburban yards—almost anyplace that offers fruiting trees or shrubs. In winter, they often frequent swamps. They avoid densely forested areas.

Cedar waxwing nests vary considerably in form, structure, and site. This bird is one of our latest breeders, often not beginning to nest until early summer.

Nests vary in placement, height, materials used, and even general form. Some are large, loose, and bulky, others relatively neat and compact. I have found them on red pine branches built against the trunk about eight feet high, but often they build much higher on horizontal limbs, away from the trunk or in an upright fork. They use twigs in the nest foundation, as well as grasses, weed stems, and string or twine if available. They line the nest with fine grasses, pine needles, plant down, and sometimes wool. Waxwings often raid nests of other birds for nesting materials.

This is one of our most *frugivorous,* or fruit-eating, birds, with an annual diet consisting of some 70 percent fruits. Highly favored are the berrylike cones of eastern red cedar (commonly called juniper), wild cherries, and flowering dogwood fruits. Blackberries, hackberries, chokeberries, mulberries, grapes, and hawthorn and viburnum fruits also rank high, but waxwings are essentially fruit opportunists, taking whatever nature offers in abundance. Apple blossom petals are especially relished in spring.

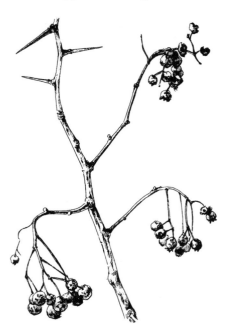

Waxwings perched on a wire often pass a cherry, petal, or caterpillar one to the other, a similar behavior to their courtship display. The birds are often gluttonous; after gorging on overripe, fermented berries, they may droop like sodden couch potatoes or become comically tipsy. On their southern winter range, waxwings consume mistletoe, privet, and persimmon fruits in abundance. North-wintering flocks seek out wetland shrubs that hold their fruits for long duration. Insect consumption is also important; waxwings are efficient predators of foliage-eating geometrid moth caterpillars (cankerworms) and also consume many leaf beetles.

Food competitors include other frugivores, such as Ameri-

Hawthorn apples, which often remain attached after the leaves drop, provide a major winter food for cedar waxwings, whose diet consists mainly of fruits.

can robins, northern mockingbirds, and European starlings. Occasionally waxwings also compete with berry and orchard farmers. Predators are relatively few, although accipiter hawks probably capture some waxwings. Waxwings vary in response to brown-headed cowbird parasitism; most waxwings eject cowbird eggs, especially during early incubation stages, but some 8 percent of waxwing nests raise one or more cowbirds.

Focus. Cedarbird, cankerbird, and cherry bird are common nicknames. The dropletlike red dabs on the tips of adult secondaries are pigmented extensions of the feather shafts. Astaxanthin, the red carotenoid pigment found mainly in red fruits, originates in the diet. Research confirms that these color markings are age related and probably confer some breeding and status advantage. Since the 1960s, a color variation in the tail band—orange instead of yellow—has been observed in many northeastern juvenile waxwings. This variation seems to have coincided with the introduction from Japan of an ornamental fruit-bearing shrub, Morrow's honeysuckle (*Lonicera morrowii*). The fruits contain the carotenoid pigment rhodoxanthin, which remains unsynthesized in the waxwing's orange tail band. The second-year molt brings normal yellow-banded tail feathers; whether this is from age-related changes in fruit diet or digestive efficiency remains unknown.

Cedar waxwings were once hunted for food; Audubon described them as "tender and juicy." Their wide habitat and food tolerances have made cedar waxwings common to abundant throughout most of their range.

16

THRUSH FAMILY (Muscicapidae)

Thrushes include some of our most melodious vocalists. Several are known for their *amphoric* tones—song notes that sound similar to hollow tones produced by blowing into a bottle. Thrushes occupy many habitats, feeding mainly on invertebrates and fruits. They are almost cosmopolitan, numbering more than three hundred species worldwide, fourteen of which breed in North America. In addition to the three species accounts that follow, with their mentioned relatives, northeastern thrushes include eastern bluebirds (*Sialia sialis*) and northern wheatears (*Oenanthe oenanthe*). More than thirty thrushes, including the nightingale (*Luscinia megarhyncos*), reside in Europe. The plumage patterns of American forest thrushes provide good examples of countershading. All American thrushes lay blue eggs. The word *thrush* is Anglo-Saxon in origin, apparently always having referred to birds of this family.

THRUSH FAMILY (Muscicapidae)

Hermit Thrush (*Catharus guttatus*)

This seven-inch-long woodland thrush can be identified by its olive-brown upper parts, reddish tail, and spotted breast. When perched, it frequently hitches its tail and flips its wings. Flutelike songs of hermit, wood, and Swainson's thrushes sound much alike; each hermit song, however, begins in a different key from its preceding song. Sexes look alike.

The hermit thrush, one of our most melodious songbirds, inhabits ground and low shrub levels of northern forest habitats. (From The Atlas of Breeding Birds of Michigan.*)*

Close relatives. Other northeastern *Catharus,* or nightingale-thrushes, include the veery (*C. fuscescens*), Swainson's thrush (*C. ustulatus*), gray-cheeked thrush (*C. minimus*), and Bicknell's thrush (*C. bicknelli*), all woodland birds.

Behaviors. This bird of the northern forest understory remains inconspicuous except when voicing its melodious, tremolo song, usually given from a low perch in dawn and evening twilight. The hermit concert can be heard only on their breeding range, which spans the continent across forested Canada to the northern United States and farther south in the Rockies and Appalachians, or on their southern winter range, where they also sing occasionally. As migrants, they are sometimes seen but seldom heard as they travel. Their alertness and secretive habits, which account for their name, make hermits difficult to approach; it's easier to bring them to you by making pishing or squeaking noises, as they are always sneakily curious. Hermits are well known for anting behavior, rubbing ants into their plumage; the formic acid released by the ants is a possible defense against external parasites.

Spring. Hermits are early migrants, traveling at night, often in large numbers, and resting during the day. Northward movement peaks in April. Previously mated pairs probably return to former territories, though data are skimpy. Courtship and territorial displays include male singing, wing flicking, crest raising, and erect posturing with uptilted bill. Nesting usually begins in May, extending into summer.

EGGS AND YOUNG: three or four; eggs pale blue. INCUBATION: by female, which is fed by male; about twelve days. FEEDING OF YOUNG: by both sexes. FLEDGING: about twelve days.

Summer. Hermits raise second broods in July and sometimes August, with song continuing well after many other bird species have fallen silent. Adults molt their feathers in August and September, while juveniles acquire their first winter plumage. Buffy spots on the wing coverts identify fresh-molted juveniles.

Fall, Winter. Hermits migrate in late fall, most moving south in October and early November. Small numbers, however, often settle north of their winter range wherever food is available. Even these birds, however, usually remain south of long-lasting snow cover. Most hermits winter south of the fortieth parallel to the Gulf Coast, the Bahamas, and Guatemala.

Ecology. Hermits favor relatively dry coniferous and mixed forests, but they show wide latitude and versatility in habitat use. Pine-oak woodlands, pine plains and plantations, forest edges, and even wooded bogs host many hermits. On their winter range, they frequent swamp borders, river bottoms, and other forest habitats.

Hermit females usually nest on the ground but occasionally nest low in a tree. Road banks and other slopes are frequent sites. Often the nest lies in a slight ground depression canopied by dense, low vegetation. Twigs, bark fibers, and grasses form the bulky outer portion, and finer plant materials line the cup.

Like most thrushes, hermits primarily consume insects in spring and summer, fruits in fall and winter. Beetles, ants, caterpillars, spiders, earthworms, snails, and small salamanders are chief food items. Migrating and wintering thrushes eat large quantities of

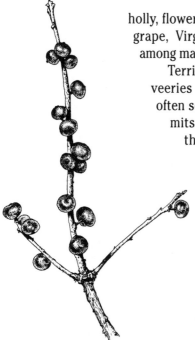

holly, flowering dogwood, greenbrier, sumac, wild grape, Virginia creeper, and poison-ivy fruits, among many others.

Territorial competitors sometimes include veeries and wood thrushes, both of which often select moister forest habitats than hermits favor. Range expansion of wood thrushes during the past several decades, however, has apparently displaced hermits and veeries in some areas. Hermit and wood thrushes do not often coexist in a woodland; their breeding ranges coincide only in a relatively narrow band across the northern United States and southern Canada.

Like all ground nesters, hermits are vulnerable to predation from such prowling mammals as foxes, raccoons, skunks, and weasels. Accipiter hawks and owls sometimes capture the birds, and snakes consume eggs and nestlings. Brown-headed cowbirds occasionally parasitize hermit broods.

*Fruits of holly (*Ilex*), shining bright red in autumn swamp thickets, are common food items for many thrushes during fall migration.*

Focus. The hermit is North America's nightingale, a "singer bashful and tender," wrote Walt Whitman. Its musical song, in many esthetic opinions, rivals or surpasses that of the famed European songster. Mohawk tradition relates that the hermit once outflew all other birds to heaven and there learned its song. The hermit's notes are not as amphoric as those voiced by the veery and some other thrushes. Early American ornithologists Alexander Wilson and John J. Audubon were never in the right place at the right time to hear this bird sing, and Audubon even declared that hermits had no song. Even Thoreau failed to distinguish its song from that of the wood thrush.

The hermit thrush is Vermont's state bird.

Closer look. Tehanetorens and J. L. Hutchens. *Sacred Song of the Hermit Thrush.* Summertown, TN: Book Publishing Company, 1993.

THRUSH FAMILY (Muscicapidae)

Wood Thrush (*Hylocichla mustelina*)

This eight-inch-long forest thrush can be recognized by its rusty red back and top of head, brownish wings and tail, dark-spotted white underparts, and piping, flutelike song ("ee-o-lay"). Sexes look alike.

Close relatives. All five northeastern brown thrushes were formerly classified in the *Hylocichla* genus; the others, listed under Hermit Thrush, have been renamed *Catharus.*

Behaviors. With its more southern distribution—New England and Great Lakes to the Gulf—the wood thrush resides nearer than hermit thrushes to where most people live. Thus it is more often heard and observed, although it shows less adaptability to various habitats than hermits. Like its *Catharus* cousins, it dwells low in the understory. Its song, similar to and fully as melodic as the hermit's, is the best revealer of its presence. Along with the red-eyed vireo and ovenbirds, the wood thrush is *the* characteristic bird of mature deciduous forests. It feeds mainly on the ground, bill-sweeping the forest litter. Alarmed wood thrushes often raise their crown feathers, giving the appearance of a crest.

Spring. Wood thrushes arrive on their breeding range in April and early May. Previous nesters return to their territories, often less than an acre in size. Traveling at night, males usually precede females by a few days, engaging in circular courtship chases when the latter arrive. Males sing mainly in the early morning and in the evening after sunset. Females choose the nest site and build the nest.

EGGS AND YOUNG: three or four; eggs bluish green. INCUBATION: by female; about two weeks. FEEDING OF YOUNG: by both sexes; insects, berries. FLEDGING: about twelve days.

Summer. Fledglings remain in the nest vicinity for up to a month or so. In July, adult females build a second nest, usually near the first one, and this nesting sometimes extends into August. Molting occurs shortly thereafter, and the birds become silent and secretive as they lose and replace their body and flight feathers.

Fall, Winter. Flying at night, most wood thrushes migrate in October and leave the continental United States, though small numbers remain along the Gulf Coast. Wood thrushes winter from Mexico to Panama and northwestern Colombia. As spring migration approaches, males occasionally sing.

Ecology. Wood thrushes reside in moist deciduous and mixed forests with large trees and dense shade and undergrowth. They often favor woodlands containing streams or springs. Frequent associates in such habitats include ovenbirds, ground warblers that resemble brown thrushes in plumage. Around 1890, wood thrushes began nesting in parks and woodlots near human habitations, and they remain fairly common in such sites. For at least half the year, however, wood thrushes reside in Neotropical rain-forest habitats. Living solitarily, at least some of them establish small feeding territories in lowland undergrowth and wet thickets. Others wander extensively, occupying a variety of habitats, including cacao and banana plantations.

Wood thrush nests, usually placed about ten feet high in the fork of a sapling or shrub, are made of leaves, grasses, and mosses, with a middle layer of mud or leaf mold, and lined with rootlets. Often the birds insert pieces of cellophane, white paper, or cloth; though this would seem to make the nest more

Wood thrush nests are fairly distinctive. They usually show a foundation of dead leaves and contain a layer of leaf mold and a lining of rootlets.

conspicuous to predators, it may actually help conceal it by breaking the nest's outline.

Spring and summer foods consist mainly of spiders, caterpillars, beetles, ants, and flies. Sowbugs, snails, and earthworms are also consumed, as are mulberries and blackberries. In fall and winter, the diet changes to a variety of wild fruits, including those of spicebush, dogwoods, and Virginia creeper, as well as cherries, grapes, and elderberries.

Foremost wood thrush competitors in the North are probably veeries. More than any other forest thrush, veeries share the same foods, feeding habits, and habitat needs of dense shade and moisture, though veeries favor somewhat cooler microclimates than wood thrushes. Each species defends its territories from the other; where territorial conflicts occur, wood thrushes usually win out. This also helps explain the latter's northward expansion of breeding range, sometimes at the expense of veeries, all through this century.

Domestic cats are frequent predators where wood thrushes nest near human dwellings. Blue jays, American robins, and common grackles sometimes puncture wood thrush eggs, and gray and flying squirrels also raid nests. The bird's main enemy, however, is probably the brown-headed cowbird, which frequently parasitizes wood thrush broods; often a cowbird nestling becomes the only survivor of a parasitized nest. Some wood thrushes try to cover or eject the cowbird egg, but most tolerate it and feed the nestling as one of their own.

Focus. For melodic beauty of song, wood and hermit thrushes are in the same league. Identification is aided by the fact that both species seldom occupy the same woodland, even where their ranges overlap. "Whenever a man hears it he is young," waxed Thoreau, who never distinguished the two species by song.

Wood thrushes have been known to survive six years, but probably most do not approach that age. Despite their trend of northward expansion, wood thrush populations are declining at an alarming rate in several eastern and midwestern states. This is an area-sensitive species, severely affected by both habitat loss in the Neotropical rain forest of its winter range and forest fragmentation in its breeding range. Increased predation and cowbird parasitism result from the subdivision of large forest tracts.

The wood thrush is the official bird of the District of Columbia.

THRUSH FAMILY (Muscicapidae)

American Robin (*Turdus migratorius*)

Measuring about ten inches long, this thrush is dark on top with a brick red to orange breast. Males have blacker heads and tails and redder breasts than the grayer females, and juveniles have speckled breasts. The male's "cheeriup, cheerily" is one of spring's most familiar bird songs.

Close relatives. More than sixty *Turdus* species exist worldwide. Nine European species include the blackbird (*T. merula*), the fieldfare (*T. pilaris*), the song thrush (*T. philomelos*), and the mistle thrush (*T. viscivorus*). The European robin (*Erithacus rubecula*), though a red-breasted thrush, is smaller and does not closely resemble the American robin.

Behaviors. One of the most common residents around human dwellings, the robin is a true yard bird. Its characteristic hop-and-stop gait in the grass, head cocking, and sudden thrust for an earthworm are familiar sights. After years of controversy, researchers have finally established that robins locate earthworms primarily by sight, not by sound. The bird can detect slight movements, undiscernible to our eyes, of a worm in its near-surface burrow. Wet lawns attract robins because saturated soil drives worms to the surface for air.

Robins are gregarious for most of the year. Even during breeding, when pairs aggressively defend their nests, one robin's territory, about one-third of an acre, often overlaps with another's, and feeding and roosting sites are often shared. Night communal roosting, most prevalent in fall and winter, also occurs among male robins during the nesting season; they resume their territories in daytime.

Robin breeding range spans most of the continent from northern Canada and Alaska to the Gulf and southern Mexico. Robins are migrators, though small populations often remain on the breeding range in winter.

Spring. Breeding robins remain faithful to their previous territories, and their arrival in force occurs in late March and early April. In moving northward—as far as Alaska and northern Canada—flocks closely follow the advancing daily temperature mean of 37 degrees F., although harsh early-spring weather can rapidly deplete robin populations. Males precede females by a few days, and territorial formation is marked by hostile chases, attacks, and various courtship rituals—"robin racket," as naturalist John Burroughs called these behaviors. Nesting begins shortly after arrival. Watch for "mustached" robins as they gather dead stems of long grasses, holding them crosswise in the bill, for nesting material. Females, which do most of the nest building, often display a mud line across the breast where they have shaped and pressed against the damp soil rim of the new nest. Sometimes they use the previous year's nest, adding materials. Male robins sing most conspicuously just before hatching time. Robin pair bonds, despite territorial fidelity, often last through only one breeding season.

EGGS AND YOUNG: typically four; eggs blue. INCUBATION: by female, which is attended by male; about two weeks. FEEDING OF YOUNG: by both sexes; insects. FLEDGING: about two weeks or slightly longer.

Summer. Usually females have begun incubating a second brood by early summer, often on the same nest. The male is the main feeder of the fledged first brood, some of which follow him about on the ground for two weeks or so. Listen for the loud, screechy "seech-ook!" of fledgling robins calling for parental attention. About the time second broods hatch, first-brood birds are becoming independent. In July and August, the annual feather molt occurs. Now robins begin to gather and roam in large flocks for both feeding and roosting. This diet and behavioral shift is evidenced by the gradual disappearance of pairs from the lawn. Watch for anting behavior—the rubbing of ants, which release formic acid, into the plumage—especially in summer.

Fall. October is the primary month of robin migration southward, often in large flocks. Most flocks travel by day to the milder, generally snowfree climate of the southern states and Gulf Coast. Some robins range as far south as Guatemala.

Winter. Nighttime roosting areas sometimes hold thousands of robins, often mixed with European starlings, common grackles, and brown-headed cowbirds. Observers have noted winter territorial behaviors as robins defend individual fruit trees from other robins. In recent decades, robins seem to be extending their winter range northward.

Ecology. American robins are true habitat generalists, able to occupy almost any land area that provides enough food. During the breeding season, they favor the artificial parklands so prevalent in shady residential suburbs. Away from town, their frequent haunts include orchards, forest edges, and lake and stream margins. Unless severe weather forces them to move elsewhere, wintering flocks both north and south favor swampy areas for feeding and roosting. The first robins of spring in many areas may actually have been residing in nearby wetlands all winter and are simply beginning to shift habitat.

For nesting, robins usually select a semisheltered tree fork, horizontal limb, building ledge, or, often, an eave pipe beneath a roof overhang. Conifers are favored sites in some areas. The nest, which may appear unkempt and not very well camouflaged,

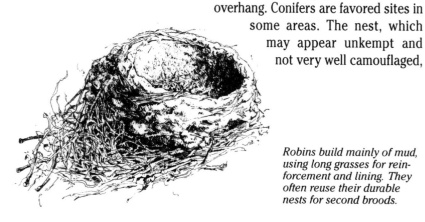

Robins build mainly of mud, using long grasses for reinforcement and lining. They often reuse their durable nests for second broods.

is distinctive for its mud construction, with grass binding and lining. One observer reported the use of earthworm castings.

Except for the required protein-rich diet of earthworms when feeding young, robins are mainly frugivores, or fruit eaters, sometimes to the fury of commercial fruit growers. Earthworms are the most conspicuous food we see robins take in spring and form about 15 percent of the total diet, but robins also abundantly reside in areas where earthworms are few or lacking. Ground, snout, and scarab beetles constitute about 40 percent of the diet. Caterpillars also rank high, but other insects, spiders, and snails are also consumed. Wild fruit foods include just about any available, with heavy summer emphasis on rose family plants. Fruits of dogwoods, sumacs, red cedar, and Virginia creeper, as well as wild and domestic cherries, blackberries, and grapes, are all favorites, as are fruits of the cabbage palm in the southern winter range. Robins rarely consume grains or other dry plant seeds.

The robin's adaptability to human environs gives it a competitive edge over many other birds, though wintering robins must compete for food with other frugivores, including northern mockingbirds, cedar waxwings, and European starlings. These same environs, however, expose fledgling robins to that notorious yard predator, the domestic cat. In rural habitats, sharp-shinned hawks occasionally capture robins, and American crows, blue jays, and snakes sometimes raid nests, consuming eggs or nestlings. Robins rapidly eject brown-headed cowbird eggs.

Focus. Their adaptability to human environs has made robins far more abundant today than in presettlement times; many Native Americans and pioneers probably saw them rarely, if at all. During the nineteenth century, robins were widely hunted and consumed for food, especially in the South; Audubon called them "excellent eating." At fruit trees where robins fed, gunners shot them day-long by the bagful. A more insidious killer later appeared in the form of DDT pesticides. Spraying for Dutch elm disease during the 1950s resulted in high concentrations of the poison in earthworm tissues, followed by the death and reproductive failure of many birds. This widely observed lawn avicide formed the basis for Rachel Carson's furiously maligned but scientifically dead-on warning in her classic 1962 book, *Silent Spring.* It took a decade for the United States to ban the use of lethal DDT. U.S. companies, however, still manufacture it and sell it to other nations that continue to use it, including those in which most of our Neotropical birds winter. U.S. robin populations rebounded, and in many areas they are now the most numerous bird species.

The word *robin* is actually a nickname for the French name Robert. Colonists transferred the name of the European robin to the American species.

The robin is the state bird of Connecticut, Michigan, and Wisconsin.

Closer look. Eiserer, L. A. *The American Robin: A Backyard Institution.* Chicago: Nelson Hall, 1976.

17

STARLING FAMILY (Sturnidae)

This family includes both starlings and a group recently demoted from family status (Mimidae), the mimic thrushes: catbirds, mockingbirds, and thrashers. Birds of this family show highly developed vocal characteristics marked by large song repertoires and often mimicry of other birds.

Most starling species are highly gregarious, feeding and roosting in flocks, and are cavity nesters. The mynahs of Asia and oxpeckers of Africa are also starlings.

Thirty-two species of catbirds, mockingbirds, and thrashers range solely in the Western Hemisphere. Most have long tails and long, slightly down-curved bills.

STARLING FAMILY (Sturnidae)

European Starling (*Sturnus vulgaris*)

A short-tailed, seven- or eight-inch-long black bird is probably this species. Sexes look alike, except that

Profiles of the mimic thrushes (gray catbird at top, northern mockingbird in the middle, and brown thrasher at bottom) show similarities of head and bill shapes through progressive size differences.

females have a yellow iris ring in the eye, but the dark plumage patterns vary seasonally. With practice, one can instantly identify starlings aloft by their triangular shape; short, pointed wings; and swift, direct flight. Starlings voice numerous sounds; common songs and notes include a squealing "tseeer," a breathy "hooee," clear whistles, chuckles, gargles, and rattles.

Close relatives. More than one hundred starling species range throughout Africa and Eurasia. Two European species are the spotless and rose-coloured starlings (*S. unicolor, S. roseus*). The crested mynah (*Acridotheres cristatellus*) and hill mynah (*Gracula religiosa*), introduced to western Canada and Florida, respectively, are Asian imports whose North American populations have remained localized.

Behaviors. Like blackbirds, starlings are gregarious, have black plumage, feed mainly on the ground, and walk instead of hop. Starlings often associate with blackbirds in mixed flocks but are not closely related to them. Starling body shape is stubbier; its flight is steady and direct, unlike the hill-and-dale flight of blackbirds; and its vocal capacity is far greater. Starlings are also more abundant, probably numbering upwards of two hundred million in North America alone. Flocks in flight often maneuver as a single unit, raising some intriguing questions about how they communicate. A foraging flock moves steadily across a field by leapfrogging, as birds in the rear fly over the vanguard, and by spreading out in radial circles and arcs.

Starlings forage by probing bill length into the soil. Their jaw muscles work the bill in a reverse fashion called *gaping*. As the bird inserts its closed bill into the sod, the bill snaps open, prying apart grass roots and often exposing hidden and winter-dormant grubs. At the same time, the eyes move forward, giving the bird a narrow range of binocular vision as it probes. Some researchers attribute much of the starling's winter survival success to gaping.

This is a sociable bird at all seasons. Though it displays territorial behaviors when nesting, a pair, unless incubating eggs or brooding young, typically joins other starlings at night to roost at fixed sites, usually tree groves or ivy-covered buildings, where they noisily screech and babble. Though not as frequent or convincing a mimic as the mockingbird (a statement with which some ornithologists disagree), a starling may voice brief snatches of other bird song—some sixty species imitations have been listed—plus sounds of dogs, cats, and machinery. Males sing during the breeding season, but both sexes do so at other seasons and when roosting.

Starling migration is peculiar; some migrate and some don't. Current breeding range extends across the continent from southern Canada into Mexico and throughout temperate regions around the globe.

Spring. By early spring, starlings exhibit their glossy blue-black plumage, a result of feather tip erosion. Also by this time, the male starling has usually established his territory, the area immediately surrounding a potential nesting cavity in a tree or building. Often he preempts cavities excavated by other birds, frequently evicting the occupants. When another starling flies overhead, perchance a female, he waves his wings in a circular motion and utters squeal calls. An attracted female views his suggestive behaviors of repeated entry and exit of the prospective nest hole. When the two begin to fly and forage together, pairing has occurred. The male soon begins bringing materials into the nest cavity, but the female cleans out his contributions and collects fresh materials.

Starlings use a number of breeding strategies. Sometimes, where several cavities occur close together, they breed colonially. Bachelor nest helpers may feed nestlings and guard the nest tree. Males, which tend to outnumber females, occasionally exhibit polygyny, breeding with more than one female. Females may dump eggs in other starling nests, and a solitary, intact egg found on the ground is often a starling's—presumably the bird was unable to get back to the nest in time.

Night roosts in spring are mainly occupied by unmated and yearling males, later by paired males during female incubation. Females join the roosts after nestlings no longer need brooding for warmth.

EGGS AND YOUNG: four to six; eggs bluish or greenish white. INCU-
BATION: by both sexes (female at night); about twelve days.
FEEDING OF YOUNG: by both sexes; caterpillars and other insects.
FLEDGING: about three weeks.

Summer. Starlings often raise two broods, beginning the second
in midsummer. A male may renest with his previous mate or shift to
another while continuing to feed first-brood fledglings. These soon

join with other young starlings to
form all-juvenile flocks that forage the countryside, often in
huge numbers. This age segregation occurs only in summer. In
August, after breeding, starlings
undergo their annual molt,
replacing their worn iridescence
with light-tipped feathers that
give the birds a duller, speckled
appearance. Starlings are one of
the few American birds in which
juveniles replace all their
plumage, including flight and tail
feathers, at this time. The yellow
bills of adults also change to
grayish. A common behavior in
summer is anting—the rubbing of
ants, which release formic acid,
into the plumage. This is often
done in company with American
robins. This period also marks

*Starling plumages vary seasonally.
In late summer, the birds molt into
light-tipped feathers (top), giving
them a speckled appearance. The
light tips wear off by spring, producing the black iridescent breeding plumage (bottom).*

the formation of the largest starling assemblages, when birds of
all ages gather, sometimes by the
thousands, to roost each night in
the communal site. Often they

share these roosts with common grackles, brown-headed cowbirds, and American robins. They also join grackles, cowbirds, and redwinged blackbirds in large daytime feeding flocks.

Fall. For those starlings that migrate, seasonal timing (late September through November) and directional movements closely follow the migrational patterns of starlings in Europe, their native continent. West of the Appalachians, the directional pattern is northeast to southwest in fall, and the reverse in spring. Movements of young and nonbreeding birds seem more random and nomadic.

For the nonmigrators, concurrent with flocking behaviors comes a renewal of nest cavity territoriality by single birds, both males and females. Most of these birds are probably previous breeders.

Winter. This most stressful season results in much starling mortality. Studies indicate that about half of all the starlings alive in January, and 60 percent of first-year starlings, will die during the coming year; one-third of that mortality occurs in February and March. Yet huge numbers survive the winter because of their omnivorous diet and their feeding and behavioral adaptations. During the coldest weather, rooftop starlings often group around chimneys or near hot-air vents. Observers in Europe have noted starlings smoke bathing on chimneys—a behavior that some suggest may serve similar functions to anting.

Starling flocks decline in size and the birds split off in pairs beginning in February. In midwinter, perhaps because of energy deficits, nest site defense diminishes, but it increases again in late winter. By now, feather tips of the starling's speckled plumage are wearing off to reveal the bird's iridescent breeding plumage, and the bills are turning yellow, brighter in males. Migrants are winging north in February and March. Upon arrival, older birds usually choose nest sites located within a half mile of the previous year's nest cavity.

Ecology. The starling's abundance owes much to its success in exploiting a variety of human environs. Equally at home in urban, suburban, farm, and edge habitats, it needs tree cavities or building crevices for nesting, lawns and open meadows for foraging, and tree groves or urban structures for communal roosting. About the only places starlings do not thrive are extensive woodlands and marshes.

Starlings cannot enter cavity entrance holes one and one-half inches or less in diameter. Almost any cavity with a hole larger than this, even if already occupied, may be claimed for a nest site. The birds load the cavity with coarse plant materials plus feathers, pieces of cloth, and other items, lining the nest cup with fine grasses and feathers. Throughout incubation, starlings also bring in sprigs of green plants that may repel mite and insect parasites, often aromatic mints such as wild bergamot, spearmint, and catnip, as well as parsleys. Starling nestlings produce excessively wet fecal matter; fecal sacs are removed by parent birds only until the nestlings begin to develop feathers, when nest sanitation ceases. The nest quickly becomes a sodden, swarming, "pest-ridden compost," as one observer noted.

Though birding protocol seems to demand that we revile these

nonnative birds wherever they appear, their omnivorous food habits often prove highly beneficial to humans. Starlings feed on root parasites in lawns and short-grass fields, primarily the larvae of ground beetles, snout beetles, and scarab beetles, including the infamous Japanese beetle (*Popillia japonica*), plus ants and earthworms. They also devour many irruptive hairy caterpillars, including gypsy and tent moths. Age segregation in feeding habitats occurs in summer; juveniles, apparently less able to find soil invertebrates, forage largely on seeds and fruits in weedy fields, whereas adult flocks seek insect larvae in short-grass areas. But in later summer, as roosts approach maximal size, a diet shift occurs

This typical nest cavity used by starlings was probably originally excavated by a woodpecker. Few native cavity-nesting birds can compete with the starling's aggressive invasion of available cavities.

in many adult starlings, and wild cherries, berries, and many other fruits are now sought.

The chief source of the starling's vast unpopularity among birders is its aggressive takeover of nest cavities, thus depriving our native cavity nesters of available sites. Woodpecker cavities rank high as favored nest sites, but starlings also compete with American kestrels, great crested flycatchers, tree swallows, purple martins, house wrens, and eastern bluebirds for cavities. In spring, because of their early-timed first brood, starlings often occupy many unspoken-for cavities. Later, as they seek new cavities for second broods after royally fouling their own nests, they often attack other cavity occupants. Few native birds can withstand a determined starling onslaught. Starlings also compete with themselves, not only for nest sites but also by brood parasitism, often laying an egg or two in each other's nests. Food competition becomes significant mainly in fall and winter, when the diet turns largely to fruits. Starling flocks may vie with American robins, cedar waxwings, and other frugivores for survival nourishment during these seasons.

Though vulnerable to predation by accipiter hawks in daytime and roost-raiding owls at night, plus domestic cats, raccoons, and a few other nest robbers, starling populations are hardly dented by predators. Human efforts to break up the enormous starling roosts that sometimes invade and foul urban areas—using all sorts of explosives, noisemakers, and ingenious technological scarecrows—have shown only partial success at best. The average adult starling lives for about a year and a half, although the maximum life span is about twenty years.

Focus. It was no lack of sweet intentions that brought European starlings to America. Blame William Shakespeare, the inspiration if not the boneheaded instigator. New York businessman-dilettante Eugene Scheifflin decided to show his love of country by acclimating to America all sixty-odd bird species mentioned by Shakespeare (Bible birds having already been unsuccessfully done). The enterprise required persistent efforts to achieve, for several previous tries had not worked. In 1890, Scheifflin released sixty starlings at Central Park in New York City, and the following year, forty more.

From these hundred starlings arose the multiple progeny we see about us. Starlings reached the Midwest by the 1920s, the West Coast by the early 1940s. Scheifflin's act led directly to the establishment of federal laws restricting introductions of other wild exotics.

Despite the anathemas hurled at them by American bird lovers (for starlings remain a "respectable" species in Europe), starlings are here to stay. And they have taught us much. Working with starlings in wind tunnels, researchers discovered possible functions of the *furcula,* or wishbone, in many birds. This U-shaped bone, with each of its free ends attached to a shoulder, bends and recoils with great flexibility, pulling apart each time the wings press down. Its movements may help push airflow between the lungs and air sacs of the bones, ultimately aiding the bird's respiration, heat control, and buoyancy in flight.

Ecologists rightly voice concern about starling abundance and what it may signify regarding trends toward less diversity and more uniformity of species in our increasingly urbanized environments. Yet again, without applauding Eugene Scheifflin, one may find much to admire about starlings. Watching their behaviors, hearing their mimicry, noting their complex social interactions and plumage changes—all offer a condensed ornithology course in your backyard.

Closer look. Feare, C. *The Starling.* Oxford: Oxford University Press, 1984.

STARLING FAMILY (Sturnidae)

Gray Catbird (*Dumetella carolinensis*)

This nine-inch-long mimid can be identified by its gray-black plumage, black head cap, rusty undertail coverts, or *crissum,* tail-flicking habit, and catlike mewing notes. Sexes look alike. Partially albino catbirds are sometimes seen, usually showing white patches or banding.

Close relatives. The black catbird (*Melanoptila glabrirostris*), a resident of Mexico and Central America, is the only other catbird.

Behaviors. Its curiosity and conspicuous sounds and behaviors make this smallest, most common North American mimid easily observable in its habitats. Catbird breeding range spans almost the entire continental United States. Although not so frequent or accomplished a mimic as some of its family relatives, the catbird has been known to imitate songs and calls of at least thirty-five bird species, plus occasional tree frogs and wagon wheels; its familiar mewing note, however, is not mimicry. Ornithologist James Granlund has observed that the birds seem to increase their song repertoires with age. The catbird also sings a sweet song of its own, consisting of jumbled musical phrases always interspersed with a few harsh squealing notes. Catbirds feed both on the ground, where they often forage by bill-sweeping, and in shrub and tree foliage. Most catbirds migrate.

Spring. Traveling at night, many of them directly over the Gulf of Mexico, catbirds arrive on their breeding range in late April and early May. Male catbirds precede females by a week or more and immediately establish territories by loud singing and chasing of other catbirds. Territories average one to three acres in size, usually in a previous nesting area. Males pursue females on their territories; they strut and fluff, erecting their tails to exhibit their only real color marking, the rusty crissum. Females construct the nests, and males cease singing when incubation begins. A pair never leaves its initial territory, even to feed, until nesting is completed. As nesting progresses, however, the vigorously defended area shrinks in size to the nest vicinity. Some catbirds remain paired over several breeding seasons.

EGGS AND YOUNG: usually four; eggs blue-green. INCUBATION: by female, which is fed by male; male also guards the nest; about twelve days. FEEDING OF YOUNG: by both sexes; insects and spiders, berries in late nestling stages. FLEDGING: ten or eleven days.

Summer. While first-brood fledglings remain in the nest vicinity, fed mainly by the male parent for about two weeks, the male also resumes singing, and a shift in territorial size and shape occurs. The female begins building a second nest in early summer, usually in the vicinity of the first. In a few areas, catbirds may even raise third broods. Then the birds congregate in heavier lowland cover. The annual feather molt occurs in August.

Fall. Listen now for the catbird's whisper song, a soft soliloquy version of the spring song, uttered anytime but most frequently in autumn. Most catbirds move south in September and October, but small populations remain on parts of the breeding range during most winters.

Winter. Catbird winter range includes the southern coastal states, the Caribbean islands, and Central America to Panama. Often they feed in flocks, but they remain mostly silent.

Gray catbird nests, built in dense shrub thickets, look bulky and unkempt. They resemble the nests of a competitor species (see illustration, Northern Cardinal).

Ecology. On their breeding range, catbirds favor wetland edge habitats, especially dense thickets bordering swamps, ponds, and other lowland areas. Willow-dogwood shrublands are favored sites, but almost any thicket habitat, including hedgerows and yard shrubbery, may host a resident pair. On their winter range, catbirds forage in dense rain-forest habitats, banana plantations, and thickets.

The crucial element for catbird nesting is foliage density. Tartarian honeysuckle, hawthorns, and grape tangles are commonly used sites in drier thickets. Usually the bulky, ragged-looking nest, seldom placed higher than ten feet, occupies the densest, innermost heart of the thicket. Leaves in the foundation plus twigs, weed stalks, grapevine bark, and often pieces of paper or cellophane form the nest's outer construction; its deep cup is lined with dark rootlets. The otherwise similar nests of northern cardinals show few if any leaves in the foundation and a lining of fine grasses. Vacated catbird nests are frequently recycled by other creatures. White-footed mice pile additional materials on them for their own nests, and red squirrels and American robins also sometimes build on catbird nest foundations. Chipmunks, mice, and squirrels use the nests as storage and feeding platforms.

The catbird's diet is roughly half animal, half vegetable. Ants, beetles, caterpillars, grasshoppers, and spiders constitute much of its spring and summer food; its seasonal consumption of blackberries, cherries, elderberries, and grapes, among other fruits, makes the catbird one of our foremost fruit eaters, or frugivores. Occasionally it raids cultivated fruit crops but usually causes few losses. Economically, the catbird's consumption of irruptive cankerworms, armyworms, cicadas, and sawfly larvae more than compensates for its orchard forays.

Its foremost nest-site competitors are northern cardinals and brown thrashers, both upland thicket dwellers. Where numerous enough, catbirds are usually territorially dominant over both species, but either may usurp catbird nests on occasion. In areas of habitat overlap, red-winged blackbirds may also conflict with catbirds. Catbirds may compete with other frugivores at certain times and places for food, but except for north-wintering catbirds, food competition is probably negligible.

Nest predators include red squirrels, chipmunks, raccoons, domestic cats, American crows, house wrens, and several snakes: blue racers and black rat, fox, garter, and milk snakes. Catbirds share with thrushes two parasites of the nasal passages, both rhinonyssine mites. I will never forget reaching overhead one day to feel into a catbird nest and experiencing the peculiar sensation of a wave moving down my arm from the empty nest—an almost invisible swarm of mites. Brown-headed cowbirds do not effectively parasitize catbird broods; catbirds quickly pierce and eject cowbird eggs.

Focus. The catbird's song, or perhaps its harsh mewing notes, seemed like mourning sounds to the Chippewa, who named it "the bird that cries with grief." The only other mewing bird of the Northeast is the yellow-bellied sapsucker.

Records of seven-year-old catbirds exist, but the average life span is probably two or three years. Catbirds have amply benefited from the creation of edge habitats and fruit culture, and it is likely that their current numbers vastly surpass their presettlement populations. Their trend of increase continues in many areas.

Closer look. Nickell, W. P. *Habitats, Territory and Nesting of the Catbird.* Notre Dame, IN: University of Notre Dame Press, 1965.

STARLING FAMILY (Sturnidae)

Northern Mockingbird (*Mimus polyglottos*)

This conspicuous, long-tailed, robin-size bird is drab grayish with large white wing and tail patches, which are best seen when it flies. A frequent mimic of other bird species, it utters snatches and phrases of various songs in its own musical, repetitive phrasings. Sexes look alike.

Close relatives. Nine other *Mimus* species plus some seven mockingbirds of different genera reside in Mexico, the West Indies, and South America.

Behaviors. Ornithologist Frank M. Chapman called the Northern Mockingbird our "national songbird." One of the most accomplished vocal mimics in the bird world, the mockingbird advertises its presence loudly and incessantly, often from a conspicuous perch. Its song largely consists of multiple plagiarism, bits and pieces lifted from the repertoires of almost any other bird it has heard, plus frog croaks, dog barks, cat meows, gate squeaks, and tire squeals. One Indian tale, however, reverses the sequence: The mockingbird taught all the other birds to sing, so *they* are the plagiarists. In any case, no two mockingbirds ever sing exactly alike. A single song bout may last up to ten minutes, a medley that itself may differ from the bird's next or past performances. It may repeat particular notes up to a dozen times before switching to another arrangement. Some male mockingbirds, writes researcher Randall Breitwisch, "have repertoires in excess of two hundred songs, certainly the acoustic equivalent of the peacock's tail." Probably their repertoire has no upper limit, as the birds add new songs and sounds throughout their lives. For birders, mockingbird medleys of stolen song offer a postgraduate course in listening. Human ears are easily fooled by mimicry, but most bird species that mockingbirds imitate seem to ignore them (although this is a subject that may bear further investigation).

Note the mockingbird's wing action. In flight, the bird plows through the air like "oaring an old rowboat," as one observer wrote. As it drops to the ground, where it forages much of the time, it often holds its wings aloft for an instant after landing, much as some shorebirds do. While foraging, it slowly elevates and spreads its wings, displaying its white patches. Some researchers suggest that this wing-flashing behavior may startle insects into movement, making them easier to capture.

Highly aggressive toward territorial intruders, mockingbirds seem to relish diving upon dogs, cats, and snakes, with other mockers often joining in. They also attack blue jays and other birds, and occasionally even people, that venture too close to a nest.

Mockingbirds reside most abundantly in the southern United States. Since about 1920, however, their breeding range has expanded northward to southern Canada, but northern populations remain sporadic and local. Many of these northern birds migrate in fall to the South. Most mockingbirds, however, remain on or near their breeding territories year-round.

Spring. Seasonal timing of mockingbird breeding varies with latitude; northern populations may not begin nesting until early summer. Males precede females on the breeding territory—usually one or two acres—in late April and May, or earlier southward. Loud song uttered from conspicuous perches plus aerial loop flights mark the male's initial territorial behaviors. Singing peaks as females arrive and nesting begins, then rapidly declines during incubation and the nestling period. Male mockingbirds that fail to find mates continue singing on their territories into midsummer, often into the night. Mockingbirds usually form long-term pair bonds, though pairs occasionally split between successive nestings. Polygyny, in which one male mates with two or more females, also may occur.

EGGS AND YOUNG: usually four; eggs blue-green, heavily brown spotted. INCUBATION: by female; about twelve days. FEEDING OF YOUNG: by both sexes; insects, fruits. FLEDGING: about twelve days.

Summer. Males continue to feed fledglings for up to a month on the territory as the pair builds a new nest and females begin a second brood. Should a nesting fail through predation, the male immediately begins singing again, signaling his mate to start over—but sometimes, in that event, she deserts to another male's territory. "Females may be programmed to try a new [perhaps more protective?] mate when no young are fledged," suggests Breitwisch. The annual molt, as juveniles finally disperse and territories are abandoned, occurs in late summer.

Fall. Individuals of both sexes plus mated pairs again become territorial in the fall, and now both sexes sing. These territories are centered around a food source, usually a fruit-bearing tree or shrub, and are vigorously defended. They tend to fluctuate in size, depending on the durability of the food source and on the weather; often they roughly coincide with the breeding territory. Wandering flocks of mockingbirds, mostly unpaired juveniles, often intrude on these territories and are aggressively chased. After fall territory formation, often in November, you may see the border dance, which might be described as an exercise in bird diplomacy: Two mockingbirds of adjacent territories meet on the ground, strutting, darting, generally aping each other's behavior. Sometimes this action provokes a brief scrap, but usually the birds simply fly off to their own territories, their borderlines apparently reaffirmed. In many areas, pair bonding of previously unmated birds probably occurs in fall and winter. Mockingbird migration consists mainly of females and juveniles; many males tend to remain in their northern range.

Winter. Mockingbirds sing infrequently now; their only defensive behavior consists of chasing other fruit-eating birds from their food territories.

Ecology. Mockingbirds occupy open and semiopen edge habitats, mosaics of plant cover and open space, including pasture thickets, orchards, and hedgerows. They have adapted especially well to urban and suburban gardens, parks, and yard shrubbery, seeming to favor sites near houses. A tall sentry tree or perch from which to sing and survey the territory seems essential.

Mockingbirds typically place their nests up to ten feet high in a shrub, small tree, or vine. In the Northeast, they favor red cedar, spruces, hawthorns, privet hedges, and osage orange and multiflora rose thickets for nest sites. The male usually builds the nest foundation of thorny sticks, forming a bulky mass; then the female lines the nest with grasses, plant stems, and brown rootlets. Mockingbird nests are virtually identical in site, size, and appearance to gray catbird nests.

The mockingbird's diet, like the catbird's, closely balances between animal and vegetable, with fruits holding a slight edge. Spiders and insects—mainly beetles, ants, and grasshoppers—are consumed most abundantly during the breeding season. Nestlings are fed animal matter for about a week, until they have developed *endothermy,* or body temperature control; then they consume increasing amounts of fruit. Summer, fall, and winter diets include fruits of hollies, greenbriers, sumacs, and pokeweed, as well as blackberries, common elderberries, and grapes. Where sufficient wild fruits exist, mockingbirds seldom invade orchards or berry farms. Mockingbird range expansion in northern states since the 1950s has closely paralleled the spread of multiflora rose (*Rosa multiflora*). This thorny alien shrub, once widely touted for wildlife plantings, has become an aggressive nuisance in many areas. Its high-nutrient fruits remain on the plant through winter, however, and in the North it now ranks as the mockingbird's chief winter

The spread of multi-flora rose thickets probably accounts for mockingbird range expansion in the northern United States. Mockingbirds not only consume the rose hips but also nest in this thorny hedge plant.

food source. In some areas, the birds nest in multiflora rose thickets, so this plant-bird association extends year-round.

Mockingbird territorial behaviors reveal strong competitiveness with other mockingbirds for nest sites and food sources. Though precise data are lacking, potential nest site competitors in areas where breeding ranges coincide include gray catbirds, some of the forest thrushes, and northern cardinals. Food competitors include all other frugivorous, or fruit-eating, birds—blue jays, American robins, European starlings, and common grackles, among others. A food tree claimed by a mockingbird, however, often becomes strictly off-limits to other frugivores.

The mockingbird's innate pugnacity drives off many would-be predators, yet most mockingbird nesting failures apparently result from predation. Snakes (kingsnakes, racers, and rat snakes), accipiter hawks, blue jays, American crows, opossums, raccoons, and domestic cats are the foremost threats. Brown-headed cowbirds rarely parasitize mockingbird nests.

Focus. Mockingbirds in the wild have been known to live for twelve years. Many Native American legends treated the mockingbird with awe, often associating it with the divine gift of language. English naturalist Mark Catesby, exploring in the Carolinas, first named it the mock-bird in 1731. Audubon associated the bird mainly with Louisiana, where he first saw it. Today, five other southern states—Arkansas, Florida, Mississippi, Tennessee, and Texas—

honor it as their state bird. Some regional writers have proclaimed its music the ultimate "song of the South" or the "voice of the realm." The mockingbird's symbolism extends to such works of American literature as Walt Whitman's poetry and Harper Lee's 1960 novel, *To Kill a Mockingbird.*

Bird-song analyst Charles Hartshorne expressed the interesting idea that each mockingbird's song is, in a sense, an autobiography—a record of the bird's exposure to the sounds, and thus the environs, of its lifetime.

Closer look. Doughty, R. W. *The Mockingbird.* Austin: University of Texas Press, 1988.

STARLING FAMILY (Sturnidae)

Brown Thrasher (*Toxostoma rufum*)

The brown thrasher's long, red-brown tail makes up about half of its twelve-inch length. Our largest and shiest mimid also has red-brown back and wings, heavy brown breast striping, and yellow eyes. It voices its loud, musical song in paired phrases, and often utters the smack call, which sounds like a loud kiss, when it is alarmed. Sexes look alike.

Close relatives. Six other *Toxostoma* species reside in the western United States. Most, like the sage thrasher (*Oreoscoptes montanus*), are desert birds. Some ten other species reside mainly in the West Indies.

Behaviors. Thrushlike in plumage and wrenlike in behaviors, brown thrashers are slimmer than thrushes and much larger than wrens. The thrasher's conspicuous behaviors, long tail, and twice-repeated song pattern make it easy to identify. This bird spends most of its time on or near the ground except when singing—often from a high, conspicuous perch—and migrating. Mainly a ground forager, it bill-sweeps dead leaves and other debris as it feeds. Its breeding range spans the continent, corresponding closely with that of its relative, the gray catbird. Also like the catbird, it occasionally includes mimicry of other birds—northern flickers, tufted titmice, wood thrushes, and northern cardinals, among others—in its song phrases. Unlike the catbird, however, it tends to shun human proximity. Brown thrashers are migrators, but a few often linger on the breeding range over winter.

Spring. Brown thrashers usually arrive on their northern breeding range in April, males preceding females. Territories may cover two to ten acres, depending on the habitat and thrasher abundance. The male's loud treetop song gives way to softer versions on lower perches as pairing begins. Few courtship behaviors have been observed. In May, both sexes collect nesting materials, but females do the actual building. Males, unless unmated, seldom sing conspicuously after nesting begins.

EGGS AND YOUNG: four or five; eggs bluish white, thickly dotted with brown. INCUBATION: by both sexes, sometimes singing on the nest; about two weeks. FEEDING OF YOUNG: by both sexes; mainly insects. FLEDGING: about ten days.

Summer. Despite bold thrasher defense of their nests, predation apparently causes many nesting failures in this species. Because of first-nest failure or double brooding, many, if not most, brown thrashers renest in early summer. Males continue feeding the fledged first brood while females begin the second nesting. Many thrashers apparently do not pair for life and may even switch mates between nestings. By late summer, when the annual feather molt occurs, young thrashers are on their own, and the birds become silent and secretive.

Fall, Winter. Southward migration occurs mainly in September. Most brown thrashers winter south of the Ohio River to the Gulf states. These birds are site faithful to both summer and winter territories. In parts of Texas, they share their winter range with long-billed and curve-billed thrashers (*T. longirostre, T. curvirostre*).

Ecology. Brown thrashers favor thickets, the denser and thornier the better. Dry forest edges and brushy undergrowth are common breeding habitats, as are conifer plantations.

Brown thrasher nests, despite their loose construction, are often visibly layered with various plant materials. These birds frequently build on the ground.

Nests vary in height. In New England, thrashers often nest on the ground; elsewhere, they usually build less than seven feet high in such shrubs as hawthorns and viburnums, often placing late-season nests higher than earlier ones. The bulky nests are typically four-layered: large foundation sticks; dead leaves and grapevine bark; grass stems and dirt-encrusted rootlets; and a clean rootlet lining.

During the breeding season, thrashers feed chiefly on beetles, as well as ants, caterpillars, crickets, and other insects. Spiders, earthworms, and frogs are also consumed. At other seasons, blackberries, wild cherries, common elderberries, dogwood fruits, blueberries, corn, and acorns rank high in the diet.

Gray catbirds and northern cardinals compete with brown thrashers for breeding habitat. Somewhat less opportunistic than these species in diet and habitat use, thrashers may sometimes be driven out of areas where one or both are numerous. In their western winter range, brown thrashers occupy dense riverbottom thickets; the other two thrasher species with which they may share their winter range favor chaparral scrub.

Predators are generally the same as for gray catbirds. Brown-headed cowbird parasitism occurs, but usually at low levels. Thrashers may eject cowbird eggs. Research suggests that cowbirds may mistakenly eject their own eggs from thrasher nests, on the basis of size; thrashers are the largest passerines victimized by cowbirds, and unlike eggs in most host nests, thrasher eggs are larger than those of cowbirds.

Focus. While the related northern mockingbird has a large song repertoire, the thrasher's is larger—indeed, with an estimated three thousand or more song types, the largest of any North American bird's. The names *thrasher* and *thrush* derive from the same Anglo-Saxon root. Brown thrush is a colloquial label for this thrasher.

Unlike catbirds and most other edge species, brown thrashers appear to be declining in most of their breeding range. Causes remain unclear. Individual thrashers have been known to survive almost thirteen years, but most probably live less than half that long.

The brown thrasher is Georgia's state bird.

18

White-breasted Nuthatch
(*Sitta carolinensis*)

Common nuthatch family (Sittidae). This five-inch-long bark climber can be recognized by its white underparts, dark-capped head (black in males, grayish in females), pearl gray back, stubby tail, and chisellike bill. Its nasal "ank ank" notes are distinctive, as is its habit of spiraling head-downward on tree trunks.

Close relatives. All seventeen worldwide *Sitta* species range in the Northern Hemisphere. The three other North American nuthatches are smaller by an inch or more. They are the red-breasted nuthatch (*S. canadensis*), with an exclusively northern breeding range; the brown-headed nuthatch (*S. pusilla*) of southeastern coastal states; and the pygmy nuthatch (*S. pygmaea*), western counterpart of the brown-headed. Most

The white-breasted nuthatch (right) and brown creeper (left), both in characteristic postures, show resemblances but are not closely related. Nuthatches typically forage downward on trees; creepers move up the trunk.

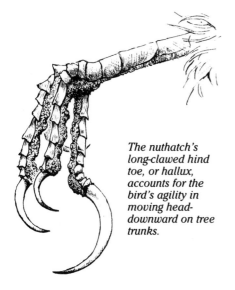

The nuthatch's long-clawed hind toe, or hallux, accounts for the bird's agility in moving head-downward on tree trunks.

common of four European species is the Eurasian nuthatch (*S. europaea*).

Behaviors. This small bird, built like a chunky dart, usually zigzags headfirst down a tree trunk; a brownish bird spiraling *up* the trunk is probably the unrelated brown creeper (*Certhia americana*). A foraging nuthatch typically flies from the base of one tree to the top of another, working the trunks from the top down, although nuthatches occasionally go up the trunk as well. Unlike woodpeckers, nuthatches do not need stiff, bracing tails for support; their antigravity device is a long, clawlike hind toe on each foot that anchors them to the trees. When feeding on a nut or seed, nuthatches do not hold it with their feet like jays and chickadees but wedge it tightly into a crevice, where they hammer it open. At night, each bird roosts separately in a tree cavity, always removing its feces from the hole in the morning. White-breasted nuthatches maintain a year-round pair bond, remaining on a home range of twenty-five to forty-five acres.

These birds are nonmigratory throughout most of their range, which coincides generally with the lower forty-eight states. Portions of the eastern population, however, often shift southward in fall and northward in spring.

Spring. Nuthatch courtship and territorial behaviors are usually in full swing by the end of winter or before. Pair bonds become explicit, with male feeding of females and bowing, chasing, and singing from treetops or conspicuous perches. The defended territory, some twenty to fifty acres, is usually a slightly smaller portion of the home range. Though nuthatches seldom remain silent for long, the pair becomes uncharacteristically quiet during incubation.

EGGS AND YOUNG: typically eight; eggs white, brown spotted. INCU-BATION: by female, which is fed by male; about twelve days. FEEDING OF YOUNG: by both sexes; insects. FLEDGING: about two weeks.

Summer. Nuthatches raise only one brood in their northern range. Parents continue to feed the young for two or three weeks after fledging, and families often remain together for several months. In late summer, adult nuthatches undergo their annual feather molt.

Fall. Young birds disperse from the original home range by late fall, some of them apparently migrating southward, presumably to areas of more abundant winter food.

Winter. This is the season when nuthatch nasal nagging may persist for minutes at a time in the woods. The birds can easily be spotted high in the trees or hitching down trunks. A resident pair forages throughout its home range during winter, often not close to one another but maintaining aural contact. Often, too, they temporarily join mixed feeding flocks of black-capped chickadees, tufted titmice, downy woodpeckers, and brown creepers. Nuthatches frequently visit yard feeders but seldom consume seeds there; like chickadees, they grab and fly. Nuthatch behaviors become most conspicuous and vocal during February and March as the birds begin to renew courtship and territorial activities.

Ecology. Beech-maple woodlands are favored habitats, but this species inhabits other deciduous and mixed forest types as well. It also frequents shady residential areas, orchards, and parks.

For nest sites, white-breasted nuthatches seek large knotholes or natural cavities in mature deciduous trees. They also use old woodpecker holes, preferring an entrance hole double or triple their body size, in contrast to woodpeckers, which usually favor a close fit.

A characteristic nuthatch habit is bill-sweeping the bark around the nest hole, usually with a crushed insect held in the bill, or with wads of plant material or fur. Both sexes sweep with great vigor, sometimes for several minutes. Sweeping is done before actual nest building—"as one might paint a house prior to moving in," wrote one observer—and may continue at intervals until nestlings fledge. At least one of the insects used in this activity is a large black beetle found on flowers and foliage, the blister beetle (*Meloe angusticollis*). When disturbed, this insect releases an oily, corrosive fluid called cantharidin from its leg joints. A squirrel in the nest vicinity often inspires a bout of bill-sweeping, and most observers believe that cantharidin or other odorous substances smeared around nest holes may repel predators or mammal competitors for a tree cavity. Sometimes the birds also stuff bits of fur in crevices around the nest hole, another possible mammal deterrent. Females collect most of the nesting materials: bark shreds, grasses, rootlets, and pieces of fur.

Spring and summer foods consist almost entirely of insects and spiders, many of them foraged from bark. Weevils, ants, adult moths, and caterpillars, including the irruptive larvae of forest tent and gypsy moths, are commonly taken. Fall and winter diet shifts to almost 70 percent vegetable foods, mainly acorns but also corn, beechnuts, pine, and other seeds. Food caching is frequent, usually in bark furrows or crevices of such trees as elms, oaks, and hemlock, and beneath the loose bark shingles of shagbark hickory (also beneath rooftop shingles). In winter, bark-foraging nuthatches consume huge numbers of spiders, insect eggs, and hibernating scale insects.

Red, gray, and flying squirrels are probably the foremost nuthatch competitors for both nest cavities and food. Other contenders for nest cavities include tufted titmice, European starlings, and house sparrows. Bird and mammal competition for acorns in the fall is always keen, and squirrels sometimes raid bark-cached items placed by nuthatches. In winter, competition among birds in mixed feeding flocks seems offset by the benefits of this association for food finding and predator detection.

Focus. This bird's name is a corruption of *nuthack,* so named because it hacks at nuts. White-bellied nuthatch is an old name for the white-breasted. The nuthatch has been nicknamed the upside-down bird because of its typical posture on a vertical surface.

Nuthatches are among the few regular talkers in the silent winter woods as pairs forage and maintain contact. "The moment comes in almost everyone's life when a nuthatch is needed," wrote naturalist Rick Marsi. They "rocket you out of the doldrums" by their feeding antics and steady self-commentary. They inform us, in short, that an upside-down way of life is perfectly normal.

19

House Wren (*Troglodytes aedon*)

Creeper, wren, and gnatcatcher family (Certhiidae). All wrens have slender, slightly down-curved bills and often cock their tails upward. At five inches or less, the house wren, the most common North American wren, ranks midway in size among other wren species. It can be identified by its gray-brown color, lack of a pronounced white eye line, and stuttering, bubbling song. When alarmed or aggressive, it often voices a staccato chatter. Sexes look alike.

Close relatives. The only other northeastern wren of the same genus is the winter wren (*T. troglodytes*). Other eastern species include the Carolina wren (*Thryothorus ludovicianus*), Bewick's wren (*Thryomanes bewickii*), marsh wren (*Cistothorus palustris*), and sedge wren (*C. platensis*). Western U.S. species include the canyon wren (*Catherpes mexicanus*), rock wren (*Salpinctes obsoletus*), and cactus wren (*Campylorhyncus brunneicapillus*). More than sixty wren species range worldwide. Other northeastern family members include the brown creeper (*Certhia americana*) and the blue-gray gnatcatcher (*Polioptila caerulea*).

Not a good neighbor to other birds, the house wren often disrupts the nests of other species on or near its own territory.

Behaviors. The male house wren's loud, gurgling song often sounds incessantly in spring and summer.

Females sing occasionally, too. Native Chippewas, saddling this bird with even more syllables than its Latin name, gave it a name meaning "making big noise for its size." For its size, it also manifests extremely aggressive behaviors toward other birds; to a house wren, almost any other nesting bird in its territory threatens competition. It often claims all nest cavities anywhere near its own. If these cavities are occupied by any bird smaller than woodpeckers, punctured eggs or dead nestlings are the common result. House wrens may likewise attack open, noncavity nests. What one observer called this "Nazi trait" of house wrens may distress some bird lovers who discover wren mayhem in their bluebird boxes. Some studies suggest that unmated wrens are the main egg-destroying culprits.

House wrens are migratory birds with strong site fidelity to their previous breeding territories. Their breeding range spans the continent from southern Canada to the southeastern United States.

Spring. Older males arrive on the breeding range in April, preceding females (which precede yearling males) by a week or two. By song, a male establishes, or reestablishes, his territory of about half an acre or more. He explores every potential cavity site in his territory—in trees, fence posts, nest boxes—and clears them of old nesting material. Then he begins preliminary nest building in up to seven cavities. In nest boxes already occupied by such residents as tree swallows or eastern bluebirds, he may build atop the nest. Sometimes he lays only a base of dead twigs and other times almost fills

The house wren's nest is a deep cup pocketed in a mass of stiff twigs, feathers, insect cocoons, bits of snakeskin, and other materials. This one, viewed from above, was crammed into a birdhouse.

the cavity with them, often leaving a single twig protruding from the entrance hole. Females, when they arrive, inspect all of these dummy nests. In mid-May, they select one for the actual nest, finishing it off with a deep cup of finer materials: grasses, plant fibers, feathers, insect cocoons, and bits of rubbish.

EGGS AND YOUNG: six to eight; eggs white, thickly speckled with reddish brown dots. INCUBATION: by female; about two weeks. FEEDING OF YOUNG: by both sexes; insects. FLEDGING: about seventeen days.

Summer. Most breeding house wrens raise two broods in a season. The male may exhibit polygyny, mating with two or more females that nest in his territory. Pair bonds also may shift to new partners between broods. After the first brood fledges in June, parent birds continue feeding the young for about two weeks. Then the female begins another nesting cycle. The male continues caring for the first brood while maintaining his territory and sometimes attracting new mates. Second broods usually fledge by early August, male singing declines, and the birds become much more secretive. The annual feather molt occurs in late summer; new plumage is darker and grayer than the breeding plumage.

Fall. Skulkers now in dense woodland underbrush, house wrens still voice an occasional, more subdued version of territorial song. Most depart their breeding range in September and early October.

Winter. House wren winter range extends from the Carolinas south along the coastal states into Mexico and northern Central America. The birds remain mostly silent and inconspicuous, foraging singly or in pairs, usually in dense thickets and undergrowth. As spring nears, the males begin to vocalize brief snatches of song. The lighter brown breeding plumage results from erosion of the darker feather tips acquired during the fall molt.

Ecology. House wrens favor edge habitats—thickets, open woodlots, orchards, and forest openings. Palmetto thickets, brushy tangles, and swampy undergrowth are typical winter habitats.

For nesting, the birds prefer open edge areas with extended visibility. It isn't Mister Loudmouth that persuades Jenny to linger but the aspect of his acre. The quality of a male's territory—that is, its insect resources and amount of properly spaced vegetation—also may determine whether, and how often, polygyny occurs. House wrens are noted for the variety of nest sites they may improvise; tin cans, flowerpots, car radiators, boots, hats, and pockets in hanging clothes are only a few of the many places they may choose.

House wrens feed almost entirely on insects and spiders; grasshoppers, beetles, bugs (including negro bugs, stink bugs, and leafhoppers), and caterpillars rank high in their diet.

Nest-site competitors include woodpeckers, great crested flycatchers, eastern bluebirds, European starlings, black-capped chickadees, tree swallows, house sparrows, deer mice, and even paper wasps. Relatively few of these can withstand house wren persistence in claiming a cavity.

Foremost predators include cats and other house wrens, which occasionally raid nests outside their territories.

Focus. To wrens we owe the institution of the annual Christmas bird count, conducted by the National Audubon Society since 1900 to offset the then-widespread practice of Christmas bird shoots. Naturalist Charles L. Horn described these shoots as "the connecting link between the modern Christmas count and the medieval Hunting of the Wren," an annual rite in which a wren, symbolizing the king, was slain for good luck. Wrens remained untouchable at all other times of year. In Germany, the wren (*T. troglodytes,* our winter wren species) is still called *zaunkönig,* "hedge king." Why such a small bird—rather than a large raptor, for example—was chosen to represent royalty may have conveyed a message in itself.

House wrens are probably much more abundant today than in presettlement times because of the increase in edge habitats created by lumbering and farming. Where forests regrow, house wren populations usually decline.

20

TITMOUSE FAMILY (Paridae)

Short, sharp bills and strong legs that enable them to glean food from branch tips characterize these small, acrobatic birds. Some fifty species exist worldwide, almost all of them in the genus *Parus*. Eleven species of chickadees and titmice reside in North America. North American chickadees have black or brown caps and black bibs; titmice are grayish and crested. All are cavity nesters, and most are nonmigrators.

Black-capped Chickadee (*Parus atricapillus*)

This five-inch-long parid is marked by a black cap, throat, and bib; buffy flanks; and a white belly. Commonly heard sounds are a clear, whistled "fee-bee," the first note a full tone above the second, and a buzzy "chick-a-dee-dee-dee" or variations thereof. Sexes look alike.

Close relatives. Of the six North American chickadees, two besides the black-capped reside in the East: the Carolina chickadee (*P. carolinensis*) of the southern states, and the boreal chickadee (*P. hudsonicus*), which inhabits northern coniferous forests across the continent. Western species include the Mexican chickadee (*P. sclateri*), the mountain chickadee (*P. gambeli*), and the chestnut-backed chickadee (*P. rufescens*). The genus *Parus* also includes titmice. England's twelve *Parus* species are called tits.

Behaviors. Most people see black-capped chickadees at winter yard feeders. Typically a chickadee rushes in, snatches a seed, and flies to nearby cover, where it vigorously attacks the seed by holding it down with a foot and hammering it to pieces.

Chickadees operate in small territorial flocks of about ten birds for most of the year. Their social relations are rigidly stratified, with a dominant pair forming the nucleus of the group. This system of status and precedence may easily be seen at the yard feeder, where a low-ranking chickadee invariably gives way to a higher-ranking bird. Males are dominant over females in most flocks, but older females rank over younger females and occasionally over young males as well. Relative size of the bird and seniority in the flock are other rank-determining factors. Apparently a chickadee can spot the flock ranking of another chickadee from some distance away, so some degree of individual recognition is involved. Various vocal signals in a feeding flock maintain contact among birds and warn of possible predators.

Their well-known curiosity makes chickadees easy to attract by pishing or by playing owl tapes. Watch them watch you while they "pretend" to be exploring a twig, "as if they were minding their own business all the while," observed Thoreau. Researchers believe that

Chickadee dominance systems may be readily observed at yard feeders. Birds perched on the rims and above are probably subordinates that will be chased if they venture onto the feeding tray.

this *displacement behavior,* common in many bird species, provides an outlet for surplus energy generated by curiosity—interest in an observer, for example. Chickadees also quickly respond to distress calls of other birds, and they frequently mob predators with incessant "dee-dee-dee" calls.

Black-capped chickadees mate for life. They inhabit the northern two-thirds of the United States plus much of Canada. In most of their range, they remain on year-round flock territories, but portions of northernmost chickadee populations migrate.

Spring. Most chickadee pairing has already occurred by late winter and early spring. Winter flocks are now breaking up as high-ranking pairs become territorially aggressive, driving away lower-ranking birds. The latter disperse to nearby areas, usually within the flock range, some to establish breeding territories of their own. The size of chickadee territories often fluctuates depending on local abundance of breeding chickadees, habitat quality, relative social rankings, and time progression of the breeding cycle. A pair that begins defending a ten-acre territory, for example, often decreases its territory size as nesting progresses—until, at fledging time, the territory disappears altogether. No courtship behaviors have been identified in this species. Instances of both *polyandry* (one female, two males) and *polygyny* (one male, two females) sometimes occur.

Black-capped chickadees utter at least fifteen kinds of notes or note patterns. Most often heard in spring are the whistled "fee-bee" notes, given mostly by males when establishing breeding territories. Softer "fee-bee" calls from either sex usually indicate incubation or brood-rearing stages of nesting. Gargle notes, a kind of musical sputter, often occur during territorial skirmishes. A common behavior when threatened by an intruding finger or pencil in the nest cavity is a startling hiss and swaying motion followed by a sudden lunge at the intruder. This so-called snake display has been cited as an example of *Batesian mimicry,* in which a prey species mimics the appearance or behaviors of a predator. To see a chickadee mimic a snake can be a bit unnerving even to a human observer.

EGGS AND YOUNG: about seven; eggs white, dotted with reddish-brown spots. INCUBATION: by female, which is fed by male; about twelve days. FEEDING OF YOUNG: by both sexes; insects. FLEDGING: about sixteen days.

Summer. Most pairs nest only once a year. After nestlings fledge, family groups move off their territories and wander about, rarely challenged by still-territorial pairs. Loudly begging juveniles remain dependent on food brought by parent birds for up to a month, then suddenly disperse in random directions, often to areas several miles away. Chickadee mobbing of such predators as owls reaches a peak in summer; perhaps, one researcher suggests, this is how the juveniles (as well as other birds such as warblers, which often join late-summer chickadee feeding flocks) learn to recognize predators. The annual feather molt begins in July or early August, lasting into fall. Molting chickadees become secretive and sedentary during this period.

Fall. In late summer and fall, a major shift in chickadee social organization occurs. Dispersing juveniles join flocks consisting of local breeding pairs. A typical flock numbers six to ten birds. Pair formation of singles occurs in the flocks, which persist over winter. Most chickadee flocks begin with equal sex ratios, though mortality factors eventually tip them either way. A hierarchy of pairs rather than of individuals dominates the flock. If both members of a pair survive until spring, they will then mate. The flock range, occupying twenty or more acres, usually encompasses the former breeding territory of the dominant pair in the flock. Flocks often vigorously defend their ranges from other chickadee flocks.

Southward migrations of black-capped chickadees appear irregular, both in frequency and in numbers. Most chickadee migrants are young birds. In some years, hardly any southward movement occurs; in irruption years, thousands of chickadees travel. Irruption years in the Northeast seem to correlate strongly with seasons of low conifer seed production.

Winter. Food resources grow leaner as food needs become greater in winter, the only real crunch time for most chickadees. Many of them do not survive this season. Young birds appear most vulnerable to predation and starvation. Up to 25 percent of a post-fledgling population may die before their first winter; more than 70 percent do not survive their first year. "To the chickadee," wrote Aldo Leopold, "winter wind is the boundary of the habitable world." During cold winter nights, black-capped chickadees roost singly, often in dense conifers or tree cavities. "One of the most amazing adaptations they possess," one researcher noted, is *regulated hypothermia,* the ability to decrease body temperature at night by about half—from about 108 degrees F. to about 50 degrees—thus preserving energy. Hummingbirds, swifts, and whip-poor-wills also become hypothermic at night.

Chickadee researcher Susan M. Smith found that two sorts of chickadees populate winter flocks: *regulars,* consisting of pairs, and *floaters,* unpaired birds that freely range between three or four flocks. Floaters are always subordinate birds except when a high-ranking pair member dies, in which case a floater fills the empty slot, thus leaving intact the pairings of the other regulars. Although complex shiftings and variations occur, floaters essentially provide the key to flock stability. Floaters that find no missing pair slots to fill remain unpaired but always available flock switchers. Young chickadees usually enter the flock system as floaters or low-ranked regulars. The "chick-a-dee-dee-dee" call, commonly heard in winter, serves to hold the flock together and coordinate movements.

Mixed-species flocks are another characteristic grouping in winter. Individual downy woodpeckers, tufted titmice, brown creepers, nuthatches, or kinglets may join chickadee foraging flocks for short or long periods, moving along with them as they feed and responding to chickadee alarm calls. In such transient groups, larger species such as tufted titmice usually outrank chickadees, which in turn are dominant over kinglets. Food availability apparently determines to what extent mixed flocking occurs; the multiple eyes of a mixed flock may increase the birds' foraging efficiency.

As flocks begin to break up in late winter, the "fee-bee" territorial call becomes increasingly frequent.

Ecology. Black-capped chickadees reside mainly in forest and edge habitats. They inhabit almost any sort of woodland or thicket, plus swamps and urban residential areas. The main habitat requirements are for nesting sites and plenty of bark and shrub microhabitats that contain an abundance of insect food.

Black-capped chickadees excavate their own nests, usually a new one each year, in stumps and dead tree stubs. Their bills are not adapted for powerful wood excavation like those of woodpeckers, so they must select sites that are soft-rotted and far advanced in decay. They usually excavate in the side of a trunk about four to eight feet high, sometimes higher. Dead birches, their tough, intact bark holding in the rotted wood tissue, are favored sites. Alders, aspens, cherries, and willows are also commonly used. Both sexes excavate the nest hole, carrying away the wood chips and dropping them; a litter of wood chips on the ground away from a tree base often indicates a chickadee nest cavity nearby. Sometimes the pair excavates two or more cavities before settling on one.

Females collect most of the nesting materials. Mosses often form the base of the cavity; on this bed the female builds a cup lined with soft plant fibers, fern down, cottony seed fluff, insect cocoons, rabbit fur or other hairs, and feathers. Occasionally, instead of excavating, chickadees use natural cavities, old woodpecker holes, or nest boxes.

Although animal matter constitutes about 70 percent of the total diet, seasonal diets vary considerably. In early spring, chickadees show a fondness for maple sap icicles, formed on broken branches as the sap begins running. But spring and summer foods consist mainly of moth and butterfly caterpillars and spiders, both gleaned from vegetation. Irruptive hairy caterpillars, such as gypsy and eastern tent moths, which remain untouched by many birds, are frequently consumed in their smaller growth stages by chickadees. Experiments have demonstrated that black-capped chickadees use a range of insect leaf-damage clues when foraging, and that they can associate these clues in various foliage types with the presence of palatable caterpillars.

Seeds and fruits supplement the insect fare in late summer and fall. Ragweed, goldenrod, staghorn sumac, and tulip tree seeds are common food items, as are blueberries, blackberries, and wild cherries. Chickadees cache seeds and other food items mainly in the fall. Common caching sites include bark crevices, leaf and birch bark curls, needle clusters, knotholes, and branch undersides. About half of the winter diet consists of seeds. Waxy berries such as those of poison-ivy and bayberry are favorites, as are birch, pine, and hemlock seeds. The birds also glean spider and insect eggs and cocoons from bark crevices.

*Durable seed heads of staghorn sumac (*Rhus typhina*) provide a common (though not preferred) winter food item for chickadees and almost one hundred other bird species. The seeds are rich in provitamin A.*

Research indicates that chickadees survive winter in about the same flock abundance whether or not yard feeders are provided. Only during periods of extremely cold or harsh weather, when the birds' energy needs are greater than usual, may yard feeders make the difference between survival and starvation. Although yard feeding may be expanding the winter ranges of some seed-eating birds, the weight of evidence suggests that, on the whole, yard feeding is more important to people than to birds. Indeed, an argument exists for *not* feeding chickadees in winter: A chickadee well provided with sunflower seeds may seek and consume fewer hibernating insects and insect eggs than it normally would; thus, in the spring, the unthinned populations of foliage-eating insects may produce a larger-than-normal abundance of plant pests.

In any hierarchical flock, food competition bears hardest on the subordinate members, which must give priority access to the dominants. Studies of winter chickadee flocks confirm that the survival rate of dominants exceeds that of low-ranking birds in the same flock. Food competition seems offset to some extent, however, by the advantage each bird derives from the multiple eyes and ears of the mixed or unmixed flock in detecting food and potential predators. The chickadee's omnivorous diet also works to its advantage.

Nest site competition is often from other chickadees, as territorial contests evict subordinate pairs and floaters from prime habitats. Most of these evacuees must settle for inferior habitats, and many do not breed at all. Tufted titmice, whose range expansion has brought them into increasing contact with black-capped chickadees, may contend for nest sites. House wrens often invade chickadee nests on or near wren territories, puncturing eggs, killing nestlings, and removing nesting material.

Frequent chickadee predators include sharp-shinned hawks, American kestrels, eastern screech-owls, and, in the far north, northern shrikes. Raccoons, squirrels, and snakes sometimes raid nests. Domestic cats are the foremost predators around yard feeders. Brood parasitism on chickadees by brown-headed cowbirds is negligible, probably because of the small entrance holes of chickadee nest cavities.

Focus. Chickadees are favorites of people who like to watch their antics and feed them in winter, and few other passerine species have received more attention from field researchers. Hundreds of scholarly papers have inspected and analyzed almost every aspect of chickadee existence, and more appear each year. Yet new questions about their territorial and flock behaviors, their reproduction, and their group dynamics continue to arise. We are far from knowing everything about these feisty little parids.

For example, recent research suggests that chickadee food caching and retrieval in the fall is an amazing complex of behavior and anatomy. The birds apparently regenerate new cells in the hippocampus, a brain area associated with spatial memory. Although this process occurs year-round, its peak occurs in October, when about 2 percent of the neurons are replaced daily. This peak coincides with the chickadee's main period of seed caching, when short-term memory of deposit sites becomes vital. The memory cells later die when the information they contain is no longer needed. Such cell economy ensures that the brain remains at a consistently small size, important in an airborne creature.

Black-capped chickadees have been known to survive more than twelve years, but average longevity is about two and one-half years.

Closer look. Smith, S. M. *The Black-capped Chickadee: Behavioral Ecology and Natural History.* Ithaca, NY: Cornell University Press, 1991.

TITMOUSE FAMILY (Paridae)

Tufted Titmouse (*Parus bicolor*)

At about six inches long, the tufted titmouse is the largest parid and the smallest crested bird of the eastern United States. It can be identified by its gray upper parts, black forehead patch, tufted crest, and rusty flanks. Its whistled songs and buzzy call notes are also distinctive. Sexes look alike, but juveniles lack the dark forehead patch.

Close relatives. Plain and bridled titmice (*P. inornatus, P. wollweberi*) are southwestern species. Other North American parids of the same genus include the chickadees.

Behaviors. Tufted titmice, which much resemble chickadees in their agility and foraging behaviors, are likewise familiar visitors to yard feeders. The clarion sounds that emanate from this plain little bird in spring—most typically a clear "peter peter peter"—are altogether disproportionate to its size. Its less musical notes resemble those of chickadees but sound more nasal and grating. Like chickadees, titmice are cavity nesters and gregarious for most of the year, but unlike chickadees, their flocks consist mainly of family groups. Few birds display such abruptly contrasting styles of behavior in a breeding season, from loudly conspicuous exhibitionism to utter stealth and silence. Titmice are also more sedentary and range less widely than chickadees and are not so adaptive to various habitats.

Titmouse range spans most of the continental United States east of the Great Plains. During the past fifty years, observers have traced this bird's remarkable northward range expansion, a movement that somewhat parallels that of the northern cardinal but is slower paced. Since about 1965, however, this expansion has slowed and halted in many areas. Tufted titmice are year-round dwellers and do not migrate.

The tufted titmouse, like all members of its family, holds a seed with its feet while hammering with its bill.

Spring. By early spring, titmouse flocks have largely dispersed into pairs and solitary birds. Breeding territories typically comprise about two to five acres, depending on habitat. Territorial skirmishes and incessant singing of males, with males often chasing females and feeding their mates, mark this period. As nesting commences in April and May, titmice fall silent and become difficult to detect.

EGGS AND YOUNG: five or six; eggs white with fine speckles. INCUBATION: by female, which is fed by male; about two weeks. FEEDING OF YOUNG: by both sexes; insects. FLEDGING: about eighteen days.

Summer, Fall. Where second nestings occur (mainly in the birds' southern range), juveniles of the first brood may help feed second-brood nestlings. The noisy fledglings continue to be fed by the parents for a month or more after leaving the nest. In contrast to the young of most passerine species, which disperse from their birth areas in late summer or fall, titmouse juveniles remain in family groups for several months, often on a home range of fifteen to twenty acres. The annual feather molt occurs in August.

Winter. Titmice become most visible in winter as they forage in plain sight and visit yard feeders. Small family flocks remain together through much of the winter, sometimes joining temporary mixed flocks of black-capped chickadees, downy woodpeckers, nuthatches, and kinglets. The pair bond apparently lasts all year, as in chickadees, but details of titmouse flock behaviors, dispersion, and pairing are not well understood. As territorial impulses quicken in late winter, the yearling birds finally disperse widely, many to form their own pair bonds. Listen in February for the ringing songs of male titmice as they begin to establish or reestablish their breeding territories. In many places, titmice are the first vocal songbirds of the year, providing the first loud, sure forecast of spring.

Ecology. Primarily a woodland bird, the tufted titmouse favors deciduous and mixed forests, moist bottomlands, and swamps. Dead trees with suitable cavities for nesting are important habitat needs. For feeding, titmice range outside these habitats to edges, thickets, suburban yards, and parks.

Unlike chickadees, titmice do not excavate their own nest cavities but use natural cavities or vacant woodpecker holes. The female brings huge billfuls of mosses, grasses, and often wet dead leaves, as well as bits of fur, string, cloth, and cast snakeskins, packing them into the cavity and lining the cup with finer materials. Occasionally a pair uses the same cavity for succeeding years.

Spring and summer foods consist mainly of caterpillars, plus wasps, scale insects, ants, beetles, and spiders. Like chickadees, titmice also forage on twigs and bark for insect and spider eggs and insect pupae. In fall and winter, the diet turns mostly vegetarian. Apple fragments, blackberries, elderberries, blueberries, and wild grapes are favored fruits; acorns, beechnuts, and corn become staple winter items. Observers believe that this bird's heavy use of yard feeders in the North accounts at least in part for its range expansion. Like chickadees, titmice often cache food items for short periods in such places as bark crevices, among foliage, or under moss or soil.

Small cavity-nesting species such as downy woodpeckers, chickadees, nuthatches, and house wrens may contend with titmice for nest sites. In areas where dead or dying trees are few, titmice may use nest boxes. Food competition probably becomes significant only in winter. The many bird and mammal consumers of acorns and beechnuts often strip these trees in the fall; competition becomes even tighter in years when nut production is poor. In areas where titmouse and chickadee ranges overlap, the potential for competition between these close relatives seems likely, but field observations thus far are inconclusive.

Raccoons are probably the foremost nest predators on titmice. Around yard feeders, sharp-shinned hawks and domestic cats often menace the birds. Brown-headed cowbirds rarely parasitize cavity-nesting birds.

Focus. The tufted titmouse longevity record is thirteen years, but most titmice probably survive only two or three years. If only half the amount of research lavished on chickadees had focused on titmice, we would know much more than we do about these birds. Many of their flock patterns and behaviors may be found to parallel those of chickadees; other parid species vary extensively in certain social and behavioral features, however, so maybe this common bird holds some distinctive surprises for us.

The name *tit* originated in England (where the name *titmouse* is unknown), apparently from the Icelandic word *tittr*, which meant anything small; the Anglo-Saxon *mase* signified "a small bird." Another explanation is that the bird's large black eyes, supposedly mouselike, account for its mammalian moniker. Tomtit is a common local name.

21

SWALLOW FAMILY (Hirundinidae)

Some seventy-five swallow species occur worldwide, six in eastern North America. Short, flattened bills, long-pointed wings, weak feet, gregarious behaviors, and swift, agile flight characterize these insect predators. Their anatomy and aerial feeding habits give them some resemblance to swifts, an unrelated family. Most swallows are colonial or semicolonial nesters. In addition to the two swallow accounts that follow, other northeastern species include the tree swallow (*Tachycineta bicolor*), bank swallow (*Riparia riparia*), northern rough-winged swallow (*Stelgidopteryx serripennis*), and cliff swallow (*Hirundo pyrrhonata*). All are migrants.

SWALLOW FAMILY (Hirundinidae)

Purple Martin (*Progne subis*)

At about eight inches long, the purple martin is the largest North American swallow. It can be identified by its notched tail and circular, gliding flight. Males two or more years old have blue-black plumage; females and yearling males are grayish with light bellies. The martin's throaty, gurgling song is distinctive.

Close relatives. Almost twenty-five swallow species are labeled martins in various parts of the world, but the genus *Progne* is exclusive to the New World. It includes the Cuban martin (*P. cryptoleuca*), gray-breasted martin (*P. chalybea*), and southern martin (*P. elegans*), all Neotropical species.

Behaviors. Purple martins have become popular yard birds because of colonial martin houses, often erected by homeowners on the mistaken notion that the martins are voracious consumers of mosquitoes. Much of the North American martin population now nests exclusively in these and other human-made structures. Martin colonial nesting is apparently not an inherent social system but results from the birds' adaptation to the condominium style of martin houses; martins, though socially oriented, are highly territorial, often claiming more than one nest compartment. Flock behaviors become most evident when martins gang up to chase potential predators from the martin house. Martins feed, bathe, and drink on the wing, often skimming over water with alternate flapping and soaring in long, graceful arcs. Often vocal in flight, voicing rich "cher-cher" notes, martins also make great hubbub in and around the nest box.

Purple martins breed throughout almost the entire continent from Canada to Mexico.

Spring. Martins arrive on their northern breeding range in late March and early April. Older males precede older females, followed by yearling birds. The birds are highly vulnerable to spells of severe weather at this time, and die-offs of migrating or just-arrived martins are not uncommon; one study estimated an annual return of only 23 percent of yearling birds. Older birds return to the colonial box where they have nested before, but yearlings usually are not site faithful, though they may return to the same general area. A male often begins defending several nest compartments, which decrease to about two as breeding activities commence. Arriving females, attracted to nest holes by male singing and flight displays, inspect every available compartment, finally choosing one and the male to go with it. If she selects a hole in an already paired male's territory, the resident male will mate with both females and defend both nests. Males apparently instigate nest building by carrying twigs hither and yon; the females, trailed by their mates, actually construct the nests. Nest building is a sporadic activity, usually lasting three or four weeks before egg laying begins.

EGGS AND YOUNG: four or five, eggs white. INCUBATION: by female; about fifteen days; males often occupy nests during female absence but do not incubate. FEEDING OF YOUNG: by both sexes; insects. FLEDGING: about a month.

Summer. Martins raise only one brood, which fledges in midsummer, sometimes not until late August. After females brood the nestlings for about two weeks, they often roost at night in vacant nest holes or in tree roosts with other adult martins.

Purple martin parents do not differentiate their own young from those of other parents; thus fledging is often chaotic, with fledglings perching on the nest box, wandering into still-occupied nest holes, and being fed by miscellaneous adults. Over the next several days, fledglings flock together at daytime grouping perches, where the parents bring them food, then return to a nest compartment at night. Adult raider martins often attack the grouped fledglings, pecking and chasing them until parent birds return and defend them. Raider harassment may have the long-term function of discouraging the spring return of yearlings to the parental nest site, thereby reducing competition for hole space, or of reducing food stealing by fledglings from nestlings, known as *kleptoparasitism.*

As summer progresses, colonial nesting areas are gradually abandoned, and family groups merge for feeding and communal roosting. Up to one hundred thousand martins may gather in premigratory roost sites, where the annual molt begins. Yearling males acquire their full adult plumage at this time. Flocks are drifting southward by daytime flight in late August, and migration is well advanced by early September.

Fall, Winter. All but stragglers have left the continent by early October, arriving on their winter range soon after. Purple martin populations concentrate in the Amazon valley of Brazil, plus areas of northern Bolivia and Argentina. Martins complete their annual molt of body feathers on the winter range. By late January, they are leisurely moving northward.

Ecology. Martins favor open or semiopen breeding areas, preferably near water. Birds of eastern populations, if given a choice, often nest within one hundred feet of a human dwelling. "Martins have 'learned,' through natural selection," writes one researcher, "that the closer they nest to man, the safer they are from their predators." Wet meadows and open shorelines of ponds and lakes also attract them. On their winter range, they frequent open areas around towns and oilfields, as well as savannas and scrubland.

Martins originally nested in tree cavities and crevices in cliffs and loose rocks; in the western United States, these are still the foremost sites. Eastern and midwestern populations, however, mainly nest in wooden or aluminum nest boxes erected for the purpose. Box placement is crucial to a successful invitation. It should stand near water in an open, grassy area with no surrounding trees or shrubbery. Erected on a fifteen- or twenty-foot pole, the box, which may contain ten to thirty compartments, attracts martins best if painted white. Nest materials, which the birds bank toward the rear of the compartment, include twigs, grass stems, paper, string, and mud. The nest cup, lined with fine grasses, is topped by green leaves, which the birds continue to bring until egg hatching; the decomposing leaves may deter the growth of feather mites or help cool the hot compartment by leaf moisture evaporation.

Flying insects, mainly hymenopterans (wasps and bees), flies, and dragonflies, are the major food items. Martins also occasionally feed on the ground, chiefly on ants. Mosquitoes are negligible items in the diet; many other predators, both insects and birds, consume a greater number of mosquitoes than martins do. The oft-touted pitch of martin house sellers that "a martin eats two thousand mosquitoes per day" remains unsupported by stomach analyses. Since most mosquitoes are active mainly at night, mosquito and martin working hours seldom coincide. Moreover, no evidence exists that birds can successfully control any insect pest at peak abundance. The martin's avid consumption of dragonflies, which are among the foremost mosquito predators, further weighs the case against the commercial propaganda. Well documented, however, is the martin's consumption of crushed eggshells and bits of gravel, presumably for mineral nourishment and digestive purposes.

House sparrows and European starlings often invade martin houses. House sparrows, in fact, usually occupy one or more compartments of most nesting boxes. Sometimes box owners must evict the nests of these invaders at periodic intervals until the martins establish their nest hole territories. Great crested flycatchers, tree swallows, eastern bluebirds, and house finches also use martin houses on occasion. Martins are rarely intimidated from nesting in a box where they have nested before, but competitors easily repel them from newly erected boxes. In areas where martins still nest in tree cavities, competitors include woodpeckers and other hole nesters. Food competition appears negligible except in cases of kleptoparasitism.

Hollowed gourds once provided popular housing for purple martins. Today the martin house industry builds rectangles full of compartments similar to human housing.

House sparrow invaders may destroy martin eggs and young as they appropriate nest compartments. House wrens also destroy the eggs. Screech-owls are known to reach into nest holes with their talons at night, bringing out squirming victims. Other predators include black rat snakes, great horned owls, hawks, American crows, opossums, and raccoons.

Focus. Humans have become the purple martin's foremost associates, mainly by providing housing that the birds readily accept. This association dates back several centuries at least. Native Americans and plantation slaves hung clusters of hollowed gourds to attract martins, believing that the birds drove away hawks and crows. People began erecting nest boxes in the early 1800s, fueling the martin's reputation as a "good bird." But martins achieved stardom only in 1962, when entrepreneurs in Griggsville, Illinois, "discovered" that martins consume huge numbers of mosquitoes. Martin house construction soon became the town's major industry, as Griggsville christened itself the "Purple Martin Capital of the Nation." Never has an American bird species received a bigger publicity buildup (except, perhaps, the house sparrow in 1850), and such salesmanship continues to sell thousands of martin houses yearly. Few birders can object to that—or maybe they should, since martin houses also host many starlings and house sparrows and result in no measurable decrease of mosquito populations.

Fluctuations in martin abundance, mostly caused by weather extremes, are frequent. A rapid decline during the past two decades has been attributed to overcrowding and consequent disease epidemics on the rather restricted winter range. As insect eaters, martins are also highly vulnerable to pesticides. In 1952, before Rachel Carson's book *Silent Spring* enlightened us, one federal wildlife biologist recommended "helping" the birds cope with parasites by dosing martin houses with DDT in early spring.

Closer look. Purple Martin Conservation Association, Edinboro University, Edinboro, PA 16444.

SWALLOW FAMILY (Hirundinidae)

Barn Swallow (*Hirundo rustica*)

Its deeply forked, white-spotted tail, bluish-black upper parts, cinnamon red throat, and buff-orange belly identify this seven-inch-long swallow. Female plumage is somewhat duller. It often voices soft, twittering notes in flight.

Close relatives. The cliff swallow (*H. pyrrhonota*) is its closest northeastern relative; cave swallows (*H. fulva*) reside in the southwestern United States. The red-rumped swallow (*H. daurica*) inhabits southern Europe.

Behaviors. This most widely distributed of all swallows breeds throughout the Northern Hemisphere. In North America, its summer range extends from southern Canada to the Gulf. Like all swallows, it catches food on the wing. Unlike most others, however, it usually flies without much gliding. Barn swallows are sociable, gregarious birds at all seasons. They often perch in rows on telephone lines or wire fences, their two-pronged tails easier to see than when the birds are flying. Perch dominance behaviors may be witnessed as the birds shift and rearrange positions.

Spring. Adult barn swallows are site faithful, returning year after year to the same swallow colony, sometimes to the same nest and mate. This does not apply to their progeny, however, which seldom return to their birth colony. Barn swallows are daytime migrants, and both sexes arrive together on their northeastern breeding range in April. A pair perching together signals that courtship has begun. Other courtship displays include the male's twittering song, chasing of the female, reciprocal preening, and circling communal song flights. In May, both sexes build a nest or renovate an old one. A pair's breeding territory extends two to five feet around the nest—or, as one observer stated, "in a straight line from the nest to the nearest good perch." Nests in a colony are seldom placed closer together than three feet.

Barn swallows dart and swoop as they feed on the wing. The forked tail, seen only in adult birds, aids maneuverability, making them among the most agile of swallows. (Courtesy of Kalamazoo Nature Center.)

EGGS AND YOUNG: four or five; eggs white, brown spotted. INCUBA-
TION: by both sexes, replacing each other about every fifteen
minutes; female at night; about fifteen days. FEEDING OF YOUNG:
by both sexes, occasionally also by nest helpers; insects.
FLEDGING: about twenty days.

Summer. Juveniles, recognized by their shorter tail forks, often
return to roost in or near the nest for a few days after fledging.
Then they join other juveniles to feed and perch together. The parent birds usually renest, except in their extreme northern range,
producing a second brood. They are frequently aided by nest
helpers, mainly unmated, unrelated adult males. These birds sometimes feed the nestlings, but they may also attack them or try to
copulate with the brooding female.

Most northeastern barn swallows begin migrating south in
August, with late nesters trailing in early September. Flocks travel
during daytime hours, usually quite low to the ground and often
along coastlines.

Fall, Winter. Barn swallows arrive on their winter range, from
Panama south and throughout most of South America, from September through November. Most northeastern barn swallows fly—
both going and coming—over Florida, the Gulf, and the West Indies.
The annual feather molt occurs on their winter range. By late March
and early April, the birds are again moving north.

Ecology. This is one species for which the vegetation complex
seems to have little bearing on habitat. Open farmlands and residential areas are its typical environs. Mud sources—shores, puddles, and wet spots—are vital for nest building, as are fields and
open water for feeding.

Barn swallows usually nest together in small colonies of five or
six or in larger colonies, but solitary nesting also is not uncommon.
Sheltered rafters, barn lofts, garage walls, and bridge and eave
undersides are typical nest sites. Before European settlement in
North America, barn swallows nested in caves, cliff crevices, and
bank cavities, and in some areas they still do. Site availability appar-

Durable mud nests, often placed on sheltered beams, may be reused and renovated, ultimately hosting several generations of barn swallows.

ently determines whether the birds colonize and the size of the colonies. Barn swallows construct bowl-shaped nests from mud pellets—some one or two thousand beakloads per nest. Some nests are *statant*, placed on a horizontal surface, and others are *adherent*, plastered to a vertical surface. Often the birds build upon the vertical tubular nests of mud-daubing wasps. Bits of straw and dried grass reinforce the mud, and the birds often line their nests profusely with white poultry feathers from farmyards. The birds frequently reuse previous nests of their own or of eastern phoebes, adding fresh mud and lining. A barn swallow nest may last up to seven years.

Almost wholly insectivorous, barn swallows consume many kinds of insects. Nearly 40 percent of the diet consists of the larger flies, making these birds valuable farmyard predators. Beetles, wasps, ants, and true bugs are also taken in large quantities. Swallows are more efficient insect consumers than flycatchers because they hunt on the wing and their feeding flights cover much larger areas. Flying over meadows, golf courses, and ponds, they also follow plow and cow, nabbing disturbed insects. A few berries and seeds add to the diet in summer.

Eastern phoebes and house sparrows sometimes compete with barn swallows for nest sites, occasionally usurping their nests. Food competition is negligible, since the birds' spring arrival coincides with insect abundance.

House wrens and house sparrows occasionally destroy barn swallow eggs, and sharp-shinned hawks, cats, and weasels are known predators. When a colony is threatened by a predator, barn swallows sometimes mob the intruder, driving it away. Fowl mites often infest the nests; these mites survive over winter, and the swallows usually avoid reusing infested nests. Brown-headed cowbirds rarely parasitize this species.

Focus. Prolonged cold snaps that deplete insect populations in spring probably account for most barn swallow mortality on the breeding range. Barn swallows have clearly benefited from land clearing and agriculture, and populations continue a general trend of increase. Estimated adult annual survival rate is about 40 percent.

The closely related cliff swallows, with which barn swallows sometimes forage, also are mud builders. These are the famed swallows that supposedly return to the mission ruins of San Juan Capistrano, California, on March 19 (but since the paving over of a local creek, the birds have largely abandoned the site). Many more tourists than swallows migrate there today.

Closer look. Moller, A. P. *Sexual Selection and the Barn Swallow.* Oxford: Oxford University Press, 1994.

22

Golden-crowned and Ruby-crowned Kinglets
(*Regulus satrapa* and *R. calendula*)

Kinglet family (Regulidae). The kinglets, only three and one-half to four inches long, are olive-gray with white-barred wings. Their quick movements and restless wing flicking are characteristic. Male golden-crowns bear black-bordered, bright yellow and orange crowns; females' crowns are yellow. Male ruby-crowns have scarlet crowns, visible only when erect; the females have no head markings. A broken eye ring gives both sexes of ruby-crowns a wide-eyed look. Songs of the two species also differ: Trebled "see-see-see"

notes and its song, a series of high notes descending to a chickadeelike chatter, identify the golden-crown. The ruby-crown's songs are louder and more complex, a series of notes on several pitches followed by repetitive multinote phrases.

Golden-crowned kinglets, year-round insect eaters, are among the hardiest of winter birds in some areas. (Courtesy of Russell Schipper.)

Close relatives. Six *Regulus* species exist worldwide. Two European species that closely resemble the golden-crowned kinglet are the common goldcrest (*R. regulus*) and the firecrest (*R. ignicapillus*).

Behaviors. A tiny, hyperactive bird flitting in the shrubbery is probably a kinglet. In the eastern United States, kinglets are most often seen during spring and fall migrations, when they commonly forage in association with warblers. Often curious and relatively tame, they come readily to a birder's pishing sounds, uttering high, creeperlike notes (golden-crowns) or a snapping "ji-dit" (ruby-crowns), eyeing the birder from twenty perches in a minute. Yet despite their abundance and almost constant contact notes when foraging, they are so easily overlooked that casual observers may remain unaware of their presence.

The two kinglets differ somewhat in distribution. Ruby-crowns breed farther north but winter farther south than golden-crowns. Summer breeding ranges of both species broadly overlap in Canada south of Hudson Bay to the Great Lakes and New England and span the continent west to Alaska. Golden-crowns winter from southern Canada through much of the continental United States. They remain year-round in a broad band extending from Newfoundland south through New England and the Appalachians to the Carolinas.

Spring. Golden-crowns begin drifting north from mid-March through April, generally preceding the northward movement of ruby-crowns by about a month. Ruby-crowns frequently travel with migrating warblers. Golden-crowns rarely sing during migration, but ruby-crowns often do. It is not known whether pair bonds

Aggressive or territorial situations cause the peaceful ruby-crown (top) to raise its colorful crest feathers in excitement (bottom); the crest is its emotional barometer.

are already formed by this time or await arrival on the breeding ranges. Golden-crown territories average about four acres in size; ruby-crown territories are probably comparable. Male erection and display of the colorful head crowns are probably territorial actions, as is singing, which occurs throughout the breeding period. Courtship behaviors include male feeding of females, which construct the nests.

EGGS AND YOUNG: seven to nine; eggs white, brownish spotted; golden-crowns often deposit eggs in two layers. INCUBATION: by female; about two weeks for golden-crowns, a few days less for ruby-crowns. FEEDING OF YOUNG: by both sexes; initially regurgitated insects, then whole insects. FLEDGING: twelve to nineteen days.

Summer. Kinglets raise two broods in many areas; pairs may build a second nest before the first brood has fledged. Little is known about the postfledging phase, but juveniles probably remain in the parental vicinity for some weeks. The annual feather molt begins in July, and some golden-crowns start migrating in August.

Fall. Peak migrational movements for both species occur in September and October, usually in much larger numbers than in spring because of the addition of juveniles. Golden-crowns may travel as far south as the Gulf Coast. A few ruby-crowns may linger in the northern United States, but most migrate, some as far as Guatemala. During seasonal migrations, kinglets broaden their habitat use, foraging in woods and edge areas of almost any type.

Winter. How do north-wintering kinglets deal with extreme cold? Certainly many perish, but many also seem to thrive. Researchers have puzzled how this insect eater can find and consume up to three times its body weight in food each day in order to survive subzero temperatures. Unlike black-capped chickadees, they apparently do not become torpid at night, nor do they cache food items. Zoologist Bernd Heinrich suggests that, like European goldcrests, golden-crowns may huddle and share body warmth at night in dense conifer branches.

Ecology. Both kinglet species favor coniferous breeding habitats. Golden-crowns prefer mature, dense-canopy stands of spruce, fir, pines, and northern white cedar. Ruby-crowns select more open habitats, often bogs containing black spruce and tamarack. Winter and migration habitats also include deciduous forests and shrubby edges.

Kinglet nests are deep, intricately woven, gourd-shaped structures suspended from a branch overlapped by foliage. Usually

*Fluffy seed heads of cotton-grass (*Eriophorum*), a bog sedge, are sometimes used as nest materials by golden-crowned kinglets.*

they hang high in a mature spruce or other conifer. Lichens and spider silk bind the nest walls, and mosses form the outer, thick-walled mass. Open at the top, the nest is lined with fine plant materials, bits of fur, and often ruffed grouse feathers arched over the rim. The nests of golden-crowns and ruby-crowns look identical, although golden-crowns usually build higher and near the trunk, whereas ruby-crowns often hang their nests at the end of thickly foliaged branches.

Kinglets, primarily insect eaters even in winter, typically feed high in conifers, hovering as they glean from bark, foliage, and branch tips. They consume an abundance of tiny springtails (Collembola) and many bark hibernators—pine and spruce aphids, psyllids, fly larvae, and scale insects—plus eggs of aphids and other insects. Such a diet, researchers believe, provides the major winter sustenance of north-wintering golden-crowns, which have also been observed feeding at sap wells drilled by woodpeckers. Later in the year, caterpillars (including the destructive spruce budworm), leaf and bark beetles, small wasps, and spiders become favored foods. Both kinglets consume small amounts of weed seeds and fruits, often elderberries, in fall and winter. Kinglets seldom come to yard feeders. Often two or more kinglets join small, mixed-species feeding flocks consisting of black-capped chickadees, tufted titmice, nuthatches, and downy woodpeckers.

For north-wintering golden-crowns, food competition with other bark gleaners could be significant, but it is probably negligible at other seasons. Red squirrels are the foremost nest predators; blue and gray jays also raid kinglet nests, which are occasionally parasitized by brown-headed cowbirds. Kinglets have been known to become fatally tangled in the hooked burs of common burdock.

Focus. Next to the ruby-throated hummingbird, kinglets are the smallest northeastern birds, yet they provide enormously important controls on plant-eating insects, mainly in egg and larval forms. Golden-crowns suffer periodic drops in population because of harsh winter weather, but the large broods raised by kinglets help compensate for these losses. Much more research has been lavished on European goldcrests than on our American kinglets, about which many life history details await discovery. English and generic names both mean "little king," referring to the bright crowns in all but the female ruby-crown.

23

House Sparrow (*Passer domesticus*)

Old World sparrow family (Passeridae). This ubiquitous, six-inch-long sparrow thrives almost everywhere people live. Males have a gray cap, white cheeks, and black throat and bib. Male bills are blacker in spring and summer. Females and juveniles are dingy brown with no distinctive markings. The unmemorable song voiced by both sexes is a two- or three-part phrase of chirrups, background noise to a busy street; single-note chirps are also common.

Close relatives. The total of twenty-three *Passer* species are all native to Eurasia and Africa. In North America, the Eurasian tree sparrow (*P. montanus*), also an introduced species, resides in areas of Missouri and southern Illinois. Other family members include the pipits (*Anthus*), wagtails (*Motacilla*), and weavers (*Ploceus*).

Behaviors. Birders of a certain age grew up knowing this bird as the English sparrow. Although

Male (top) and female (bottom) house sparrows show different plumages, unlike nonrelated native brown sparrows. The amount of black on males also differs with the season.

219

it was indeed introduced to America from England, it was also an immigrant there, having arrived from the European continent some two thousand years ago. Today, because of natural dispersion and deliberate introductions, it abundantly inhabits almost every temperate region of the globe. Superbly adapted to utilize habitats created by people, it has shadowed the spread of humankind through history and continues to rival rock pigeons, starlings, and dandelions as one of humanity's foremost biotic associates. Yet house sparrow distribution, though widespread, is patchy: These birds, once established, become relatively sedentary and seldom fly across areas of unsuitable habitat, such as wetlands or dense forests.

The hallmark of house sparrows is gregariousness. They feed, dust-bathe, water-bathe, roost (both day and night), and sometimes nest in communal flocks. Their sociability becomes most conspicuous—especially from summer through midwinter—at roost sites. Immense flocks often gather at these locales before sunset, noisily chirping and shifting positions. Birds may arrive from three or four miles away to settle communally for the night, often gathering at preroosting sites before approaching the primary roost in small groups. As relatively late sleepers, they seldom leave the night roost until after sunrise. Midday roosting of smaller congregations for an hour or so is also common. Unlike most gregarious birds, house sparrows show no rigid social structure or peck order; though aggressive interactions do occur, they seem largely circumstantial and inconsistent. A common habit is tail-flicking when perched, a sign of apprehension.

House sparrows reside year-round throughout most of their range, though northern populations often shift southward during periods of extreme cold. Nest building or repair occurs more or less continually except for a brief period in late summer.

Spring. Many house sparrows pair and use the same nest site for life. By early spring, light tips of the male's throat feathers have worn off to reveal the black bib breeding plumage, and courtship activities are well advanced. Small male flocks chase single female birds, performing hop-and-bow displays in front of them, and single males loudly chirp from perches near a nest site. These behaviors, though most prevalent in spring and fall, may be seen at any season. Pairs set about repairing previously used nests or rebuilding new ones. Territories average about two hundred feet or less surrounding the nest. Most actual nesting begins about April in the North, March in the South, but many February nesting dates are also on record. Human antipathy toward the house sparrow, especially earlier in this century, often extended to the birds' frequent copulations. Describing their "conspicuous venery," one sparrow hater fumed that "the male suffers from satyriasis, the female from nymphomania."

EGGS AND YOUNG: usually four or five; eggs white or greenish white, brown speckled. INCUBATION: by female; about thirteen days. FEEDING OF YOUNG: by both sexes; insects. FLEDGING: fifteen to seventeen days.

Summer. Fledglings continue to be fed, often by the male parent, for a week or so while the female begins renesting. Accounts differ as to whether females always reuse the same nest or sometimes move to a vacant one. Typically a pair raises two or three broods through September, occasionally more and later into fall. All-juvenile flocks feed and roost together through summer. After nesting ends, house sparrows molt into new plumage; males acquire light-tipped throat feathers, obscuring their new black bibs. Adult birds now join the juvenile flocks, deserting their nest sites to feed in grainfields and weedy, overgrown pastures.

Fall. In northern populations, a resurgence of territoriality occurs in late fall, with pairs and widowed mates returning to their spring and summer nest sites. Most juveniles disperse a mile or so from their birth sites, but some may return to the original colony to compete for available nesting space.

Winter. House sparrows use their nests through winter for roosting and shelter, defending them vigorously from neighboring sparrows. Juveniles continue to roost communally. As days begin to lengthen, nest site prospecting, courtship activities, mate replacement for widowed birds, and pairing of unmated birds begin to occur. A second dispersal of the previous fall's juveniles, as they seek nest sites and mates, may also occur. House sparrow females are dominant over males in winter, a behavior visible at yard feeders.

Ecology. Human and house sparrow habitats are virtually the same. Birds residing in urban areas usually look grayish and dingy, quite unlike rural house sparrows, which often appear neater and cleaner, with considerably lighter plumage. City air pollution presumably accounts for the difference.

For nesting, house sparrows favor outside crevices and crannies in houses, barns, and other buildings. Tree nesting usually occurs only when other sites are lacking. Nest sites are often located near a dependable food source, such as a barnyard or trash bin. Almost any sort of cavity can be used. Birdhouses, including colonial martin houses, are quickly claimed. Dense ivy growth on vertical walls and thick-foliaged ornamental plantings provide both

nesting and roosting cover. Both sexes load the cavity with dried grasses and weeds, and sometimes cloth and string as well. Nest lining often consists of poultry feathers or fine grasses. Observers have reported that some house sparrows bruise and place pieces of tansy leaves, a possible parasite repellent, in the nest. Vine and tree nests are bulky, globular masses of vegetation with side openings. Occasionally house sparrows

Dense ivy growth on buildings is commonly occupied by house sparrows for nesting and roosting. House finches also favor these sites.

adopt swallow nests or build nests in the exterior walls of large, occupied hawk nests.

House sparrows are primarily ground-feeding seed eaters, despite the nineteenth-century propaganda extolling their virtues as a biological control on insects. A single house sparrow, it is estimated, consumes six to eight pounds of food—mostly grains—per year. Insects and spiders form only about 10 percent of the diet, mainly during the lengthy nesting season. Prey includes the Japanese beetle, a pervasive yard pest, caterpillars, and cankerworms. Grasshoppers, crickets, and ants are also frequently consumed.

In the spring, house sparrows often feed destructively on fruit tree buds. They also consume flower and grass fragments, shredding petals of apple blossoms, peas, beans, and others; in England, they seem to favor yellow flowers. In summer and fall, the diet becomes almost wholly granivorous, as the birds move into fields— seldom more than two miles from the breeding area. There they consume ripening wheat, oats, and sorghum and scavenge much waste grain, such as cracked corn. Field feeding occurs in tight flocks, usually within five yards of the field edge near hedgerows or other cover. In lawns and weedy fields, house sparrows also consume large quantities of ragweed, crabgrass, bristlegrass, and knotweed seeds, among others. Occasionally they raid orchards, pecking at fruits. Birdseed, elm seeds, organic garbage, and chickenfeed are common yard and barnyard foods.

Field borders near edge cover provide common feeding sites for house sparrow flocks, especially in summer and fall.

House sparrows compete with almost all other cavity-nesting birds for tree holes, nest boxes, even using the ground holes of bank swallows. Their invasion and destruction of eggs and nestlings in already-occupied cavities are common occurrences; one observer compiled a list of seventy bird species that have been molested at times by house sparrows. Unless placed in suitable habitats, but sometimes even then, nest boxes erected for eastern bluebirds or purple martins may quickly attract house sparrows. House finches, recent invaders over most of the northeastern United States, have probably become the house sparrows' foremost competitors for food, though in most one-on-one competitive situations the more aggressive sparrows usually win. Summer and fall competitors in grainfields include blackbird and European starling flocks.

Raptors, American crows, and common grackles sometimes attack house sparrows. Nest predators, including black rat snakes and raccoons, take a toll as well. Many house sparrows are killed by heavy rain or sleet storms and collisions with automobiles. Because of their long occupancy, nests frequently become ridden with mites. The birds acquire and transmit other parasites in poultry yards and hog pens, where house sparrows often hang out. Persistent removal of nests and water spraying of roosts are probably the best human means of controlling house sparrow populations.

Focus. The record longevity for a wild house sparrow is thirteen years, but the average life span is probably two years or less. Nobody professes to like the little tramps—or can doubt that they are here to stay. Yet house sparrows have declined along with their food sources since their period of greatest abundance (1910–20) in North America. Animal feed and horse manure, a staple source of undigested grain, no longer litter city streets.

Multiple house sparrow introductions and establishment of house sparrow populations across North America occurred over a thirty-six-year period (1850–86). Many so-called experts initially hailed the bird as a biological weapon that would soon wipe out irruptive, foliage-eating inchworm caterpillars, especially the elm spanworm (*Ennomos subsignarius*). Once introduced, the sparrows quickly dispersed along highways and railroads, where waste grain and human garbage invited them to thrive. By 1890, the house sparrow's aggressive habits, omnivorous diet, competition with native birds, and increasing abundance had developed into a colossal ecological headache. Thus began the Great Sparrow War, a conflict marked by loud verbal fireworks. Die-hard sparrow defenders, led by Thomas Brewer, and the "I-told-you-so" camp of Elliott Coues, both prominent ornithologists, radi-

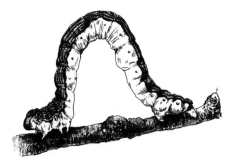

The elm spanworm, also called the linden looper, is a geometrid moth caterpillar. Its abundance in 1850 provided the rationale for the introduction of house sparrows to North America.

cally overstated their cases while science took a backseat. Brewer's arguments consisted mainly of denying the overwhelming data; Coues, a master of withering invective who labeled house sparrows "animated manure machines," and others blamed the birds for all sorts of hardly relevant environmental and social problems, including the scarcity of reliable household servants. Contrary to Coues's dire predictions, house sparrows never stripped the vast grainfields of the Great Plains; they remained most numerous in the cities, close to their human benefactors. And contrary to Brewer's optimism, the elm spanworm remains abundantly with us. In 1931, the prestigious American Ornithologists' Union finally allowed that this species had become a North American bird.

The Great Sparrow War amounted to a vastly entertaining show of sound and fury—but something else, too. Its surprising effect was a kind of national consciousness raising. Only rich people could afford to buy copies of Audubon's splendid bird folios, but two scholars with attitude enlivened the curiosity of the man in the street, where most house sparrows were. More people started looking at birds as creatures worthy of study and interest. Thus this dingy, disreputable immigrant helped democratize an eccentric specialty into the passion and pastime of increasingly numerous observers. The house sparrow, in some sense, trailed environmental awareness in its messy wake.

House sparrows also give us insights into the process of speciation, the way evolution works. Since its introduction to America, the bird has developed many geographical variations in size and plumage patterns, illustrating the operation of natural selection on sparrow gene pools.

Closer look. Summers-Smith, D. *The House Sparrow.* London: Collins, 1963.

24

FINCH FAMILY (Fringillidae)

This is the largest bird family, comprising more than nine hundred species worldwide, some one hundred fifty in North America. It includes the rest of the species accounts in this book. This family lumps several large groups that not so long ago held family status in their own right but are now classified as tribes of three subfamilies. Common traits of the entire family are difficult to generalize; kinship has been established by DNA similarities rather than by physical or behavioral likenesses. To gain a better handle on this widely diverse family, the following accounts are grouped under two subfamily headings: Fringillinae and Emberizinae.

Subfamily Fringillinae

North American fringillines are otherwise known as cardueline finches (tribe Carduelini) and are also called winter finches because most remain in the north over winter, often visiting yard feeders. In addition to the following three species accounts, northeastern carduelines include the pine grosbeak (*Pinicola enucleator*), the crossbills (*Loxia*), the redpolls (*Carduelis*), the pine siskin (*C. pinus*), and the evening grosbeak (*Coccothraustes vespertinus*). Most carduelines have small but stout, conical bills adapted for seed crushing. Many are melodious singers, and males often show brightly colored plumage. Including winter finches, some one hundred thirty species range worldwide, most in temperate zones. Also included in this subfamily are the rare Hawaiian honeycreepers (tribe Drepanidini).

Closer look. Newton, I. *Finches.* New York: Taplinger, 1973.

American Goldfinch (*Carduelis tristis*)

This five-inch-long "wild canary" can be recognized by its black wings marked with a prominent wing bar. Spring and summer males have bright yellow body plumage and a black forehead patch; females are dull olive-gray. Winter plumage of both sexes is greenish gray with yellowish tinges. Goldfinches bounce in flight, "as if skimming over unseen billows," wrote Thoreau, often uttering an accented "ac-*cip*-i-tee!" as they fly. Also commonly heard is an ascending, querulous "sweee?"

Close relatives. Some thirty *Carduelis* species exist worldwide. The nearest eastern U.S. relatives are the pine siskin (*C. pinus*) and common and hoary redpolls (*C. flammea, C. hornemanni*). Lawrence's goldfinch (*C. lawrencei*) and the lesser goldfinch (*C. psaltria*) reside in the western United States. The European goldfinch (*C. carduelis*) is one of several Eurasian relatives, including the greenfinch (*C. chloris*), linnet (*C. cannabina*), chaffinch (*Fringilla coelebs*), and brambling (*F. montifringilla*). The canary (*Serinus canaria*), native of the Canary Islands and a popular cagebird, is also closely related.

Behaviors. Gregarious in small flocks for most of the year, goldfinches are common year-round visitors at yard feeders. They become especially conspicuous in spring and summer, when the males' bright plumage and warbling, canarylike song convey a sense of exuberance.

Winter goldfinch residents may not be the same goldfinches present in summer, since wandering or south-migrating populations from farther north often supplant the summer residents. Goldfinch diet requires access to plenty of water, and these birds frequently bathe. When perched goldfinches watch other goldfinches bathing, the watchers often flutter wings and tail in imitation movements, as if bathing themselves.

Goldfinch breeding range spans the continent from southern Canada to the southern United States.

Spring. Most winter goldfinches move northward in spring, and north-migrating goldfinches arrive on their breeding areas in April and May. This is one of the few passerine birds that undergo a prenuptial plumage molt, which begins in late winter and extends through spring. Only the body and head feathers are replaced; males transform from blah to brilliant as they gain new yellow body plumage and jet-black crown feathers. Bills of both sexes turn from dull gray to yellow-orange.

Although territory formation and nesting do not occur until several months later, the birds engage in song and courtship behaviors, with males skirmishing and chasing single females. The singing male's flat flight, a high, level, rapidly flapping movement in contrast to the typical looping flight path, is often seen at this time. Previously mated males may disperse to new areas, but females usually return to an earlier nesting vicinity. Pairing soon occurs, but the birds continue to feed together in small flocks. Goldfinches typically remain faithful to one mate for the breeding season but change mates from year to year.

Summer. Goldfinches, among our latest nesters, begin establishing territories in late June or early July. Territories may extend to a quarter acre or more or, in places where the birds nest in loose colonies, to a diameter of only one hundred feet. Males sing from localized perches, chase away other males, and perform high, circular flights over the territory as females build the nests. These circle flights are good indicators of nest locations. As incubation proceeds, defensive behavior wanes and territorial boundaries shrink to the immediate nest area. Parent goldfinches often raise two broods; sometimes females lay the second clutch of eggs in a new nest before the first brood has fledged, in which case the male takes over most of the feeding chores. Nesting often extends into September.

EGGS AND YOUNG: typically five; eggs bluish white, unmarked. INCUBATION: by female, fed by male; about twelve days. FEEDING OF YOUNG: by both sexes; regurgitated seed pulp. FLEDGING: about two weeks.

Fall. As goldfinch families forsake the nest vicinity, they can be recognized by the incessant "chipee chipee" calls of the fledglings as they bounce along in the air, following a parent. Soon the young are independent, and social organization becomes flock oriented; all-juvenile flocks of several hundred often feed and fly together. Late in the fall, goldfinches undergo a complete plumage molt, including wing and tail feathers. The sexes now look much alike, with olive-gray plumage and darker bills, although females show paler yellow-ish throats and males more facial yellow and blacker wings.

Goldfinch migration is erratic and age-segregated. Many goldfinches travel long distances south in October and November, often in daytime flocks of several thousand. But others, usually juvenile flocks, may remain in or near the breeding area. Probably food abundance determines the scale and distance of migration in this species as in other so-called irruptive migrators.

Winter. Goldfinch winter range extends from the northern United States to the Gulf Coast and northern Mexico. Often a winter feeding flock advances across a field by leapfrogging, with birds in the rear continually flying to the forefront. Biologist Kenn Kaufman has pointed out the individual variations of goldfinches in winter flocks; on close examination, the amount of facial yellow and subtle differences in other plumage patterns give each bird a distinctive appearance. Yard feeders have probably influenced the winter dis-tribution of goldfinches, causing them to remain in areas they might otherwise vacate.

Ecology. Goldfinches are edge-habitat birds that have benefited from human land clearing and agriculture. They favor open areas with scattered trees and shrubs, overgrown fields, shrub wetlands, and suburban residential areas. Access to water is important, as are thistle-seed food sources; they often nest within one hundred yards or less of the latter.

Favored nest sites include dogwood, shrub willow, and hawthorn thickets. The deeply cupped nest, often attached to sev-eral upright branches in a fork, averages four to fourteen feet high. Goldfinches often use milkweed bark strips, giving the nest a yellow-ish or silvery appearance. For nest lining, they collect cottony mate-

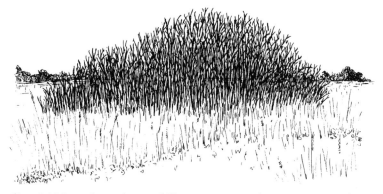

Clonal thickets of gray dogwood (Cornus racemosa) *are common nesting sites for American goldfinches, especially if thistles—a favored food source— grow nearby.*

rials, mainly thistle and cattail down. Sometimes they raid vacated nests of willow flycatchers, yellow warblers, and Baltimore orioles for nest fibers. The compact cup is so tightly woven that it even holds rainwater, yet is so flexible that it expands as the nestlings grow. In shoreline shrubs, the nests much resemble those of yellow warblers, which also build there, but goldfinch nests typically show droppings on outer edges of the rim, where nestlings have backed up to defecate. The presence of feather sheaths embedded in the nest lining probably indicates a successful nesting, revealing the first growth of juvenile plumage. Goldfinch nests often last through winter and are often recycled by various creatures. White-footed

Goldfinch nests often show bird droppings on the rim where nestlings have defecated. These nests closely resemble those of yellow warblers (compare illustration, Yellow Warbler).

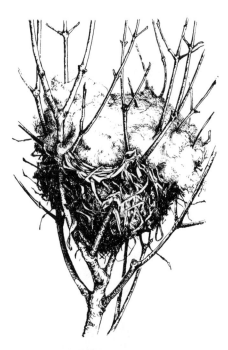

So tightly woven and durable are goldfinch nests that white-footed mice often adopt the vacated nests for their own, loading the cup with soft cattail down.

mice may pile them with cattail down, adapting them for their own nests; mice, red squirrels, and chipmunks also use them for seed storage and feeding sites; and next spring's yellow warblers may tear them apart for nesting materials.

The goldfinch's late nesting sequence coincides with its summer seed diet from maturing food plants, especially composites—thistles, dandelions, ragweeds, and sunflowers—plus grasses and many others. Thistle rings, circles of strewn thistledown around the plant, reveal that goldfinches have been there. Birch and alder catkins, elm seeds, flower buds, and berries are also consumed. In spring, goldfinches also devour many cankerworms, tree aphids, and massed aphid eggs; observers report watching goldfinch flocks work tamarack trees from the top down for insect eggs. In fields, goldfinches often alternate between seed feeding on the ground and on the plants.

Two other species—willow flycatchers and yellow warblers—nest in the same shrub habitats as goldfinches, often in close proximity. They usually breed in spring, however, so competition with goldfinches is minimal. Food competition is also insignificant at most times. Winter foraging flocks of up to three hundred goldfinches may associate with pine siskins, common redpolls, and American tree sparrows.

Nest predators include blue jays, common grackles, and weasels. Occasionally goldfinches become entangled in burdock burs and spiderwebs. Many are killed by collisions with automobiles and by salmonellosis, a bacterial infection sometimes transmitted at yard feeders. Brown-headed cowbirds find goldfinches poor prospects for brood parasitism; cowbird nestlings need much more protein than the goldfinch seed diet provides, and they often starve in the nest. Occasionally goldfinches bury cowbird eggs in their nests, reflooring them for their own eggs.

Focus. Watching goldfinches at yard feeders reveals much about their eating habits. Unlike many feeder visitors, they eat in place rather than carry seeds to another perch. They are also most methodical, neatly trimming a sunflower seed of all husk portions and finishing up the edible fragments before taking another seed.

Average goldfinch longevity is probably six years or less; banding records show a maximum of eleven years.

Iowa, New Jersey, and Washington have designated the American goldfinch their state bird.

FINCH FAMILY (Fringillidae) • Subfamily Fringillinae

Purple and House Finches
(*Carpodacus purpureus* and *C. mexicanus*)

The two species resemble each other in size (five to six inches) and red male plumage. Purple finches are burgundy or plum red, more evenly colored over head and back; house finch color varies from pale yellow to bright red, with browner head and back markings and dark streaks (lacking in purples) on the lower breast and flanks. Females of both species are brown with heavy breast streaking. The purple's characteristic flight and perch call is a bluebirdlike "cheeyew"; males voice a rich, musical warble somewhat resembling that of the warbling vireo. House finch song is also fast and lively, usually three-phrased and ending in a long, trilled "wheer."

Close relatives. Some twenty-one *Carpodacus* finches exist worldwide. Cassin's finch (*C. cassinii*) resides in the western United States. Eurasian *Carpodacus* finches are called rosefinches.

The male purple finch (top) and house finch (bottom) look much alike. House finches show streaking, however, and habitats of the two also differ.

Behaviors. Purple finches are northern birds, breeding from the tree line in Canada to the northern states and south along the Pacific coast; house finches range throughout most of the continental United States. Not so long ago, house finch range was much more restricted, a fact that aided identification of these purple finch lookalikes. Now, however, the two species' ranges increasingly overlap, so observers may see both in many areas, especially at yard feeders in winter. Both species are gregarious for most of the year and feed in small flocks, though they seldom mingle with each other. Ground-foraging *Carpodacus* flocks tend to rise "impulsively" as they vacate one feeding site for another. When flying to cover, they usually favor higher branches rather than low shrubbery. Purple finches migrate, but house finch seasonal movements remain unclear.

Spring. Purple finches migrate to their northern breeding range in April and May, often in large, day-traveling flocks. House finches, of more southern distribution, are often incubating on their nests by this time. Males of both species sing lengthily at morning and evening, purple finches from high treetop perches, and house finches from prominent singing posts near the nest. Females sing only in brief bursts. House finch singing apparently bears no strong connection with territory, since several males may sing from the same tree. Hopping and strutting courtship displays are exuberant. House finch males often feed females at yard feeders; often two males follow and flutter around a single female.

House finch territory is considered as floating, centering mainly around the female. Territorial defense around the nest, mainly by females, is often weak and sporadic. Information is lacking on purple finch territories. Purples begin nesting in May. Both species may maintain pair bonds over more than one breeding season.

EGGS AND YOUNG: four or five; eggs pale bluish green, brown spotted. INCUBATION: by females; about two weeks. FEEDING OF YOUNG: by both sexes; mainly seeds. FLEDGING: two weeks for purple finches; eleven to nineteen days for house finches.

Summer. Parent birds continue to feed fledglings for at least several days. Whether purple finches typically raise second broods remains uncertain, as some are still nesting in July, but house finches usually raise two or more broods, continuing into August. By late summer, both species have abandoned their breeding territories and gather in gregarious flocks of twenty or more. Purple finches tend to form and migrate in unisexual flocks; house finches usually flock to fields en masse with no discernible age or sex segregation, paralleling the foraging behaviors of house sparrows at this season. Both adult species acquire new plumage from July through September. Males now appear duller, reduced to pinkish hues as buffy feather tips partially mask the underlying red plumage.

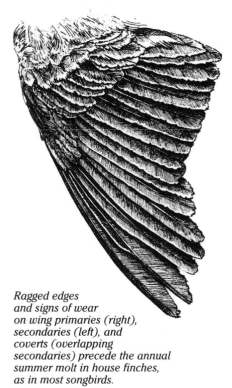

Fall. Purple finch southward migration proceeds through September and October, but movements vary in extent and abundance of birds from year to year. Banding studies indicate

Ragged edges and signs of wear on wing primaries (right), secondaries (left), and coverts (overlapping secondaries) precede the annual summer molt in house finches, as in most songbirds.

that west-to-east migration also occurs. At least some house finches shift southward in fall and winter.

Winter. Purple finch winter range extends from the northern Great Lakes and New England, where summer and winter ranges overlap, to the Gulf Coast and Texas. Flocks appear irruptively during some winters, invading in large numbers at irregular times and places, perhaps driven by low food resources in the northern range. House finches tend to remain on or near their breeding areas over winter, though extensive wandering may also occur. In northeastern areas recently colonized by these birds, yard feeders have probably aided or enabled their year-round survival. In the males of both species, the buffy feather tips erode, gradually revealing their red breeding plumage, and they sing with increasing frequency as winter advances.

Ecology. Purple finches favor northern coniferous and mixed forests and edges, as well as evergreen plantations and spruce bogs. House finches occupy generally the same habitats as house sparrows, though they increasingly appear in edge, dune, and semiopen countryside. Landscaped suburbs, nursery plantations, and building vicinities are typical habitats, as are weedy fields, for feeding sites.

Purple finches place their nests on horizontal conifer branches, often spruce, well out from the trunk at almost any height. Nests are camouflaged in needle clusters, making them almost invisible from beneath. The shallow cup built of twigs, grasses, and weed stems is lined with fine grasses, hair, and moss.

House finches build in a much greater variety of places, requiring only a stable base for the nest and at least minimal overhead shelter, such as an overhanging eave. Tree cavities, nest boxes, building ledges, ivy-covered walls, hanging planters, and ornamental conifers are all common nest sites. Open nests in trees usually abut the trunk. The open-cup nests consist of twigs, grass, debris, leaves, and other materials. House finches often appropriate vacated nests of Baltimore orioles, swallows, and other species. Sometimes they nest semicolonially within a few feet of each other.

Both finch species are primarily seed eaters, though purples depend less on weeds and ground foraging. In the spring, purple

House finches nest in a variety of places. Two favored sites are yard conifers, such as these spruces (top), and hanging planters (bottom). They also frequent dense ivy growth, as do house sparrows (see house sparrow illustration).

finches forage extensively in flowering trees and shrubs. They trim petals and consume the developing seeds and buds of many fruit trees, elms, maples, aspens, and others. Spring insect food consists mainly of aphids and cankerworms. In summer and fall, they feed extensively on the dry seeds of elms, ashes, sycamore, tulip tree, and ragweeds, as well as on the fruits of dogwoods, cherries, and many others. In winter, purples sometimes join feeding flocks of pine siskins and American goldfinches.

House finch diets consist almost exclusively of seeds and fruits. Seeds of dandelion, thistle, and other composites are highly favored, as are those of radish and field mustard in overgrown pastures or barnyards. House finches forage in almost any open, weedy area. In early spring, the birds relish dripping maple sap and tree buds. Sometimes they also pierce the bases of trumpet-shaped flowers, seeking nectar. Experiments suggest that they favor red-colored fruits, a diet that bears directly on the redness of male plumage (and thus, indirectly, on breeding success, as females of both species seem to prefer the redder males). In the western United States, house finches sometimes become orchard pests.

The foremost house finch competitors are probably house sparrows. Almost anyplace that a house sparrow nests, a house finch can do likewise, but house finches show a somewhat broader nest site tolerance and typically forage over larger areas. With the recent house finch explosion, many observers hoped that the newcomers would successfully compete with house sparrows. House sparrow declines have in fact occurred in some areas of house finch expansion, but countrywide data remain inconclusive.

The decline of purple finches in certain wooded suburban areas has been blamed on both house sparrows and house finches, but neither species' breeding habitats overlap widely with those of the purple finch. Food competition among the three probably becomes critical, if at all, in winter. At winter yard feeders, house finches often show dominance over purples, and house sparrows tend to dominate both.

Accipiter hawks likely capture some purple finches, and people once trapped them for cagebirds, but predation appears insignificant. Brown-headed cowbirds occasionally parasitize the nests of both species. House finches, more abundant than purples in urban areas, are exposed to frequent predation by domestic cats, as well as by American crows and blue jays. Mites frequently infest house finch nests, especially those that are repeatedly used. Disease epidemics, often prevalent in large populations of a species, include a widespread mycoplasma infection that affects the eyes of house finches, often encrusting them and swelling them shut.

Focus. The red pigment of both male finches is echinenone, metabolized from beta-carotene found in many plant sources, especially red fruits. Red coloring in males increases as they age.

Biologists continue to marvel at the house finch's explosive increase in the northeastern United States during the past fifty years. In Michigan, for example, none were seen before 1972. Populations grew exponentially through the 1980s until, in some urban areas today, they outnumber house sparrows. Unlike European starlings and house sparrows, this is not an alien immigrant, though its rates of increase and dispersal resemble those of alien organisms. Thus its rapid spread offers unique opportunities for study. Biologists worry, however, that the hardy, adaptable house finches may displace other, less aggressive native birds, though current data show little sign of this.

All eastern U.S. house finches are ancestrally native to southern California. Trappers illegally shipped many Hollywood finches or red-headed linnets, as they were called, to New York City in 1940 for sale as cagebirds. Threatened with prosecution there, some pet dealers released their birds, which soon began to thrive in Long Island. By 1950, the species was pushing north, south, and west, spreading across the entire eastern continent over the next forty years. This expansion has occurred by two dispersal modes: diffusion, a gradual incremental process; and jump dispersal, in which a few birds establish satellite colonies in the vanguard of parent populations. The original California population at the same time expanded eastward. Today the two populations are bridging North America in the plains states, thus achieving continentwide distribution.

How to account for such vigor? Birds go where habitats invite them, and many researchers believe that the house finch explosion reflects urban and suburban growth, which provides numerous new habitats for the birds. Yet the likewise urban-loving house sparrow is declining, a trend that cannot entirely be attributed to house finch competition. The house finch's adaptiveness may relate to its opportunism in seeking nest sites and food and to its cohesive social structure. Unlike house sparrows, house finches show rigid dominance hierarchies in which each bird knows its place in the flock.

They also show reversed sex dominance, rare in passerine birds: Winter females dominate males, and yearling males dominate older, redder males. These interactions are often visible at yard feeders.

You will find the scientific literature loaded with contradictory information about house finches. For example, they may wander as far as five hundred miles in winter, yet they are considered essentially sedentary; they are cold tolerant but adapt poorly to low temperatures; they often reuse previous nests but usually rebuild for each brood; they drive out house sparrows, but the latter are socially dominant over them; they compete with house sparrows for food but not nest sites, or vice versa; and so on. Probably all of these statements are correct for certain times and places; if so, we have only begun to measure the profile of the house finch. Clearly, this newcomer poses many questions that remain to be answered . . . or asked.

Purple finches have survived to ten years, but their life span probably averages three or four years.

The purple finch is New Hampshire's state bird.

Subfamily Emberizinae

This second subfamily of finches consists of almost eighty eastern North American species, including all the remaining accounts in this book. Emberizines are split into five tribes that were formerly considered separate families. Each tribe differs in physical and adaptive characteristics. For that reason, the following accounts are presented under their respective tribal headings.

SPARROW-BUNTINGS (TRIBE EMBERIZINI)

Sparrows and certain buntings number more than three hundred species worldwide, almost fifty in North America. These include eighteen New World sparrows that reside in the Northeast, plus juncos and towhees. Longspurs (*Calcarius*), the snow bunting (*Plectrophenax nivalis*), lark bunting (*Calamospiza melanocorys*), and seedeaters (*Sporophila*) are also emberizine finches. Birds of this tribe vary in size and form, but all have conical bills adapted for crushing seeds. Most are modestly colored as befits their mainly ground-feeding habits. Differences in sparrow plumages are subtle, usually requiring binoculars for visual identification of a species. The word *sparrow* derives from an Anglo-Saxon word meaning "flutterer."

FINCH FAMILY (Fringillidae) • Subfamily Emberizinae • SPARROW-BUNTINGS

Song Sparrow (*Melospiza melodia*)

Our most common native brown sparrow is five or six inches long and shows heavy breast streaking that converges into a large central spot. Song sparrows characteristically pump their rounded tails as they fly. Male song begins with a series of three or four introductory "sweet sweet sweet" notes followed by a variable musical trill. Sexes look alike.

Close relatives. The Lincoln's sparrow (*M. lincolnii*) and swamp sparrow (*M. georgiana*) are both North American species. Vesper sparrows (*Pooecetes gramineus*) somewhat resemble song sparrows in plumage and song but usually occupy more open habitats.

Behaviors. One bright day in the dead of every winter, the song sparrow, joined by the tufted titmouse, launches into loud, insistent song, marking for me the true if invisible turning point of the seasons.

Song sparrows breed across most of the continental United States and Canada. The large number of subspecies—thirty-four geographic forms, more than

Song sparrows incessantly voice their melodious notes from conspicuous perches in their territories. These sparrows appear less social and flock oriented in winter than most others.

for any other North American bird—reveals song sparrow populations as highly adaptive; the species is extremely sensitive to localized environmental influences and is undergoing rapid evolutionary
transition. This variability extends to migration patterns: Most song
sparrows migrate, arriving early and staying late, but many remain
on their breeding range all year. One can observe them almost year-
round in the right habitats, often as they move in short, bounding
flights between patches of cover. Thoreau remarked that "they generally bring some object, as a rail or branch, between themselves
and the face of the walker." When foraging on the ground, they
scratch simultaneously with both feet. Unlike many sparrow
species, song sparrows rarely flock together habitually, usually
appearing solitarily or in pairs.

Spring. Most male song sparrows are on their breeding range by
early spring, and territorial song is loud and frequent. Both nesting
and feeding occur within the territory, the size of which depends on
song sparrow abundance; it may range from half an acre in crowded
habitats to more than an acre in less populated sites. Territorial
males sing, chase, and display, habitually using several song
perches, but they often tolerate song sparrow intruders who don't
sing or act territorial. Females arrive one or two weeks later than
males, returning to the previous year's territory and thus frequently
to the same mate. *Pouncing* behavior, in which the loudly singing
male dives on the female, often marks pair formation at this time.
Male singing decreases when females arrive; then, as nest building
begins in late April and early May, song again becomes frequent.
The female constructs the nest—often repeatedly, for nest predation is frequent in this species. If disturbed with young in the nest
or vicinity, parent birds exhibit a showy distraction display, running
about with stiffly erect wings and dragging tail.

EGGS AND YOUNG: typically three or four; eggs greenish white,
heavily brown spotted. INCUBATION: by female; about twelve
days. FEEDING OF YOUNG: by both sexes; insects. FLEDGING: about
ten days.

Summer. Fledglings typically leave the nest before they can fly, hiding in ground cover. They begin to fly in about a week but remain in the nest vicinity, following and being fed by a parent, usually the male, for three or four weeks before dispersing. The female often renests only days after the first brood fledges, sometimes using the same nest, sometimes building a new one. She may produce two or even three more broods, nesting well into August. Most song sparrows probably remain monogamous only through a single breeding season. Polygyny, in which one male mates with two or more females, may occur when a male dies and his mate pairs with another already mated male or when females of a population outnumber males. As nesting declines toward late summer, territorial behaviors and song also cease, a signal that the annual plumage molt has begun. Molting may extend through September.

Fall. Males often become briefly territorial again after molting, but song is seldom heard after November. Song sparrow migrations are *partial;* portions of a population—most juveniles and adult females and about half the adult males—usually migrate, but individual males may migrate one year and remain on their breeding range the next. Some juvenile males establish territories in the fall, then migrate and return to them the following spring. Fall migration usually lasts into November, as individual birds drift away.

Winter. A broad overlap of breeding and winter ranges extends across the northern United States south to the central tier of states. Winter residents on the breeding range consist of birds remaining on or near their summer territories plus arrivals from farther north. South of this range overlap, song sparrow winter range spans the southern United States, extending into central Mexico. Song sparrows never become actually gregarious, but they often form small foraging flocks during migrations and in winter, especially during severe weather. They frequently mix with dark-eyed juncos, American tree sparrows, and northern cardinals at this season. At yard feeders, they are among the most belligerent of birds. In January and February, song commences, increasing in frequency as migrants head north in late winter. A large percentage of first-year birds, it is reported, return to areas near their birth sites.

Ecology. Song sparrows favor dense, brushy thickets, often near water, in both summer and winter ranges. Any shrubby area near a pond or stream may host one or more pairs. Hedgerows and overgrown fields are also typical habitats.

Song sparrows usually build their first nests of the season on the ground, half hidden by a tuft of grass, low shrub, or brush pile. Later nests are often placed two or three feet high in a shrub or young tree, frequently a conifer. The cup, formed almost entirely of dried grasses and lined with finer grasses, looks pocketed in the ground but bulkier when placed above ground.

Song sparrows usually feed on or close to the ground. Insect prey makes up 34 percent of the diet, chiefly beetles, plus grasshoppers, caterpillars, ants, and others, consumed mainly during the breeding season. The year-round seed diet includes smartweeds, bristlegrass and other grasses, ragweeds, oats, pigweed, and sedges, plus berries and cherries in season.

Competition with other species is probably negligible. Birds of its size that often nest in similar habitats include American goldfinches, yellow warblers, and common yellowthroats. Song sparrows often defend their territories from these species, but most competition is probably between the sparrows themselves as they conflict with unmated floaters that seek territories.

Song sparrow predators are many, but the amount of predation that occurs seems strongly correlated to density of cover. "A well-situated population is practically immune to predation," wrote ornithologist Margaret Morse Nice, "while a badly situated one suffers heavy losses." Accipiter hawks, falcons, and owls prey upon the birds; nest predators include snakes, box turtles, common grackles, opossums, raccoons, skunks, and domestic cats. One recent study found that song sparrow nesting success increased with the abundance of local coyote populations, suggesting that these canine predators may control other predators that prey on the nests. The sparrows may mob potential predators on occasion. This species is one of the most frequent hosts of brown-headed cowbird parasitism. A high percentage of the song sparrow nests I find contain one or more cowbird eggs; some studies estimate cowbird parasitism at about 40 percent. But in optimal habitat, according to Nice, the sparrows easily tolerate this parasitism, and loss of sparrow nestlings is minimal. In marginal habitat, cowbird nestlings often survive while the sparrow young die of starvation.

Focus. The song sparrow has probably been the most intensively studied of all passerine birds, mainly because of Ohio researcher Margaret Morse Nice. Working on her own time and with minimal resources, she spent years observing this species, ultimately providing a classic model for life history studies. Nice's work, conducted during the 1930s, also added vastly to our knowledge of passerine birds in general. In the roster of great American ornithologists, Margaret Nice ranks near the top.

Eleven years is the maximum recorded life span for wild song sparrows; probably two or three years is average. Nice estimated that only about 12 percent of hatched young survive long enough to breed. Adult yearly survival is an estimated 60 percent, however, and song sparrows remain one of our most abundant native birds, second only to American robins in many areas.

Closer look. Nice, M. M. *Studies in the Life History of the Song Sparrow* (parts 1 and 2). New York: Dover, 1964.

FINCH FAMILY (Fringillidae) • Subfamily Emberizinae • SPARROW-BUNTINGS

White-throated Sparrow
(*Zonotrichia albicollis*)

This seven-inch-long northern sparrow can be recognized by its white throat patch and the yellow mark between eye and bill, in the area known as the *lore*. Its clear, plaintive song begins with two or three long, whistled notes followed by a series of three-note phrases: "Oh-h-h swee-e-et Canada Canada Canada Canada." A cardinal-like "chink" note is also characteristic. Except for morphic differences in pairs, sexes look alike.

Close relatives. The white-crowned sparrow (*Z. leucophrys*) is the white-throat's nearest northeastern kin. Harris' sparrow (*Z.*

querula) resides in the west-central United States; the golden-crowned sparrow (*Z. atricapilla*) is a Pacific coastal species.

Behaviors. Its ringing, melancholy song heard from afar voices the northern wilderness as hauntingly as loon, raven, and wolf but is more commonly heard than all three. White-throats breed from the upper Great Lakes and New England throughout much of forested Canada. Like ruffed grouse and screech-owls, they are *polymorphic,* showing two distinct color forms: birds with black and white head stripes, and birds with brown and tan head stripes. Unlike grouse and screech-owls, however, white-throats tend to pair with their opposite-colored morphs. Research by James K. Lowther in 1962 indicated that behavioral differences may account for this tendency: White-striped males are more aggressive than tan-striped males toward singers of both morphs, driving them off; since white-striped females sing and tan-striped females do not, the upshot is that white-striped males monopolize tan-striped females, leaving white-striped females to mate with the less aggressive tan-striped males. This system, called *negative assortative mating,* sounds more complex than it is.

White-throated sparrows nest on the ground and in low shrubs. These birds, like many, show countershading (inset), in which lighter underparts help camouflage the plumage in low-light habitats (see Cuckoos).

Most white-throats migrate, though some, especially adult males, remain in the breeding range year-round. These birds are most commonly seen as they forage in flocks during spring and fall migrations.

Spring. A prenesting molt occurs in early spring as the birds arrive on their breeding range. Only head and body feathers are replaced; the white-striped morph acquires its black and white coloration at this time. Males arrive one or two weeks ahead of females in April and May, often returning to their previous breeding territories. Females return less often to the same sites, so most pairs remain monogamous only for the season. The male's territorial song seldom interrupts the song of a neighboring male, as if by mutual agreement to grant each other solos, thereby enabling each to vocalize its claim to the fullest. Not uncommonly, males also sing at night. Song decreases when the female arrives but usually recommences if predation or other failure causes renesting. She builds the nest, and the pair becomes silent and secretive. White-throats are excitable, easily aroused by a birder's pishing sounds, especially near the nest. Even then, however, they usually remain hidden in the underbrush. An incubating female may not flush from her nest until almost stepped on.

EGGS AND YOUNG: four to six; eggs glossy, whitish, heavily brown spotted. INCUBATION: by female; eleven to fourteen days. FEEDING OF YOUNG: by both sexes; insects. FLEDGING: eight or nine days.

Summer. I have found white-throat nests containing nestlings in July, and nesting may even continue into August. Since pairs seldom attempt to raise two broods, however, these later nestings probably result from one or more previous nest failures. Renesting white-throats usually rebuild more than one hundred feet away from the previous site. The relatively short duration from hatching to fledging may relate to the low placement of nests and their consequent vulnerability to predators. Parents continue to feed fledglings for about a month. Then females and juveniles often depart the territory, while males may remain there until fall. White-throats molt their entire plumage in late July and August; both morphs acquire tan-striped head plumage that lasts until the following spring.

Fall. White-throats migrate, usually in small flocks and at night, through September and October. During the day, they settle in brushy areas to feed. Occasionally they sing during these layover periods in both fall and spring. White-throats exhibit differential migration, with the females and the heavily streaked juveniles traveling farthest south, while many adult males remain on or nearer the southern breeding range.

Winter. Most white-throats winter from the lower Great Lakes south to the Gulf Coast and northern Mexico. Individuals often return to the previous winter's site, which, in optimal habitats, may encompass less than an acre. Rigid dominance hierarchies govern white-throat flocks in winter. The flock, averaging five to fifteen birds, often forages in association with other ground-feeding sparrows and dark-eyed juncos. "The [eastern] towhee is the white-throated sparrow's best friend," wrote one old-time birder; although breeding ranges of the two species coincide only in a relatively narrow band, they often occupy similar winter habitats. North-wintering white-throats often appear at yard feeders.

Ecology. The white-throat's primary habitats are natural openings in northern coniferous or mixed forests, often in or near wetlands. Such areas include bogs, swampy alder and shoreline thickets, edges of burnt-over clearings, shrubby ravines, and windfall gaps. These favored edge habitats often border stands of large coniferous trees. The birds also frequent dense lowland and upland thickets and brush piles in both summer and winter. During migrations, however, they may appear in almost any habitat, including marshes, suburban lawns, and deciduous forests.

White-throats usually nest on the ground, occasionally two or three feet high in shrubs or small trees. Extremely well concealed in the low vegetation, the small, cuplike nests are usually sited at edges of clearings, though I have also found their nests in sphagnum bogs. Often the nest lies within several feet of a lookout perch such as a stump or small tree. Coarse grasses, bark fibers, pine needles, and rootlets form the nest, which the female lines with finer grasses and sometimes hair.

White-throats forage from the ground to treetops, seldom far from cover. Foraging methods likewise vary. On the ground, the birds scratch with both feet; in trees, they hop systematically along one branch after another. At times they also hawk insects in flight. In early spring, the birds devour several kinds of tree buds and blossoms (staminate flowers of beech are favorites), plus elm and maple seeds. The breeding-season diet consists mainly of insects, many gleaned from leaves and branches. Ants, small wasps, beetles, caterpillars, and spiders are the foremost items. In late summer and fall, the diet shifts to seeds—ragweeds and smartweeds alone may provide some 25 percent of the annual food intake—and pulpy fruits, minus skins and large seeds, including wild grapes, blueberries, bunchberries, and dogwood and poison-ivy fruits. White-throats are probably the foremost fruit-eating sparrows.

Its feeding adaptability probably gains the white-throat a degree of competitive advantage in its habitats. In many areas, it shares similar ground-nesting habitats with song sparrows and dark-eyed juncos. One study indicated that it favors a density of nesting cover midway between the sparser preferences of the song sparrow and the denser preferences of the junco.

Hawks and owls sometimes capture white-throats, but most predation probably occurs at the nest. As with all ground-nesting birds, white-throat eggs and nestlings are vulnerable to many mammal predators, such as raccoons, skunks, squirrels, and red foxes. Brown-headed cowbirds occasionally parasitize the nests, but white-throats are not common cowbird hosts, probably because most nest in remote areas outside typical cowbird habitats.

Focus. Vernacular names include Canada bird and Peabody bird, both referring to its characteristic song. The oldest white-throat on record survived almost ten years, but average longevity is probably less than half that.

White-throats seem to be declining throughout much of their breeding range. As edge dwellers, they probably benefited from lumbering, increasing their abundance from presettlement times.

As north-country breeders, however, they seem caught in a habitat squeeze of sorts: Both extensive clear-cutting and the aging of mature forests deprive them of optimal habitat (though early-stage regrowth of clear-cut areas attracts them), and both continue to occur in numerous areas of the breeding range.

FINCH FAMILY (Fringillidae) • Subfamily Emberizinae • SPARROW-BUNTINGS

Dark-eyed Junco (*Junco hyemalis*)

This sparrow-size bird is dark hooded down to its breast, with a whitish belly, pinkish bill, and white outer tail feathers, its most conspicuous feature as it flushes from the ground. Males have blacker heads than the grayer females. The junco's trilling song resembles that of the chipping sparrow, and junco flocks often utter twittering notes as they fly up. They also voice musical, finchlike "tew tew tew" notes.

Close relatives. Not so long ago, ornithologists recognized ten separate *Junco* species. All were North and Central American residents, and each varied somewhat in plumage. In 1983, these were demoted to races or subspecies of just two species: the dark-eyed junco and yellow-eyed junco (*J. phaeonotus*). Five distinct races, often hybridizing where their ranges overlap, are now lumped as the dark-eyed junco. The most widely distributed race, formerly known as the slate-colored junco species, is the typical junco of eastern North America. The other races are the Oregon, white-winged, gray-headed, and Guadeloupe juncos.

The dark-eyed junco in typical plumage (inset) exhibits strong countershading as befits ground nesters. Partially albino juncos (left), showing odd patches of white, are not uncommon.

Behaviors. Most of us see dark-eyed juncos only in winter, when their twittering flocks populate the hedgerows and the ground beneath yard feeders; they only occasionally venture as high as the feeder itself. This ground-loving habit characterizes juncos throughout most of the year. A distinctive junco feeding characteristic is its double-scratching in leaf litter or snow; it jumps forward and back with both feet, a quick hop-step observable wherever the birds are foraging. Like most flocking birds, juncos show rigid dominance hierarchies, an evolutionary adaptation that apparently maintains social stability.

Junco breeding range spans the continent from Canada's tree line south to the upper Great Lakes, New England, and the Appalachians to Georgia. Juncos are migrants.

Spring. Males precede females on the breeding range by a week or more in April and early May. Adult males probably return to their previous territories; a junco territory may span two or three acres or, in prime nesting habitats, may be much smaller. Males often sing from the tallest trees in their territories; this is the only time of year when juncos spend much time high off the ground. As in many songbirds, male singing contrasts with initially hostile behavior when a female actually arrives; he chases, but she lingers. Male song decreases, and soon the birds are reciprocally displaying with drooping wings, fanned tails, and a nodding head dance. Females build the nests, mainly in June.

EGGS AND YOUNG: typically four; eggs bluish white, brown speckled, especially at the larger end. INCUBATION: by female; about twelve days. FEEDING OF YOUNG: by both sexes; regurgitated insects at first, then soft-bodied insects. FLEDGING: nine to thirteen days.

Summer. Many junco pairs raise two broods, nesting into early July. The female builds a new nest for the second brood soon after the first brood fledges, and the male feeds the first-brood fledglings. One or both parents feed the brown, streaked young for up to a month before the latter disperse. From mid-August into September, adult juncos undergo their complete annual molt.

Fall. Juncos move southward in flocks through September into early November, with the largest numbers traveling in October. This species demonstrates a movement pattern called differential migration, also seen in several other passerine species. Adult females migrate farther south than young females. Young males remain farthest north, and adult males may winter with, or slightly south of, young males. Thus most juncos in a flock often consist of same-sex, same-age birds (though mixed flocks do occur). Such sex and age segregation probably relates to the birds' rigid dominance hierarchies.

Winter. Dark-eyed juncos winter from southern Canada to the Gulf states and northern Mexico. They narrowly overlap their breeding range in the upper Great Lakes, New England, and Appalachia. Adult juncos usually return to their previous wintering areas. At night the flock, generally fifteen to thirty birds, roosts in a habitual place, usually a densely foliaged conifer. Winter flocks are fixed but flexible units, each with a foraging range of ten to twelve acres that seldom overlaps into another flock's range. A junco flock may subdivide and reform at irregular times through the day, but all birds of a flock remain in the flock range, associating with American tree sparrows, black-capped chickadees, white-throated sparrows, and other weed- and ground-feeding species. Each junco in the flock knows its place in the pecking order; in mixed flocks, males tend

Junco nests, well camouflaged in ground vegetation, are often built on slopes or against banks. Eggs are heavily wreathed with brown at one end.

to dominate females, and adults dominate juveniles. By March, males are beginning to sing, and some flocks are moving northward.

Ecology. Dark-eyed juncos breed in the drier coniferous and mixed forest regions of North America. They seldom inhabit dense forests, however, favoring brushy edges and natural openings. During migrations and winter, they frequent hedgerows, brush piles, thickets, and weedy fields.

Juncos typically nest at the edge of forest clearings, along woodland roads or power lines, rarely in deeply shaded sites. Nests are built on the ground, occasionally in low vegetation, often in slight depressions against a vertical bank or in upturned tree roots overhung by sod or plants. I have also found them sheltered amid grass clumps or small shrubs on hillside slopes. Occasionally juncos build in such untypical sites as trellises, open cans on the ground, and semiopen cavities in stumps or walls. The nest of dried grasses lined with pine needles, bark strips, rootlets, and sometimes hair much resembles the nests of its ground sparrow relatives.

Juncos are mainly ground-feeding seed eaters, but they consume about 50 percent animal matter—mainly caterpillars, beetles, ants, and spiders—during the breeding season. Even in winter, they feed avidly on winter gnats and springtails ("snow fleas"). Most of their diet, however, consists of weed and grass seeds. Ragweeds plus foxtail, crab, panic, timothy, and dropseed grasses rank high, as do smartweeds and pigweed.

Competition with other species is probably negligible. Poten-

*Seeds of annual crabgrasses (*Digitaria) *are relished by juncos and many sparrows.*

tial users of similar bank or tree-root nesting sites might include yellow-bellied flycatchers, winter wrens, and waterthrushes. Competition between sexes for food may provide impetus to differential migration.

Accipiter hawks and northern shrikes occasionally capture juncos. In some areas, garter snakes are the foremost nest predators. Others include red squirrels, chipmunks, weasels, skunks, and raccoons. Brown-headed cowbird parasitism appears infrequent.

Focus. Flocking in birds has been described as a mixture of "gregariousness and intolerance, a compromise of costs and benefits"—as is evolution itself. So it is with juncos and many other flocking species. Many people know juncos as snowbirds, since in most areas of the United States their arrival forecasts winter. Wrote Thoreau, "You see them come drifting over a rising ground just like the snowflakes before the northeast wind." Another writer described junco coloration as "a sort of meteorological microcosm of a snowy winter day (leaden sky above, snow below)."

The name junco, from the Latin *juncus,* meaning "rush," resulted from the bird's supposed marshland habitat, a misnomer sanctified by time and conservatism. Audubon, who often recycled his artistic models by eating them, reported junco flesh as "extremely delicate and juicy." The junco's maximum recorded life span is ten years, a longevity that most never approach.

FINCH FAMILY (Fringillidae) • Subfamily Emberizinae • SPARROW-BUNTINGS

Chipping Sparrow (*Spizella passerina*)

This five-inch-long sparrow can be recognized by its unstreaked pale gray breast, bright reddish brown cap, white line over the eye, and black line through it. Its song is a rattling trill on one pitch. Sexes look alike.

Close relatives. Other northeastern *Spizella* species include the American tree sparrow (*S. arborea*), field sparrow (*S. pusilla*), and clay-colored sparrow (*S. pallida*). Brewer's sparrow (*S. breweri*) and the black-chinned sparrow (*S. atrogularis*) are western U.S. species. These six species form the entire genus.

Behaviors. Before the unrelated house sparrow's invasion of North America, the "chippy" was widely regarded as the most domestic of all the sparrows. It remains one of the most common summer residents of suburban yards, always voicing its monotonic trill, which varies in tempo and pitch among individual males but remains consistent for each. Some males emit a relatively slow succession of "chips" or almost cricketlike trills; others sing faster and sound drier and more staccato. Though mainly ground foragers, chipping sparrows always sing from elevated perches and occasionally at night.

Chipping sparrows breed across the continent from the tree line in Canada south to Nicaragua. Northern populations migrate.

Spring. A molt of head and throat feathers in early spring gives chipping sparrows their breeding plumage of reddish crown and white brow line. Males arrive on their breeding range in April a week or so before females; in my yard, their arrival coincides with daffodil flowering). Singing establishes the territory, ranging from half an acre to more than an acre in size. Few courtship displays greet the arrival of females, but copulation on the ground or a perch is frequent and conspicuous, often in the morning. Females, often interrupted by these couplings, collect materials and build the nest, usually in early May.

EGGS AND YOUNG: usually four; eggs pale blue, brown spotted at the larger end. INCUBATION: by female, which is fed by male; about twelve days. FEEDING OF YOUNG: by both sexes; insects. FLEDGING: seven to ten days.

Summer. Chipping sparrows usually raise two broods, sometimes three, and nesting may extend into mid-August. Most pairs probably remain monogamous for the entire season, though polygyny, in which the male mates with an outside female, sometimes occurs as incubation begins; usually few extra females are available, however. Renewed singing by males and nest building by females herald the beginning of each new breeding cycle. Older nestlings may fledge a few days early if the nest is disturbed. Last year, as I observed an early-August nest, one of four nestlings fledged directly into my face, scrambling all over me before dropping to the ground—a case of instinctual offense as best defense or of utter confusion? Well pummeled in any case, I retreated.

One researcher estimated that about 60 percent of chipping sparrow nests prove successful—that is, fledge birds—a relatively high proportion among passerines. Parents continue to feed the fledglings for several weeks even as renesting commences. Family flocks desert their territories in August and wander widely, often combining with other family groups, as well as with song and field sparrows. In late summer, the birds molt, acquiring a duller plumage of brown-streaked crowns and tan eye stripes. They rarely sing after August.

Fall. Chipping sparrows travel southward through September and October, usually in nighttime flocks of about thirty, resting and feeding during the day.

Winter. A few chipping sparrows may remain on the northern breeding range through winter, and some travel as far south as Central America, but most settle inland in the Gulf states. Typically the

Typical nesting habitat of chipping sparrows includes small conifers in fairly open density. Many suburban yards duplicate this type of habitat.

birds forage in flocks of twenty-five to fifty, sometimes mixing with field sparrows and dark-eyed juncos.

Ecology. Optimal habitat for this upland edge resident is a mixture of shrubs, small conifers, and open ground—exactly the landscape of many suburban lawns. Chipping sparrows also favor pine groves and plantations, orchards, and shrubby, overgrown fields. Before humans provided these kinds of habitat, the birds, much less abundant then, probably inhabited dry pine and oak savannas (often the result of fires), plus a variety of mixed open-edge sites.

Chipping sparrows usually nest three to ten feet high, often on an outer horizontal branch of a pine, red cedar, spruce, or hawthorn. The small, compact cup formed of dead grasses, weed stalks, and rootlets is lined with fine grasses and hairs. "In our rural past," wrote ecologist Richard Brewer, "[this bird] was known for lining the nest with horsehair and, even today, the birds usually find some type of hair for the lining." This led to the birds' former name of hairbirds. Often they remove and reuse the hair lining from the previous nest when rebuilding.

Chipping sparrows forage on or near the ground, as well as in low shrubs and trees. Like most seed-eating birds, they feed mainly on insects during the breeding season, when nestlings require a high-protein diet. The June diet may consist of some 90 percent insects, with large proportions of grasshoppers, caterpillars (including destructive gypsy moth larvae), and beetles.

Chipping sparrows favor low conifers for nesting. Usually the nest lining contains mammal hairs, which the birds may recycle for later nesting.

After the nestlings fledge, the seeds of many grasses and weeds become the staples, including those of oats, chickweeds, pigweed, ragweeds, and crab, foxtail, timothy, and panic grasses. Chipping sparrows apparently obtain most of their water from their diet and may survive without drinking for up to three weeks, a useful adaptation for their dry-habitat preference.

Competition appears negligible. In earlier decades, chipping sparrows may have declined in some areas because of seed competition with house sparrows; the decline of house sparrows plus the widespread growth of suburban habitats since World War II have apparently offset this effect, however. Blue jays, snakes, and domestic cats are probably the foremost chipping sparrow predators. Brown-headed cowbirds often parasitize their nests, especially those containing first broods; since subsequent sparrow nestings extend beyond the period of cowbird breeding, however, long-term negative effects on chipping sparrows appear minimal.

Focus. Chipping sparrow song bears close similarity to that of several other passerine birds, notably the pine warbler, worm-eating warbler, dark-eyed junco, and swamp sparrow, each of which has deceived me at times. The differences are subtle and, because of the chippy's individual variations in speed and pitch, not invariably distinctive. Differences in typical breeding habitats help narrow voice identification where summer ranges of two or more of these species coincide. Together with American robins and house finches, chipping sparrows have probably become our most common native birds in suburbia.

FINCH FAMILY (Fringillidae) • Subfamily Emberizinae • SPARROW-BUNTINGS

Eastern Towhee (*Pipilo erythrophthalmus*)

This seven- or eight-inch-long bird can be identified by its long tail and distinctive pattern of robin-red sides, white belly, dark upper parts, white tail corners, and red irises. Male heads and upper parts are black; those of females are dark brown. The contrasting solid-color patterns of towhee plumage provide effective camouflage in the light-and-shadow mosaic of its habitats. The towhee's song is likewise distinctive: a loud, three-part phrase— "drink-your teee"—the last syllable higher and trilled. The two-note call, "too-WHEE," is also commonly heard.

Eastern towhees noisily rummage on the ground for food. This male shows the finch bill characteristic of the sparrow-bunting tribe.

Close relatives. The four other North American towhees—spotted towhee (*P. maculatus*), green-tailed towhee (*P. chlorurus*), brown towhee (*P. fuscus*), and Abert's towhee (*P. aberti*)—reside in the western United States. Two others are Mexican residents.

Behaviors. The towhee spends most of its time on or near the ground. It often reveals its presence, when not singing, by its vigorous rummaging in the leaf litter, where it double-scratches in a manner similar to juncos. Towhees display much tail action, pumping, spreading, and flicking their white-splashed rectrices as they move about, accenting the fact that this is our longest-tailed northeastern finch. A lover of bathing, it often flutters in dew-heavy foliage, thoroughly drenching itself, then fluffs and preens on a perch.

Eastern towhees range east of the Great Plains, breeding from southern Canada to the southeastern states. The northern population migrates.

Spring. In the northeastern range of this species, peak migration occurs in late March and early April. Males precede females, remaining in small flocks for a few days before establishing territories of half an acre to two acres in size, probably on or near previously held territories. They sing from low perches or on the ground. When the females arrive, there is much chasing, usually in triads of two males and a female, before pairing occurs on the territory. A common courtship display by both sexes while perched is a brief spread of wings and tail, exhibiting the birds' white markings. The female builds the nest, often accompanied by male song from an overhead perch as she collects materials. About mid-May, both song and territory diminish somewhat as nesting begins. Unmated males continue to sing, however.

EGGS AND YOUNG: three to five; eggs grayish, brown spotted, especially at the larger end. INCUBATION: by female; about twelve days. FEEDING OF YOUNG: by both sexes; mainly insects, some fruits. FLEDGING: about ten days.

Summer. Fledglings begin flying a week or so after leaving the nest. They continue to be fed for about a month on the territory. Towhee parents remain monogamous for the entire breeding season, often raising two broods in the original territory. A week or more after the first brood fledges, the female begins building anew, and this nesting may extend into July or August. The independent young often form small flocks with other juvenile towhees and wander widely, usually ignored by the still-territorial adults. Juveniles are heavily brown streaked until their first molt in midsummer, and the males possess brown wing primaries until their second-year molt. Song largely ceases by August, when the adult towhees also acquire new plumage.

Fall. Migration from the northern range proceeds leisurely in September and October, mainly at night with daytime rest stops. Most towhees travel to the southern United States, many leapfrogging past year-round residents of the central states. Females travel the farthest south, an example of differential migration.

Winter. Most towhee migrants join year-round resident towhees, whose range extends from south of the Great Lakes and New England to the Gulf. Flocks of fifteen to twenty-five birds forage over areas of twenty to thirty acres, often mixing with northern cardinals, various sparrows, and dark-eyed juncos. Small numbers of male towhees spend the winter on the northern breeding range, and males also outnumber females on the northern winter range.

Ecology. Towhees are not as tolerant of humans as American robins are and rarely reside in suburban yards or farmland. Yet their favored habitats result mainly from human activities. Dense, shrubby edges and deciduous and mixed open woodlands with heavy leaf litter characterize both summer and winter habitats.

A female scratches a depression in the litter, building the nest rim flush with the ground surface. She lines the bulky cup of leaves, grasses, twigs, and bark strips (especially grapevine bark) with fine grasses, pine needles, and sometimes hair. Nests usually lie sheltered beneath a grass tuft, low shrub, or brush tangle. Occasionally, especially for later nestings, towhees build a foot or two high in a dense, low shrub.

Towhees consume almost any sort of invertebrate they can find in the leaf litter, chiefly beetles, plus caterpillars, ants, spiders, and snails. In the spring, they relish blueberry flowers and glean many insects from tree foliage. Towhees are foremost predators of late-stage gypsy moth caterpillars and the adult moths. The diet turns mainly vegetarian in summer and fall, and they consume many kinds of fruits and seeds. Seeds of ragweeds, smartweeds, sedges, and foxtail grasses are favored, as are corn, blueberries, and blackberries. The birds also eat acorns in fall and winter.

Although towhees inhabit the same upland thicket sites as cuckoos, brown thrashers, and white-throated sparrows, among other edge dwellers, competition for nest sites and food appears minimal, except for north-wintering towhees.

Ground nests are always vulnerable to foraging predators, including pilot black snakes and mammals such as weasels, skunks, and raccoons. Probably the towhee's foremost nemesis, however, is the brown-headed cowbird, which often deposits eggs in towhee nests. The towhee's tolerance for forest fragmentation places it on a collision course with cowbirds, which favor patchy forest tracts and edges. If not for the fact that many towhees nest into summer, when most cowbirds have ceased breeding, probably fewer towhees would exist.

Focus. The name towhee is one of many transliterations of this bird's call notes. Vernacular names include chewink, red-eyed towhee, and ground robin. Banding data show a longevity record of ten years; four to six years, one researcher judged, "is not an uncommonly long life span for this species."

As edge habitats are transitional, towhee abundance varies locally over time. A dramatic trend of decrease in New England— some 8 to 10 percent per year since 1966—has been attributed mainly to forest regeneration.

WOOD WARBLERS (TRIBE PARULINI)

The parulines—about one hundred fifteen species—are all birds of the Western Hemisphere. Forty warbler species (most in the genera *Dendroica, Vermivora,* and *Oporornis*) breed in eastern North America, but most of these reside for all but a few months of the year in the tropics. Small in size (four to six inches long), they have slender, sharp-pointed bills. In the spring, most, though not all, show brilliant yellow plumage on some part of the body. Songs are distinctive for each species. Warblers "lisp, buzz, hiss, chip, rollick, or zip," wrote one observer; few actually warble, a trilling song description better ascribed to finches.

Migrant warblers are usually among the last bird arrivals in spring. Seldom remaining still for long, they hyperactively forage in well-defined *niches*—specific subdivisions of a habitat particular to each species. Their niches range from ground surface to treetops, as well as in particular stages of plant succession from transitional edges to mature for-

This yellow warbler male shows the typical warbler needle-pointed bill, adapted for insect foraging. Warblers, with few exceptions, feed almost exclusively on foliage insects.

est. Warblers can be classified by foraging sites into three broad categories: those that feed primarily in trees (most warblers), in brush, and on the ground. Several species that nest in conifers are known as spruce woods warblers. Unfortunately, space permits inclusion of only a few members of this diverse, colorful tribe in the following pages.

Today many wood warbler species are profoundly at risk, showing steadily decreasing abundance in areas where not so long ago they thrived. Severely affected by habitat fragmentation in their breeding range and probably by Neotropical rain-forest destruction as well, our dwindling warbler populations express alarming indicators of environmental decline. The four species included here, however, remain relatively common in their habitats.

Closer looks. Harrison, H. H. *Wood Warblers' World.* New York: Simon and Schuster, 1984.

Morse, D. H. *American Warblers: An Ecological and Behavioral Perspective.* Cambridge: Harvard University Press, 1989.

FINCH FAMILY (Fringillidae) • Subfamily Emberizinae • WOOD WARBLERS

Yellow Warbler *(Dendroica petechia)*

This bird is the most extensively yellow of all warblers, from crown to tail tip. Males show rusty streaking on breast and sides. The high-pitched song typically ends with a quick, up-slurred "tee-tee-weet"; some researchers postulate two main song types based on accented or unaccented endings. Parts of the song sometimes resemble notes of our other, though not closely related, "wild canary," the American goldfinch.

Close relatives. Twenty-one *Dendroica* warblers breed in North America; twelve of these are northeastern species. They include the chestnut-sided warbler (*D. pensylvanica*), magnolia warbler (*D. magnolia*), yellow-rumped warbler (*D. coronata*), and pine warbler (*D. pinus*).

Behaviors. Plainly marked and easily observed, the yellow warbler shows the largest breeding distribution of any paruline species, spanning the continent across northern Canada and Alaska south to Mexico and the southeastern United States. Since it resides for only about three months of the year in most of this range, however, its reproduce-and-run schedule matches that of some shorebirds. Not as hyperactive as most warblers, yellows also seem much less shy of humans, sometimes permitting close observation—a main reason, no doubt, for the large amount of research focused on this species.

Spring. Warblers migrate at night, often in mixed warbler flocks, stopping in daytime to rest and feed. Most northbound yellow warblers begin moving from their southernmost winter range in late March. Before or during migration, they acquire their breeding plumage by undergoing a partial molt, replacing all but wing and tail feathers. They arrive on their breeding range from late April to mid-May, depending on latitude; typically their arrival coincides with the first spring insect hatches but occurs before most leaves have emerged. Males precede females by a week or so and immediately begin territorial singing from exposed perches. Watch for chasing, circling, and slow, fluttering flights by males as they establish their claims. Territories range from about one-half to three acres, though the birds may also range up to a quarter mile from the territory to feed. Each territory must contain a suitable nest site, concealment cover, song perches, and tree foraging sites. Males with larger amounts of reddish breast streaking apparently possess greater territorial advantage, and possibly higher sexual status, than males with dimmer streaking.

Females, upon arrival, as in most species that do not pair for life, are first treated as intruders; but after selecting a territory to her liking (and with it, incidentally, the male claimant), the female resists being chased off. Soon she begins nest building, and copulation occurs as the nest nears completion. Males continue singing until the eggs hatch, then become less vocal. If disturbed at the nest, the birds commonly flutter along the ground in vigorous distraction displays. Males occasionally exhibit polygyny, breeding with two females, but most yellows remain monogamous for the season.

EGGS AND YOUNG: usually five; eggs whitish, brown spotted or blotched, especially at the larger end. INCUBATION: by female, which is attended by male; ten to twelve days. FEEDING OF YOUNG: by both sexes; insects. FLEDGING: nine to eleven days.

Summer. Parents continue feeding the juveniles for several days near the nest and do not often raise second broods. As soon as the young can feed themselves, usually in July, females and juveniles desert the territories; adult males may remain and occasionally sing. The birds soon undergo a feather molt. Females and juveniles acquire a dull yellowish plumage, but males renew their breeding brilliance. Yellow warblers seldom linger once breeding is finished and usually begin migrational movements in July, sometimes while still molting. Through August and September, their populations, swollen in number by juvenile birds, wing southward nightly across a broad front. Most of the eastern migrants apparently travel from the southeastern states directly across the Gulf to landfalls on the Yucatán coast—a five-hundred-mile nonstop route.

Fall, Winter. Most yellow warblers have arrived on their winter range by early fall. This area extends from the Bahamas and northern Mexico south through Central America into Peru, Bolivia, and the Amazon Basin. Adult yellows appear site faithful to their previous wintering areas; upon their arrival, males sing and establish territories, aggressively defending them. Females also remain solitary, whereas juveniles may mix with other warbler species in small, wandering flocks. In some coastal areas, the northern migrants join two resident yellow warbler subspecies called mangrove and golden warblers.

Ecology. The yellow warbler favors hot, humid places and climates, as befits a bird that spends most months of the year in the Neotropics. There it forages in lowland thickets and plantations, often, as in its breeding range, frequenting the sunnier, open-edge areas created by agriculture or human habitation. A habitat generalist in its breeding range, it favors early transitional vegetation, especially the dense thickets along ponds and streams; it also resides in shrubby uplands, scrub thickets, and garden hedges. But, as ornithologist Raymond J. Adams, Jr., writes, the yellow warbler "appears to respond to the habitat structure more than the moisture of the site (wet or dry), although wetlands . . . typically support the highest breeding densities."

The nest, a strong, tightly woven structure, is usually placed three to eight feet high in the upright fork of a shrub or small tree. Shrub willows and dogwoods are common shoreline nest sites, as are hawthorn trees in drier uplands. Fine grasses and milkweed

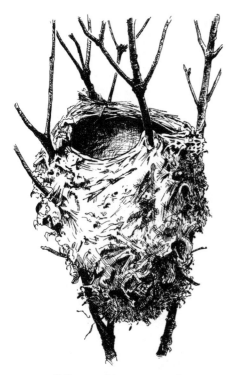

bark often give the nest a silvery gray appearance; the deep cup is lined with grasses and downy materials, such as willow and aspen seeds, cinnamon fern stems, and tent caterpillar webbing. Female yellows sometimes raid other yellow warbler nests, as well as vacated willow flycatcher and American goldfinch nests, for materials. Yellow warbler nests much resemble those of American goldfinches in both form and construction. Goldfinch nests, however, often show droppings on the outside rim, which is thinner and bent inward in many yellow warbler nests. The downy plant materials used are also indicative; the warblers nest much earlier than goldfinches, and each species uses the most available down of the season. Brown-headed cowbird parasitism often results in nest superstructures. The durable nests

Yellow warbler nests, much resembling those of American goldfinches in form, placement, and often habitat, usually show thinner rims that bend slightly inward.

become most conspicuous in fall after the leaves drop. White-footed mice pile many of them with cattail down, recycling them for their own nests.

Yellow warblers feed by two main methods: gleaning from bark and leaves on a perch; and aerial actions, gleaning while hovering and hawking flying insects. They batter their insect prey against a branch before consuming it. Foliage-eating caterpillars rank high in this bird's diet. It especially relishes cankerworms and the young caterpillars of tent and gypsy moths, making this bird a friend of the forester and orchardist. Weevils, bark beetles, midges, and spiders also are frequently consumed. Diet on the winter range remains largely unknown, though it probably differs considerably from that of spring and summer. Researchers have noted sexual differences in yellow warbler foraging behavior, as in several other warbler species. The male of a pair forages higher and in trees with less dense foliage than the female; this differential may provide territorial lookout advantage to him while keeping her less conspicuous.

Potential nest site competitors, such as willow flycatchers and American goldfinches, nest later than yellow warblers. The relatively early breeding cycle of yellows likewise gives them a head start over other habitat users with similar diets—a time-based rather than space-based partitioning of resources. A rough zonation may occur between yellow and chestnut-sided warblers in pond-side vegetation, with yellows occupying the younger successional growth. In the Neotropical winter range, where migrants join resident yellow warbler populations, the residents generally concentrate in undergrowth thickets and the migrants tend to glean in tree foliage. The yellow's ecological counterparts in the winter range include a number of small tyrant flycatcher species, which vastly outnumber warbler species as resident breeders.

Nest predators include snakes, blue jays, and squirrels. The yellow warbler is a foremost victim of brown-headed cowbird parasitism, but it is far from an ideal foster parent. If a female cowbird lays an egg in the warbler nest before the warbler has laid two or three eggs, the warbler may desert her nest or cover the cowbird egg along with her own, resulting in a two-story nest. Repeated cowbird visits may result in a several-story tenement nest, the record being ten stories. If, however, a cowbird visits after the warbler has produced three or more eggs, the female yellow often accepts the cowbird egg, incubates it, and raises the nestling as one of her own. Some 40 percent or more of yellow warbler nests are parasitized by cowbirds. Because cowbirds also remove a host egg as they lay their own, they account for a large percentage of warbler egg losses. Some studies indicate that lower-placed yellow warbler nests may be more vulnerable to cowbird parasitism than higher-placed nests.

Focus. This warbler's population status remains generally more stable than that of most warbler species, which continue alarming trends of decline. In some places, it has even increased significantly and is probably much more abundant now than in presettlement landscapes. Because of its adaptation to human-created habitats, writes one researcher, "the yellow warbler will probably never be threatened by forest clearing in the tropics the way some other species might be." The yellow's nesting success, mainly dependent on the extent of local cowbird parasitism, may range from 30 to 80 percent. Annual survival rate of adult yellow warblers has been estimated at about 50 percent, surprisingly high for a bird of its size. Probably migration hazards, including sudden weather changes, account for most mortality of the summer yellowbird.

FINCH FAMILY (Fringillidae) • Subfamily Emberizinae • WOOD WARBLERS

American Redstart (*Setophaga ruticilla*)

Adult male redstarts are black with bright orange patches on wings and tail; females and first-year males are olive-brown with yellow instead of orange patches on the same wing and tail areas plus white underparts. Redstarts voice two principal song types—with accented and unaccented endings—often alternating them during a song session. Common songs include a series of high-pitched single- or two-note phrases ending in an upward or downward slur, plus variations on this pattern.

Close relatives. This is the only warbler of its genus. The painted redstart (*Myioborus pictus*) is a southwestern species, one of ten tropical *Myioborus* redstarts. The unrelated European redstart (*Phoenicurus phoenicurus*) is one of twelve Old World thrushes called redstarts.

Behaviors. Sometimes called the most animated of our warblers, the hyperactive redstart is one of our most common woodland warblers. Sometimes it sings from a habitual perch, but often it flits constantly in the underbrush, uttering a song wherever it lands, then moving on. At peak breeding periods, male redstarts may sing three hundred to four hundred times an hour—more than six times per minute. Redstarts often droop their wings and fan out their tails in a distinctive posture and frequently launch into the air to snatch passing insects. Except for the redstart's restless movements, its foraging habits more closely resemble those of flycatchers than of other warblers. Also like flycatchers, they have flattened bills, with rictal bristles at the base, and often snap their bills in aggressive encounters. Unlike flycatchers, however, they do not return to the same perch after capturing an insect.

Redstart breeding range spans eastern North America, from Canada's boreal forest to the southeastern states, and much of the Northwest as well.

Spring. In March and April, redstarts undergo a partial molt, chiefly of head and throat feathers. Male redstarts acquire their black and orange breeding plumage only in their second year—the only northeastern warbler species that exhibits such delayed maturation. Moving northward in a broad, twenty-five-hundred-mile front, many cross the Gulf of Mexico in a nonstop, twelve-hour flight. Older males precede females to the previous breeding territory by a few days, usually in May or early June, and yearling males follow a week or so later; thus the older males obtain first choice of optimal breeding territories. Nevertheless, many yearling males, though still in femalelike plumage (but with black feather tips on throat and breast) and subordinate to older, more aggressive males, do mate successfully. Males show a highly ritualized, stiff-winged flight display—often in a perfect circle—during territory formation, and often two territorially adjacent males perform at once. Territories average about a quarter acre in size but may shrink by more than half by the end of nest building, which is done by the female. Redstarts are monogamous and may pair with the same mate in succeeding years. Apparently there is also a large population of unmated, nonterritorial male floaters, always ready to test a pair's territorial bounds or to replace a missing mate.

EGGS AND YOUNG: usually four; eggs whitish, brown spotted, especially at the larger end. INCUBATION: by female; about twelve days. FEEDING OF YOUNG: by both sexes; insects. FLEDGING: about nine days.

Summer. Usually a pair raises only one brood, but nesting may extend into July or even August. Fledglings remain in the nest vicinity for just a few days, some being fed by the male, others by the female. Juveniles then remain on or near the territory until migration. July and August are also the months of complete feather molt, with second-year males acquiring their colorful adult plumage at this time. Sporadic southward migration begins in August and peaks in September, the young of the year usually preceding the adults.

Fall, Winter. Most redstarts have left the continent by mid-October. Winter range extends from central Mexico through Central America and the West Indies to the Amazon rain forest and Andean highlands. Like all warblers, redstarts of both sexes form winter territories and remain site faithful. These territories average about a half acre per bird.

Ecology. Redstarts favor extensive tracts of contiguous, second-growth deciduous and mixed forest habitats, often floodplain and maple and aspen woodlands with an ample understory of saplings. They also inhabit a variety of edge and open-woods habitats, including roadside trees, willow and alder thickets, and even suburban parks and gardens. Winter habitats include open woods, thorny thickets, and mangrove forests.

Alders, shrub willows, white birch trees, and hanging grapevines often host redstart nests, but the birds use many other shrubs and saplings as well. Placed in a vertical fork, usually ten to twenty feet high, the nest somewhat resembles the yellow warbler's in form but is thinner walled and contains little or no silvery milkweed bark. Compactly woven grasses, bark fibers, and rootlets bound with spider silk are the usual materials; lichens, feathers, pieces of birch bark, and bud scales are sometimes added. Fine grasses and plant fibers line the cup. Occasionally, like yellow warblers, redstarts build new nest floors over brown-headed cowbird eggs. Sometimes a pair adopts an old or abandoned vireo nest for its own.

American redstarts build compact, soft-woven nests at medium height in forks of trees, vines, and shrubs.

Redstarts, almost exclusively insectivorous, often hover acrobatically to glean from leaf undersides, branches, and trunks. Sidling along a branch, they constantly pivot, often stirring up insect movement by flashing their colorful wing and tail patches. Redstarts tend to forage higher in trees during early morning, moving downward and hawking aerial insects more frequently as the day advances, a behavior probably reflecting periods of greatest insect activity. Caterpillars, including cankerworms and gypsy moth larvae, are favored items, as are leafhoppers, foliage beetles, midges, mosquitoes, and spiders. Redstarts bat captured prey against a branch before eating it or feeding it to nestlings. They rarely consume seeds and berries.

Redstarts often occupy the same thicket habitats and feeding *guild* (a group of organisms that share a common resource) as least

Redstarts (top) show bill adaptations to aerial insect foraging similar to those of flycatchers. The least flycatcher (bottom, not drawn to scale) is a frequent redstart competitor.

flycatchers, with which they often conflict. These competitors aggressively drive out redstarts from habitats where both species are present. Balancing such competition is the redstart's wider, less specialized habitat range, specifically its toleration for denser foliage.

Snakes and squirrels are common nest predators; one study found that nest predation (probably in edge habitats) may exceed 70 percent in some years. Redstarts also become frequent victims of brown-headed cowbird parasitism. Their only defense is to bury the cowbird egg in the nest along with their own and start over, perhaps accounting for the frequency of late-nesting redstarts.

Focus. No warbler has confused me so often by its variable songs, forcing me to relearn them every year. Sometimes the bird comes readily to pishing sounds; at other times it seems oblivious. *Candelita,* meaning "little candle," and *mariposa,* meaning "butterfly," are two lovely aliases for the American redstart south of U.S. borders. In French Canada, the bird is known as *paruline flamboyante.* Its fancied resemblance to the unrelated European redstart gave this warbler its American name, *start* deriving from the Old German *stert,* meaning "tail."

Redstarts that succeed in fledging show a high annual survival rate, some 70 percent. Because of their habitat adaptability, they may be less vulnerable to human-created changes in landscape than some of the more specialized warblers. Yet they thrive best in large forest tracts, away from edge-dwelling predators and cowbirds. Redstart numbers are currently increasing in the northeast-ern United States; in some western areas, however, they continue to decline.

Ovenbird (*Seiurus aurocapillus*)

This six-inch-long ground-dwelling warbler, much resembling the brown thrushes in plumage, has brown upper parts and a white breast streaked with black. A dull orange crown (most visible close up), prominent white eye rings, and pinkish legs are also distinc-tive. Males voice a loud, rising crescendo of accented notes, usually transliterated as "teach-er teach-er teach-er TEACH-ER!" but actu-ally more like "er-teach er-teach er-teach er-TEACH," with emphasis on the second syllable. Sexes look alike.

Close relatives. Northern and Louisiana waterthrushes (*S. noveboracensis, S. motacilla*) are this warbler's nearest kin, much resembling it in plumage but not habitats.

Behaviors. Despite its atten-tion-getting song, the ovenbird is a shy, secretive species. Except when singing or alarmed, it sel-dom leaves the ground. Curiosity stirred by a birder's pishing noises, however, often brings it close. It will stealthily stretch to observe the birder from a low branch, its eye rings giving it a bewildered look.

Unlike the hyperactive behav-iors of most tree-foraging warbler

The ovenbird (top) and wood thrush (bottom), though unrelated, look much alike and occupy simi-lar habitats. Ovenbirds, however, are about two inches shorter and show streaked rather than spotted breast plumage.

species, ovenbird movements are slow and deliberate. On the ground, it walks instead of hops, teetering somewhat like a sandpiper, often jigging its tail like a hermit thrush. Unlike most other ground-feeding birds, ovenbirds seldom scratch in the leaf litter.

Ovenbird breeding range covers most of eastern North America, from mid-Canada to the southeastern states, extending west to the northern Great Plains.

Spring. Males precede females on the breeding range by nine to fourteen days, arriving with great regularity each year on or near the same date in late April or early May. With both sexes often returning to the same place, wrote researcher Harry W. Hann, "there would seem to be a strong tendency for the pairs to remate in subsequent years," a situation that applies to many passerine birds. The male immediately begins singing, usually from a lower branch of the tree canopy, establishing his territory of about three acres. The arriving female probably "goes first to the old territory," wrote Hann. "If the male there already has a mate, she goes to an adjoining territory. The particular male in the territory seems to be of no consequence." Male courtship, marked by frantic chasing of the female, is spectacular. His exuberant flight song, a jumble of soft, musical notes voiced from a perch or as he flies high over his territory, begins about the time females arrive. It continues throughout nesting, usually on overcast days or in evening twilight, and occasionally thereafter. Occasional instances of polygyny, in which a male pairs with two females, occur, usually while the first female incubates.

EGGS AND YOUNG: usually five; eggs white, brown spotted, especially on the larger end. INCUBATION: by female; about twelve days. FEEDING OF YOUNG: by both sexes; insects, mainly cankerworms. FLEDGING: about eight days.

Summer. Male "teacher" singing continues until eggs hatch, then declines in frequency; sudden silence in this species invariably signals that a new phase of parenthood has begun. Most pairs raise only one brood, and nesting may extend into July. Fledglings usually leave the nest one at a time, each following a parent. They become independent as territories are abandoned in about five weeks. The annual feather molt begins in mid-July. Southward migrational movement begins in August and peaks in September.

Fall, Winter. Flying by night, most ovenbirds have vacated the continent by mid-October, but small winter populations settle on the Gulf Coast and in southern Florida. Winter range extends from these areas to the West Indies and Mexico south to Colombia and Venezuela. Ovenbirds are said to be much less reclusive on their winter range, though they occupy individual territories and occasionally sing.

Ecology. The forest floor, thickly littered with dead leaves, is the ovenbird's foremost breeding and foraging habitat. It favors mature, dry deciduous or mixed forests with large trees, open canopies, and medium-dense ground vegetation. Ovenbirds are area sensitive, thriving only in large tracts of contiguous forest, forty to some four hundred acres minimum; in isolated, fragmented patches of woodland, these birds decline. Dry thickets, shaded forest understory, and cane fields are common winter habitats.

The ovenbird's nest is a small, mounded shelter of dry leaves and other vegetation said to resemble the domelike shape of a

Thick leaf litter of mature forests provides optimal ovenbird nesting and foraging habitat.

In typical habitat, the ovenbird's dome-like nest, entered from the side, is a marvel of camouflage. (From The Atlas of Breeding Birds of Michigan.*)*

Dutch or beehive oven, hence the bird's name. To build it, the female scrapes bare a slight depression with her bill, often in a small open area or alongside a woodland road or trail. She then brings leaves, dried grasses, and other plant fibers, building from the edges in and mostly from inside, arching materials over the top for roofing. She places a slitlike entrance at or near ground level and lines the interior cup with fine rootlets and hair. The finished structure sheds rain and is extremely well camouflaged—"on the ground, yet out of sight," as Thoreau wrote. Count yourself an exceptional observer if you can spot an ovenbird nest unrevealed by a flushing female bird. Her convincing display, as she drags and flutters across the ground, may not only distract you from her nest but cause you to lose bearings on it altogether. After the birds vacate, the nest settles back into the forest floor and soon disappears.

Ovenbirds, mainly carnivorous, take most of their invertebrate food from the top of the leaf litter, only occasionally turning over a leaf to explore beneath. Choice food items include snout and carabid beetles, cankerworm caterpillars, ants, spiders, snails, and small earthworms. A strong inverse relationship exists between the size of ovenbird territories and food resources; the higher the prey density, the smaller the territory. Though ovenbirds feed mainly from the ground, also consuming large amounts of sand and fine gravel for aiding digestion, they are also well-known predators of the spruce budworm, foraging in conifers for this insect. Irruptions of this destructive caterpillar bear directly on ovenbird nesting; the birds may increase their egg clutch size and produce up to three broods during budworm outbreaks. Ovenbird fall and winter diet includes some amount of seeds, fruits, and other vegetable matter.

The ovenbird's guild (a group of organisms that share a common resource) includes several other forest floor dwellers, which are potential competitors. These include wood and hermit thrushes, waterthrushes, and Kentucky and worm-eating warblers. Thrushes, however, aggressively scratch in the leaf mold; waterthrushes and the other two warbler species seldom pick food from the ground and favor lowland sites (waterthrushes and Kentucky warbler) or slopes (worm-eating warbler). Thus these species do not usually compete with ovenbirds. Nor do such forest ground nesters as whip-poor-wills, which are aerial insect feeders, and ruffed grouse and wild turkeys, which are mainly vegetarians.

Barred owls frequently attack ovenbirds, and nest raiders include snakes, opossums, red and gray squirrels, raccoons, skunks, and weasels. Probably the ovenbird's foremost enemy is the brown-headed cowbird, which may parasitize at least half of all ovenbird nests, removing an egg as it lays one of its own. Unlike many cowbird victims, ovenbirds do not seem to perceive cowbirds as a threat or chase them off when they appear in ovenbird territory. Thus many ovenbirds become cowbird foster parents. One classic study, however, revealed that ovenbird nestlings in parasitized nests survive and thrive as well as nestlings in nonparasitized nests, apparently because of their innate vigor in competing for nestling food. The chief negative effect on ovenbirds probably results from cowbird removal of the host eggs, an estimated loss of some 15 percent each year.

Focus. In most northeastern deciduous forests, ovenbirds and red-eyed vireos are the most abundant summer bird residents. The oldest ovenbird on record survived seven years, but average life span is probably less than three, with an annual adult survival rate of 54 to 85 percent. Ovenbird populations in large northeastern forests generally appear to be thriving. Yet in other areas of their range, ovenbirds have undergone significant declines during the past several decades. Night-migratory ovenbirds seem especially susceptible to collisions with transmission towers and tall buildings; numerous records of heavy bird mortality exist at some of these locales.

The ovenbird was probably Thoreau's unidentified "night warbler," whose flight song so puzzled and entranced him. Emerson advised him not to seek out the bird lest life lose some of its mystery (a fear Thoreau never shared). Ovenbird colloquial names have included golden-crowned thrush and teacher bird.

FINCH FAMILY (Fringillidae) • Subfamily Emberizinae • WOOD WARBLERS

Common Yellowthroat (*Geothlypis trichas*)

Olive-brown upper parts and bright yellow throat and breast mark both sexes of this five-inch-long warbler. The male, "masked like a bandit," has a glossy ribbon of black extending down the sides of the head. The loud, rhythmic, chanting song consists of several repetitions, typically "witchery-witchery-witchery-wit." Harsh chattering and a husky "chip" note are also commonly heard.

Close relatives. Some eight other *Geothlypis* species reside mainly in the Neotropics. Bahama yellowthroats (*G. rostrata*) and gray-crowned yellowthroats (*G. poliocephala*) venture occasionally into the southern United States. The similarly named yellow-throated warbler is another distinct species (*Dendroica dominica*).

Behaviors. Pairs of these common, lively warblers of low thickets are easily detected, if not always readily seen. A birder's pishing sounds usually arouse any yellowthroats that are present, causing great commotion among them. Yet a loudly singing male can be almost impossible to spot in the brushy tangles of its habitat. Females are even more elusive, usually seen only in transit as they dart and disappear in the shrubbery. One may identify an individual male by learning his subtle but consistent variations in song phrasing.

Common yellowthroats have one of the largest contiguous breeding ranges of any North American warbler, spanning the continent from southern Canada to the Gulf and into Mexico. Indeed, it is probably our most abundant warbler. All but the extreme southern U.S. populations migrate.

Spring. Males arrive in late April and early May on the breeding range and immediately begin loud, frequent singing. Many probably return to the previous year's site. Territorial size varies widely, averaging one-half to two acres. Sudden silence occurs when females arrive some two or three weeks later. Few courtship displays are evident, but male singing resumes as females begin building nests in late May or early June. Later in the nesting cycle, watch for males performing song flights, often in the afternoon; they arch over the territory as high as one hundred feet, voicing a sputter of notes at the apex of flight, then drop silently to a low perch. Polygyny, in which the male mates with two or more females, sometimes occurs, but pairs usually remain monogamous for the season, and some pairs for successive seasons.

EGGS AND YOUNG: usually four; eggs white, brown spotted, especially at the larger end. INCUBATION: by female; twelve days. FEEDING OF YOUNG: by both sexes; insects. FLEDGING: about ten days.

Summer. Though becoming highly excited if an intruder approaches the nest, yellowthroats do not perform distraction displays. Second broods may extend the nesting season into early August but are uncommon north of the Great Lakes. Fledglings can fly about three days after leaving the nest, but they remain dependent on the parents for food for about twenty days, a longer period than for most warblers. Family groups range freely, ignoring territorial bounds, which may shift and become reestablished if and when second nestings begin. In early August, as singing declines, the annual plumage molt replaces and duplicates the breeding plumage. Parent birds may still be feeding juveniles as migration time approaches in August. Southward migration extends through September.

Fall. Northern yellowthroat populations move in a leapfrog migration pattern, bypassing the permanent resident yellowthroat

populations of the Gulf and southwestern United States. Flying at night, the birds probably suffer their heaviest mortality during migrations. Many perish in stormy or foggy weather by colliding with transmission towers, tall buildings, and lighthouses, becoming disoriented by lights on these structures.

Winter. Most migrant yellowthroats winter from the West Indies and southern Mexico through Central America. Not uncommonly, however, a few yellowthroats remain on their northern breeding range through winter, usually in extensive marshland or brushy swamps.

The common yellowthroat, like many songbirds, shows age-related differences in tail plumage. Older birds (top) exhibit rounded feathers; yearling birds (bottom) retain pointed juvenile feathers until their first complete molt.

Ecology. Sometimes termed our only true wetland warblers, yellowthroats favor shoreline thickets, roadside ditches, and brushy or open areas near water. But they also inhabit drier upland thickets, dense grass and shrub mixtures, overgrown fields, hedgerows, and woodland edges—basically any area of tall ground vegetation that provides thick cover. Density of low-growing vegetation rather than the presence of water is apparently the key habitat factor. Their adaptability to both wet and dry sites gives yellowthroats a far greater habitat range than most warbler species. In their winter range, yellowthroats inhabit the same general habitat types.

The bulky nest, usually placed just above ground surface and well concealed in rank vegetation, is supported on all sides by cattails, weed stalks, or grass tussocks, though not attached. Coarse grasses, sedges, and dead leaves frame a cup lined with fine grasses, bark fibers, and sometimes hair. Second-brood nests or renestings that result from early-season failures tend to be placed slightly higher.

Common yellowthroat nests, though usually placed a few inches above ground, are not attached to the surrounding plants. This one is shown in marsh vegetation.

Almost entirely insectivorous, yellowthroats forage mainly in brush vegetation but also glean from bark and occasionally from the ground. Caterpillars, including cankerworms and gypsy moth larvae, aphids, and spiders rank especially high in the diet.

Competition is probably negligible in both wet and dry habitats, given the adaptability of this species. Swamp sparrows and marsh wrens are frequent yellowthroat associates in wetland habitats.

Snakes and mammal predators raid yellowthroat nests, but this bird's foremost enemy is the brown-headed cowbird. Cowbirds may parasitize some 40 percent of early-season yellowthroat nests, often resulting in nest desertion or almost an entire brood of large, demanding cowbird nestlings. Later-season nests are less frequently parasitized; perhaps most yellowthroats that survive to adulthood are summer offspring.

Focus. Successively named the Maryland yellowthroat and northern yellowthroat before receiving a more cosmopolitan adjective, this species also has long been known as the ground warbler. Today its abundance appears to be increasing over its breeding range, probably because of its adaptability to both wet and dry edges. Adult annual survival rate in yellowthroats is estimated at about 50 percent.

Though yellowthroat song is more distinctive to human ears than that of many other warblers, many dialect variations occur across this bird's extensive breeding range. One researcher classified one hundred thirty-eight overlapping song-phrase types, each spanning up to three hundred miles cross-country. Yet the basic pattern of yellowthroat song remains essentially similar wherever you hear it. This species also shows minor plumage variations in some ten subspecies throughout the continent.

FINCH FAMILY (Fringillidae) • Subfamily Emberizinae

Scarlet Tanager (*Piranga olivacea*)

Tanager tribe (Thraupini). One of our most spectacular forest birds, the bright red summer male has jet black wings and tail. Females have a greenish back with darker wings and yellow underparts. Size is about seven inches. Tanager bills are stout and slightly notched on the sides. The robinlike song has a distinctive husky or burry quality; a "chip-churr" call is also commonly heard.

Close relatives. Sixty genera contain some two hundred forty tanager species, many of them brilliantly colored. All tanagers except four of the eight *Piranga* species are year-round Neotropical residents. Besides the scarlet, the other North American breeders include the summer tanager (*P. rubra*) in the East and the western and hepatic tanagers (*P. ludoviciana, P. flava*) in the West.

This head profile of a scarlet tanager shows its stout, slightly notched bill. Its diet consists mainly of insects, plus some fruits.

Behaviors. Scarlet tanagers spend most of their time high in the forest canopy. Yet, because males tend to remain on a single perch for long intervals while singing, careful glassing with binoculars can often trace the sound to a bird so blazing in color you wonder why you had to search for it. "It flies through the green foliage as if it would ignite the leaves," wrote Thoreau. For sighting females, more luck is required; though they too sometimes sing, their plumage blends superbly with the sunlit leaves. Tanager movements often appear leisurely, almost lethargic, like a "somewhat self-conscious personality," as one observer described it.

Scarlet tanager breeding range spans the eastern half of North America from southern Canada to Oklahoma and the Carolinas. They are migrators.

Spring. Winging across the Gulf of Mexico, scarlet tanagers travel by night in small flocks. Concurrent with spring migration, the birds undergo a molt of body feathers only. Males acquire their brilliant scarlet plumage at this time, females a duller, greenish yellow aspect. They arrive on their breeding range in late April and early May, usually just when most deciduous trees are beginning to leaf out. Males precede females by a few days, returning to the previous year's territories of two to six acres in size. They begin singing almost continually from high perches, but do so less frequently once they have attracted a mate. A common male display, done on or quite low to the ground, is to droop the wings and expose his red back to a female perched above him. Probably relatively few females pair with a previous mate. Females gather materials from the ground and build the nests. Copulation is frequent and continues into late nesting.

EGGS AND YOUNG: usually four; eggs bluish green, brown spotted, especially at the larger end. INCUBATION: by female, which is fed by male; about two weeks. FEEDING OF YOUNG: by both sexes; insects. FLEDGING: about ten days.

Summer. Scarlet tanagers raise only one brood. Fledglings, calling noisily, remain in the nest area and are fed for about two weeks before dispersing. They bear brownish and streaked plumage on breast and sides until their first molt in late July and August, which replaces body feathers with femalelike yellow-green plumage. The adult annual molt, sometimes extending into October, replaces all body, wing, and tail feathers. Males at this time often wear a red, green, and yellow patchwork of color—"like autumn foliage," wrote naturalist Emma B. Pitcher—culminating in a yellowish plumage resembling that of females but with black wings and tail.

Fall. No longer brilliant hued, scarlet tanagers wing southward at night singly or in small flocks through September. Most have departed the continent by mid-October, though late stragglers are sometimes seen.

Winter. Scarlet tanagers winter in two relatively narrow bands of Neotropical montane rain forest, one bordering the Pacific in Colombia, and the other along the east side of the Andes from Colombia and Ecuador south to central Peru and Bolivia. The birds apparently remain solitary, neither paired nor in flocks. Much remains unknown about their habits and habitats in these remote areas where they reside for most of the year.

Ecology. Early ornithologist Edward H. Forbush called this bird "the appointed guardian of the oaks . . . drawn to these trees as if they were magnets." Scarlet tanagers require extensive stands of mature trees, which are often oaks, but they also reside in beech-maple, mixed, and occasionally pine or hemlock forests. They favor dry over moist forests but reside in both habitats. More important than the type of forest, apparently, is its age and size. Forest fragmentation means habitat loss and nest failures for these birds, compressing their territories and exposing them to increased predation and cowbird parasitism. The minimal woodland size required by a pair is about four acres, with eight being optimal. Occasionally, however, pairs inhabit suburban areas with large shade trees. In their winter range, the birds inhabit evergreen broad-leaved forests.

Nests, frequently built in oak trees near a forest opening, path, or deer trail, are usually placed midway out on a forking horizontal branch, often about twenty feet high. Like the red-eyed vireo, a frequent tanager associate, tanagers commonly nest lower than they forage. The flattish, rather flimsy cup consists mainly of twigs and rootlets, thickly lined with grasses; its shallow meshwork floor sometimes reveals the eggs from beneath.

Primarily insect eaters, scarlet tanagers glean from foliage, bark, and occasionally the ground. Often they forage along a branch from trunk to outer tip. They also capture insects, mostly flies, on the wing. Females tend to forage higher in trees than males and more often hawk flying insects. Hymenopterans (wasps, bees, and ants) rank high in the diet, as do beetles, small caterpillars (including the destructive gypsy moth), and adult moths. The summer diet also includes wild fruits such as mulberries, elderberries, blackberries, blueberries, and sumacs. Fruits of the cecropia rank high in the winter diet.

In the central tier of states, where scarlet and summer tanager breeding ranges overlap, the two species aggressively defend territories from each other. Scarlet tanagers also react aggressively to great crested flycatchers and, at times, eastern wood-pewees, both forest canopy birds. While such interactions between species often indicate at least potentially competitive situations, the degree of actual competition between them remains unknown.

Predators include accipiter hawks, merlins, and several owl species. Blue jays and fox and gray squirrels, though vigorously attacked by the tanagers, succeed in raiding many nests, as do American crows, from which the parent birds usually flee. Tanagers also attack female brown-headed cowbirds, which nevertheless may parasitize up to 60 percent of tanager nests, a rate probably affected by the aforementioned habitat factors. Tanager nestlings, however, seem to compete quite successfully with one or more cowbird nestlings for food and protection.

Focus. A recent Cornell University research effort called Project Tanager has established that regional differences exist in scarlet tanager sensitivity to forest patch size. New England, eastern Canadian, and midwestern tanager populations apparently require larger contiguous forest acreage than New York and Pennsylvania populations, which tolerate considerably smaller patches. Reasons for this geographical variation await discovery. Despite tanager vulnerability to forest fragmentation in both breeding and winter habitats, trends of increase have been noted in most areas of their summer range.

Firebird is, for understandable reasons, one of this bird's colloquial names. "This and the emperor [cecropia] moth make the tropical phenomena of our zone," remarked Thoreau; he mistakenly attributed this bird's tropical home as Brazil (possibly Thoreau's generic term for the tropics). Yet the word *tanager* indeed derives from Brazil, from a Tupi Indian word meaning any small, brightly colored bird.

The longest scarlet tanager survival on record is ten years; most birds probably live less than half that long.

Closer look. Prescott, K. W. *Studies in the Life History of the Scarlet Tanager,* Piranga olivacea. Trenton: New Jersey State Museum Investigations No. 2, 1965.

CARDINAL-GROSBEAKS (TRIBE CARDINALINI)

About thirty-seven species of these heavy-billed finches range worldwide, of which ten are North American residents, including the dickcissel (*Spiza americana*), a grassland species. Males often have colorful plumage, and both sexes of several species utter melodious song. These birds' powerful jaw muscles and heavy bills are adaptations for cracking seeds. Bird banders learn to avoid the massive bills of cardinals and grosbeaks when handling these birds, for they can clamp a finger in a viselike pinch.

FINCH FAMILY (Fringillidae) • Subfamily Emberizinae • CARDINAL-GROSBEAKS

Rose-breasted Grosbeak
(*Pheucticus ludovicianus*)

The rose-breasted grosbeak is a chunky, eight-inch-long bird. The male has a black head and upper parts; white wing patches, rump, and belly; and a triangular, rose-red breast patch and pinkish underwings. Females resemble large brown sparrows, with breast streaking, white wing bars, a white eyebrow stripe, and striped crown. Both sexes have thick, whitish bills. Male song is robinlike but richer and more melodious. The metallic "chink!" call note is also distinctive.

Close relatives. The name grosbeak, referring to the bird's large, seed-crushing bill, has little taxonomic significance; worldwide, some twenty-four so-called grosbeaks occupy slots in both the cardinal-grosbeak tribe and the cardueline finch tribe.

All six *Pheucticus* species reside in the Western Hemisphere. The black-headed grosbeak *(P. melanocephalus)* is the rose-breasted's western U.S. counterpart, and the two sometimes hybridize where their ranges overlap. The blue grosbeak *(Guiraca caerulea)* is the only other closely related eastern grosbeak.

Behaviors. Rose-breasted grosbeaks appear quite sedate, deliberate, and self-contained in their behaviors, though territorial males can savagely attack other males. The male's red breast patch varies considerably in size and shape among individuals; probably no two are exactly alike.

This bird's breeding range spans the continent in Canada but notches south along the eastern Great Plains into Kansas; from there it extends eastward to the Atlantic, enclosing the Great Lakes and New England, and southward in the Appalachians. Rose-breasteds migrate.

Cardinaline finches show heavy, seed-crushing bills and spectacular plumages. From top, the northern cardinal, rose-breasted grosbeak, and indigo bunting.

Spring. Adult males arrive on the breeding range in late April and May, several days before younger males and a week or so before females. Many return to previous territories. Singing from the treetops, males chase and scrap with other singing males as they establish territories of two to three acres; they often tolerate nonsinging males, however, most of which are probably just passing through. Male song diminishes briefly with the arrival of females, few of which probably pair with previous mates. Male courtship displays include song flights and a slow, body-rotation dance with drooped wings and spread tail, often on a low branch or the ground. In some cases, at least, males aid in nest building, and both sexes may sing in the nest vicinity or while incubating. "This seems like a good way to attract unwanted attention," wrote researcher Gail A. McPeek, "but perhaps it does just the opposite and warns other grosbeaks and enemies to stay away." Nesting usually begins in late May.

EGGS AND YOUNG: usually four; eggs bluish green, brown spotted with dense wreath at the larger end. INCUBATION: by both sexes; twelve to fourteen days. FEEDING OF YOUNG: by both sexes; insects. FLEDGING: nine to twelve days.

Summer. Most rose-breasted pairs raise only one brood, but two broods are not uncommon. In the latter case, the male assumes the task of feeding fledglings while the female builds a new nest, often within fifty feet or so of the vacated one, and begins egg laying. Fledglings are fed in the nest vicinity for two or three weeks before dispersing. In August, juveniles acquire their first winter plumage and adults undergo a complete feather molt. Adult males acquire brown heads, faded rather than brilliant reds, and streaked body plumage.

Fall. Traveling southward in September to mid-October, rose-breasted migrants converge from a broad, two-thousand-mile front to a band about seven hundred miles wide as they vacate the United States. Males often travel separately from combined female-juvenile flocks. Small flocks stop to feed in treetops along their way. The birds finally cross to Mexico over the Gulf.

Winter. Rose-breasteds winter from central Mexico through Central America into northern Peru, mainly in highland areas. They often feed in flocks of up to twenty birds and do not sing in winter. From January to April, the birds replace their body feathers with the breeding plumage. Second-year males, which up to now have worn dull plumage, though they may have bred the year before, acquire their full adult breeding plumage.

Ecology. Rose-breasted grosbeaks occupy a broad range of deciduous and mixed forest habitats, especially mixtures of tall trees, saplings, and shrubs in second-growth woodlands. Forest and wetland edges, orchards, shrub thickets, and wooded yards and parks are also common habitats. In winter, the birds frequent open woods and edges, as well as tree plantations and gardens.

Rose-breasted nests are exceedingly loose, flimsy structures; so thin is the flooring that the eggs may be seen from beneath. Seldom over fifteen feet high, the nest is usually insecurely placed in a horizontal fork, often at the outer end of a branch. The birds favor white

Shallow platform nests of rose-breasted grosbeaks resemble those of mourning doves in their loose, flimsy structure.

cedars in some areas, a variety of deciduous trees and shrubs in others. I have usually found their nests in woodland edges or fairly open thickets. The birds break off and collect twigs for the nest, using hemlock when available. The shallow saucer is lined with weed stalks, twigs, rootlets, leaves, and sometimes hair, but seldom grass. Incubating females often sit tight on the nest, reluctant to move; on occasion I have briefly lifted them off to count the eggs.

Though they are primarily seed-eaters, as indicated by their seed-crushing bills, rose-breasteds also feed extensively on insects, which constitute almost half the diet in summer. Of these, beetles and caterpillars, including many plant pests, rank high. Cucumber and Colorado potato beetles, cankerworms, and gypsy and tent moth larvae are frequently taken, as are flea beetle larvae (*Blepharida rhois*) for nestlings. Grosbeaks glean insects from foliage and bark and hover-glean and hawk aerial insects. Female rose-breasteds often forage higher in trees than males and hover-glean more frequently. Both sexes also feed on the ground. I have watched the birds forage in recently burned, fresh-sprouting areas, known as green burns, which often hold abundant seeds and insects. In May, the birds often consume tree buds (white ash) and flowers (beech, hickories, cherries, and elms). Fruits become staple items in summer and fall—elderberries, wild cherries, and blackberries, among others. Elm and catalpa seeds are relished, as are smartweed seeds, corn, wheat, and garden peas, though there have been few reports of crop damage caused by these birds. A favored food in the winter range is said to be the seeds of a *Stillingia* spurge.

Competition with other species appears negligible. Common nest predators include blue jays, common grackles, and red and gray squirrels. Accipiter hawks also attack these relatively slow-flying birds. Rose-breasteds are also commonly parasitized by brown-headed cowbirds and in some instances raise broods of all cowbirds.

Focus. The rose-breasted is "our richest singer, perhaps, after the wood thrush," judged Thoreau. Occasionally an especially mellow-voiced robin may deceive the listener into calling it a rose-breasted, but usually the grosbeak tones are sweeter and more melodious.

Probably because of human land practices resulting in the creation of widespread edge habitats, rose-breasted grosbeaks have increased in abundance since 1900. Following rapid increases in the 1960s and 1970s, however, the birds began declining in many areas after 1985. This trend likely reflects the fact that edges are transitional.

This is one of the many plants and animals that pious peasants associated with the Crucifixion (the male's rosy breast being a dab of holy blood worn since a very far off-range grosbeak got splashed). A vernacular name for the male was throat-cut. On their winter range in Central and South America, grosbeaks are sometimes trapped and sold as colorful cagebirds, but relatively few birds are taken for this purpose. The longevity record for the rose-breasted grosbeak is nearly thirteen years; probably few approach that age.

FINCH FAMILY (Fringillidae) • Subfamily Emberizinae • CARDINAL-GROSBEAKS

Northern Cardinal (*Cardinalis cardinalis*)

Both sexes of this eight- to nine-inch-long finch have a prominent, pointed topknot and a heavy, reddish bill with a black patch at its base. Male plumage is otherwise all red; females are brownish, showing red tinges on wings, tail, and crest. The cardinal's loud, clear whistles, often "whoit whoit whoit," "cheedle cheedle cheedle," or "what's here, what's here, here, here," occur in several variations, some of which resemble tufted titmouse song; a loud "chip!" is also characteristic.

Close relatives. The cardinal's southwestern U.S. counterpart is the pyrrhuloxia (*C. sinuatus*). Vermilion cardinals (*C. phoeniceus*) inhabit South America. Most of the five other species called cardinals are South American and Hawaiian emberizine finches.

Behaviors. One of the most familiar and colorful of the birds that frequent suburban yards, the cardinal resides year-round in most of its continually expanding range. Its rich, pure voice makes it most conspicuous in late winter and spring, but this bird remains relatively unshy at all seasons and often becomes a reliable visitor at yard feeders. One observer described the chunky, restless cardinal as "rather a clumsy fellow" when moving on the ground with its stiff, hopping gait. Though it loosely associates with other cardinals for much of the year, males often show aggressive dominance behaviors toward those that try to share a feeder, including its erstwhile mate. Breeding season hormones work changes as the pair bond grows stronger, and the birds become extremely attentive mates and parents.

Cardinals breed throughout eastern and central North America from southern Canada to the Gulf, and westward through Mexico to Guatemala.

Spring. Many, if not most, cardinals remain monogamously paired year-round. Territorial behaviors are well advanced by early spring, with males singing loudly from high perches. Females also sing, most frequently after the territory is established but before nesting begins in March to May. Listen for *countersinging,* in which cardinals on adjacent territories, as well as paired males and females on their own territories, alternate matching songs as if in imitative "sez-you" bouts. Cardinals aggressively chase other cardinals of the same sex that venture onto their territories, which are generally three to ten acres, but they tolerate the presence of opposite-sex cardinals. Cardinals are also well known for shadow boxing, battling their own images, sometimes for lengthy periods, in reflective surfaces such as windows and auto hubcaps. Both sexes perform a lopsided, swaying courtship display when perched; males also perform song flights and often feed their mates, tilting their heads sideways to do so, on both perches and nests. Females build the nests, often accompanied by their mates as they gather materials. Nesting usually begins in late April.

EGGS AND YOUNG: usually three; eggs grayish or bluish white, brown spotted. INCUBATION: by female, which is fed by male; eggs are also occasionally incubated by male; about twelve days. FEEDING OF YOUNG: by both sexes; regurgitated insects at first, then whole insects. FLEDGING: about ten days.

Summer. Many cardinal pairs raise two or more broods, and nesting may extend into August. Females build a new nest on the same territory, leaving their mates to feed the first-brood fledglings. Fledglings achieve independence in three to four weeks, when renesting parents sometimes drive them off. The annual molt begins in late summer, extending into fall.

Fall, Winter. The new male plumage, showing feather tips edged with gray, is somewhat duller than the scarlet breeding plumage, which is acquired during winter by simple wear of the gray edging. If you examine individual feathers of a male's body plumage, you will see that most of the feather length is gray; only the upper third or so is pigmented red, giving the cardinal its brilliance.

The pair bond becomes relatively lax as the birds join other cardinals in fall and winter groupings (flocking is too social a term for most cardinal aggregations). These groups are usually small, with six to twenty birds, but occasionally many more. Some wandering groups probably consist entirely of first-winter juveniles. Many cardinals remain in the breeding locality year-round, ranging no more than a few miles during their entire lifetime. About February, males start to become more tolerant of close female presence and begin courtship behaviors and early-morning singing.

Ecology. Northern cardinals favor open-edge habitats, and originally they probably occupied forest openings. Today just about any thicket vegetation, wet or dry, in forest or suburban yard, may host cardinals. Isolated patches of dense shrubbery seem to be the vital habitat element, conditions ideally met in many human residential areas, as well as along roadsides and in overgrown fields and hedgerows.

Nests, seldom placed over six feet high, often occupy the densest part of a thicket or brier tangle. Multiflora rose and honeysuckle hedges are frequent sites, as are hawthorns, lilac and gray dogwood shrubs, and thick-foliaged conifers. Securely placed in a vertical fork or mat of vines, nests consist of four more or less distinct layers of plant materials: a foundation of stiff twigs or weed stalks, often stalks and seed bases of yellow avens (*Geum aleppicum*); leaves or bits of paper and bark strips; weed and grass stems; and a

Cardinals build in a variety of sites, often thorny hedges. Nests sometimes resemble those of gray catbirds, which compete with cardinals in some habitats.

fine grass lining. Cardinals differ extensively in their nest-building styles. Some nests are compact and thickly lined; others are loose, flimsy, and unkempt, with little lining. Gray catbird nests, found in similar habitats, may resemble cardinal nests but are usually bulkier, contain many more foundation leaves, and are lined with rootlets. White-footed mice frequently use vacated cardinal nests as feeding platforms and may also load the nest with plant down and move in themselves.

Omnivorous in diet, cardinals consume a huge variety of plant and insect foods, the latter mainly during the breeding season. Caterpillars, grasshoppers, true bugs, beetles, and other small invertebrates constitute some 60 percent of the spring diet. The birds eat almost any kind of fruit, with wild grapes, dogwood fruits, and mulberries ranking high. Smartweeds, corn, oats, and sedges provide much of the seed diet; in winter, seeds of sumacs, vervains, and tulip trees are favored, and anyone who maintains a yard feeder knows how much these birds relish sunflower seeds.

The cardinal's foremost food and nest site competitor in many areas is the gray catbird, which usually dominates any interaction, often driving cardinals to the less optimal fringes of their mutual habitats. As a relatively recent arrival in much of its present northern range, the cardinal appears still in the process of adjusting, in an ecological sense, to prior resident species. Yet its year-round presence, habitat and diet opportunism, early and lengthy nesting season, and promptness to renest after predation give it many competitive advantages.

Cardinal nests fall victim to many predators, including blue racers and black rat and milk snakes; American crows, blue jays, and house wrens; gray, fox, and red squirrels; eastern chipmunks; and domestic cats. Brown-headed cowbirds frequently parasitize the nests, and cardinals raise many cowbird nestlings.

Focus. Cardinals have expanded their original southern U.S. range northward during this century, a trend that continues. They began their northward expansion up the Mississippi valley late in the last century. Appearing first as casual visitors in the North, they rapidly increased from 1910–70, after which their range expansion slowed. Reasons for their successful northward invasion remain speculative; frequently suggested possibilities are the abundance and increase of edge habitats, a period of mild winters during the early 1900s, and a more recent climatic warming trend. Much of their range expansion has apparently occurred in winter, as the birds gravitated toward yard feeders and fruit-rich swamps, thus establishing nuclei for local populations. Despite their southern origins, cardinals apparently suffer few lethal effects from cold, though I have occasionally found a cardinal frozen on the ground beneath evergreens after an exceptionally cold night.

Often called the redbird, the cardinal, named for the red-robed princes of the church, was once commonly trapped in the southern states and sold as a cagebird.

The cardinal's spectacular color does not always make it conspicuous, as paradoxical as that sounds. "If a species evolves to become brightly colored, and if it lives in shady green places," wrote biologist Stephen Fretwell, "red or blue are good colors to be." This is because deciduous foliage absorbs most of the blue and red spectra, shedding green light that is not readily reflected by red plumage in the shade. Thus in its nesting habitat, at least, the cardinal may become relatively inconspicuous.

Average yearly adult survival rate is estimated at about 50 percent. This bird's longevity record surpasses fifteen years, but two or three years is probably a typical life span.

Seven states—Illinois, Indiana, and Ohio being the northernmost—have named the northern cardinal their state bird. The cardinal outnumbers any other bird species for this distinction.

Closer look. Osborne, J. *The Cardinal.* Austin: University of Texas Press, 1993.

FINCH FAMILY (Fringillidae) • Subfamily Emberizinae • CARDINAL-GROSBEAKS

Indigo Bunting (*Passerina cyanea*)

This common, sparrow-size finch is sexually dimorphic in plumage. The summer indigo male is our only all-blue bird; females are plain brown with indistinct breast streaking. Indigos voice double phrases on different pitches, as "sweet-sweet, chew-chew, seer-seer, sweet." Also distinctive are its sharp, buzzy "spit!" call notes.

Close relatives. Bunting, a catch-all name for numerous finches, has no taxonomic significance except in England, where the term refers exclusively to emberizine finches. Some six *Passerina* species range mainly in Central and South America. Additional North American species include the lazuli bunting (*P. amoena*), the indigo's western U.S. counterpart; the varied bunting (*P. versicolor*) of the Southwest; and the painted bunting (*P. ciris*) of the South and Southwest. The blue grosbeak (*Guiraca caerulea*) is also a close relative.

Behaviors. Highly active, energetic little birds, indigos are hard to miss. Yet, in the opinion of one observer, "people rarely see indigo buntings until they learn the song because light conditions for seeing the blue are rarely good." If you approach an indigo bunting nest within thirty or forty feet, the birds' excited "spit!" calls and tail flicking will inform you of your trespass (though finding the nest itself is another story).

The song language of indigo buntings has received much research attention. Each song typically lasts two or three seconds with ten-second pauses between. Within the general song pattern, however, the phrasings of individual birds—especially the song beginnings—are distinctive and consistent. Thus by careful listening, one can distinguish separate males by song alone. Yet the phrasings of all males in a given area often bear close similarity. Male indigos apparently learn their songs in the social context of their first breeding season. They imitate the songs of nearby older males, thus producing a song neighborhood or dialect that does not indicate blood kinship between the birds. Though hardly gregarious, breeding indigos are social to the extent that they often establish territories near other indigos in preference to settling in vacant similar habitat.

Indigos are migrators. Their breeding range covers the eastern two-thirds of North America from mid-Canada to the Gulf, plus the Sonoran region of the Southwest.

Spring. Relatively late migrants, the older males precede females and younger males on the breeding range by a few days, in late April through early June, usually in night-flying flocks of five to ten birds. By this time, the birds have completed a partial prenuptial molt; second-year and older males acquire body feathers with gray tips, which quickly wear off to reveal the new, bright blue plumage. Male indigos are among the most site faithful of all passerines, returning in spring to previous nesting locales and sometimes even continuing to occupy sites where plant succession has gradually transformed the favored edge habitat into woodland. Females are more likely to settle on a previously unused territory, sometimes even that of an already paired male. First-year birds usually occupy territories a mile or more away from their birth sites; this is probably the typical settlement pattern for most passerine species and tends to preclude inbreeding.

Territorial males begin singing conspicuously from high perches, continuing to do so throughout the breeding season regardless of mating status or phases. The territory of two to six acres, in which all feeding and nesting occur, is vigorously tested—mainly by younger males—and defended. Males perform a rapid, fluttering "moth-flight" display, voicing a goldfinchlike flight song. They often avoid the nest until the eggs hatch, their only real participation being nest defense should the need arise. Females, inconspicuous in plumage and behaviors, build the nests. "The mated pair seems to dwell in different zones," wrote ornithologist Edward H. Forbush.

EGGS AND YOUNG: three or four; eggs white, unmarked. INCUBATION: by female; twelve days. FEEDING OF YOUNG: mostly by female; spiders and insects. FLEDGING: about ten days.

Summer. Indigos usually remain monogamous through a breeding season, but sometimes only in a "social sense," as one researcher writes (a situation, researchers are finding, that applies to many so-called monogamous species). Some 15 percent of indigo males mate with two or more females, and paired females are often receptive to copulation with intruding males. Yet the original pair maintains its territorial and parental behaviors through the entire season. Many indigo females raise two broods, and nesting often extends into August. Researchers estimate that because of predation and cowbird parasitism, only 30 to 50 percent of nesting attempts succeed. Territories may shift between nestings; individuals of either sex may move from upland to lowland sites. If the female of a pair renests, males finally become parental, feeding fledglings of the first brood for two or three weeks. Second-brood juveniles often remain with the parents in family groups until migration. In August, as singing ceases, the annual molt occurs; both sexes acquire brown, femalelike plumage, though males usually show some blue on wings and tail.

Fall. Juvenile indigos often flock together, foraging in fields as migration time approaches. They and adult birds, the males now quite inconspicuous, move southward from late August through mid-October, traveling in large, night-flying flocks and feeding during the day in brushy areas. Most of the population crosses the Gulf of Mexico, reversing the spring flight route.

Winter. Although some indigos winter in southern Florida and the West Indies, the majority settle in southern Mexico and throughout Central America. They forage and roost in large, loose flocks, often mixing with lesser goldfinches, blue grosbeaks, seedeaters, and other finches. They show fidelity to winter sites, but they neither establish territories nor sing. Around February, adults again molt, the males acquiring their blue breeding plumage, although patchy blue first-year males do not attain full breeding plumage until their second winter.

Ecology. On both summer and winter ranges, indigo buntings are edge residents, favoring brushy and weedy thickets, overgrown fields, hedgerows, woodland clearings and margins, and swamps. Any semiopen area that contains blackberry, raspberry, gray dogwood, or staghorn sumac shrubs is likely to host indigos in summer. On their winter range in Belize, indigos are called riceys because of their frequent presence around rice fields.

For nesting, indigos favor dense, low shrubbery. They place the nest amid forking branches or brushy tangles, seldom higher than about three feet, and always beneath the shrub canopy. Later-sea-

Indigo buntings thrive in thickets and edge habitat mixtures such as this. Few such sites are without resident indigos in spring and summer.

Indigo bunting nests are small, grassy cups usually built on a foundation of leaves.

son nests are often relocated to tall herbs such as bracken ferns (where I often find them), dogbane, goldenrods, giant ragweed, thistles, nettles, and purple loosestrife. Females attach the nest rims to the vegetation, often at points toward the top of the rim, with no direct support from beneath. A base of leaves or sometimes a snakeskin, both useful identifying features of the indigo's vacated nests, underlies the small cup of woven dried grasses and plant fibers.

Indigos forage mainly on the ground or close to it and also glean insects from higher shrub foliage. Insects and seeds both rank high in the indigo's diet. In spring and summer, the birds especially favor cankerworms and other caterpillars, plus beetles and grasshoppers. They also consume a large variety of grass and weed seeds, farm grains, and such fruits as blackberries and elderberries.

The indigo's adaptability to various edge habitats probably gives it competitive advantage. House wrens and house sparrows sometimes raid indigo nests and destroy the contents, actions that are probably more competitive than predatory. On western borders of their breeding range, indigos sometimes conflict—and also hybridize—with their lazuli bunting counterparts.

Indigo bunting nests, usually accessible to ground predators, are attacked by blue racer snakes, opossums, raccoons, red foxes, and feral cats. Probably the major nest predator in most areas is the blue jay. In areas where research has been conducted, brown-headed cowbirds parasitize some 20 percent of indigo bunting nests, and sometimes many more. Indigos occasionally bury cowbird eggs in the nest, building over them.

Focus. The sight of a bright blue indigo singing vigorously from a perch has probably converted many a casual observer into a birder. As in the blue jay, the indigo's blue plumage originates not from pigments but from an interaction with sunlight spectra.

Using these birds as his subjects, researcher Stephen T. Emlen discovered much about bird orientation during migrations. Young indigos, it appears, are not always sleeping at night. Emlen's experiments demonstrated that they learn a sky map, especially the northern star patterns as they relate to rotation around Polaris, the North Star, and that they use these celestial cues for navigation. It is likely that many, if not all, night-flying migrants do the same, possibly also using other means of orientation.

Indigos were probably far less numerous before European settlement and forest clearing in North America. Today they thrive in abundance. Bird census data indicate that in contrast to many Neotropical migrants, this species continues to expand in both breeding range and numbers, likely reflecting the present abundance of North American edge habitats. Indigos have been known to survive ten years, but the average longevity is much less.

BLACKBIRDS (TRIBE ICTERINI)

Not all ninety-eight blackbird species are black, though most show some amount of black plumage. Icterines reside throughout the Western Hemisphere, reaching their greatest diversity in South America (the so-called blackbird of Eurasia is actually a thrush related to the American robin). Blackbirds display a broad range of physical and behavioral features. Many blackbird species walk rather than hop on the ground, and many voice harsh or shrill song and call notes, though some are melodious singers. Breeding strategies and social behaviors also vary. The sexes in many species are dimorphic, differing in plumage coloration. Most blackbirds forage by gaping, as do crows, jays, and starlings. Powerful jaw musculature enables them to open the bill against strong resistance, thus exposing hidden prey in the ground. Eye position on the head aligns with the lower edge of the upper mandible, allowing the birds direct focus into the foraging space, as well as giving them a characteristic bug-eyed appearance when viewed head-on.

Of the twenty-one blackbird species that reside in North America, eleven breed in the Northeast. Besides the three following accounts, plus the mentioned relatives of those species, northeastern icterines include the bobolink (*Dolichonyx oryzivorus*), eastern and western meadowlarks (*Sturnella magna, S. neglecta*), the red-winged blackbird (*Agelaius phoeniceus*), the yellow-headed blackbird (*Xanthocephalus xanthocephalus*), and rusty and Brewer's blackbirds (*Euphagus carolinus, E. cyanocephalus*). South American icterines include the troupials, oropendolas, and caciques. Crows, ravens, and European starlings, though black birds, are unrelated to icterines.

Closer look. Orians, G. H. *Blackbirds of the Americas.* Seattle: University of Washington Press, 1985.

FINCH FAMILY (Fringillidae) • Subfamily Emberizinae • BLACKBIRDS

Baltimore Oriole (*Icterus galbula*)

Flaming orange underparts and black head and wings distinguish the male Baltimore oriole; females are variably yellow-orange beneath and olive-brown above. Both sexes, seven to eight inches long, show two white wing bars. Piping, whistled phrases, voiced by both sexes, are distinctively unrhythmic. A short series of notes on one pitch sounds "like blasts from a tiny trumpet," as one observer wrote, and a loud chatter of alarm notes resembles the rattle notes of brown-headed cowbirds or house wrens.

Close relatives. Of the twenty-six *Icterus* species, eight breed in North America. The orchard oriole (*I. spurius*) is the only other eastern U.S. species. The western U.S. counterpart of the Baltimore is Bullock's oriole (*I. bullockii*). Other western species include Scott's oriole (*I. parisorum*), Audubon's oriole (*I. graduacauda*), the hooded oriole (*I. cucullatus*), and the Altamira oriole (*I. gularis*). The unrelated Old World orioles (tribe Oriolini) belong to the family Corvidae (crows and jays).

Behaviors. Despite the male's gaudy colors, the Baltimore is easier heard than seen. Baltimores spend most of their time in the tree canopy, though they also forage low on occasion. The song pattern of clear, slurred notes is distinctive, revealing this oriole's often common presence where one may have visually missed it. Each oriole voices its own particular pattern of song phrasing and tonal characteristics, enabling individual recognition by careful listening. Males in neighboring territories often countersing back and forth, and one bird may closely imitate the other's song.

Baltimore orioles are migrators, breeding throughout most of the eastern continent from southern Canada almost to the Gulf.

Spring. "To many of us who live in the northern states," wrote orinthologist Winsor M. Tyler, "the Baltimore oriole represents the spirit of spring." Fairly late migrators (late April through May), male Baltimores seldom appear before the trees have leafed out. They precede females by a week or more, usually returning to a previously held territory. First-year males still appear brownish on the head and wings, resembling females, but they acquire full adult plumage in a spring prenuptial molt. Chases, chatter calls, and frequent song from high, conspicuous perches mark the male's establishment of territory, usually two or three acres. When females arrive, one may see courtship displays, especially males bowing in front of females. Females build the nests, usually beginning in late May, though I have watched male Baltimores tugging on loose ends of a clothesline as if trying to collect it. Occasions of extrapair copulation, when a male invades another's territory and copulates with the paired female, are known to occur.

EGGS AND YOUNG: usually four or five; eggs bluish white, brown streaked and blotched, especially at the larger end. INCUBATION: by female; twelve to fourteen days. FEEDING OF YOUNG: by both sexes; regurgitated insects at first, then whole insects. FLEDGING: twelve to fourteen days.

Summer, Fall. Baltimore pairs raise only one brood, but nesting typically extends to late June. Song and nesting cease at the same time. Parents feed the noisy fledglings for two or three weeks, but females sometimes roam away from them, beginning their annual plumage molt a few days before the males stop feeding the young. Males often remain solitary on their territories until completing their molt; orange plumage becomes more vivid as males age. Juvenile males molt into an intermediate femalelike plumage but show a black throat patch, which they will wear until their spring molt. Females and juveniles begin flocking and drifting southward in mid-August, with males following through mid-September.

Winter. Most Baltimore orioles winter in Mexico through Central America to northern South America. Increasing numbers, however, remain in North America, especially along the Gulf and Atlantic coasts north to the Carolinas. On their winter range, the birds remain solitary or associate in small groups. They occasionally sing, and males may also defend feeding territories.

Ecology. Baltimore orioles favor open deciduous woodlands and edges. Orchards, parks, and residential areas with tall shade trees are also frequent habitats. In their winter range, these birds frequent shaded coffee, cacao, and banana plantations, as well as shady thickets and rain-forest canopies.

The Baltimore's suspended, sacklike nest is a durable marvel of tight-woven plant fibers. Usually placed thirty feet high or more at the outermost end of an arched, drooping branch, they are difficult to see when trees are in foliage but easy to spot after leaves drop in the fall. Tall American elms were frequent nesting sites before Dutch elm disease killed so many of these trees. Maples, willows, and apple trees (hosting lower nests) are also common sites, but almost any large tree with arching branches may be selected. Nest building takes the female oriole five to eight days or longer. From a snarl of loose, hanging fibers draped over supporting twigs, she goes to work on the dangling strands. Strips of milkweed, dogbane, or Indian hemp bark often provide the tough suspension fibers, along with pieces of string, grapevine bark, and grasses. She feverishly pushes and pulls in shuttlelike movements, randomly weaving from

all sides, to create a flexible, suspended pouch, open at the top.
She lines the chamber with hair,
fine grasses, and plant down.
Occasionally a female repairs and
reuses a nest of the previous
spring, but usually she builds a
new one each year. House finches
may sometimes adopt vacated
oriole nests.

Caterpillars form the bulk of
oriole diet year-round. This bird
is one of the foremost consumers
of hairy and spiny larvae, including tent, gypsy, webworm, and
tussock moth caterpillars. Orioles forage in the dense webs of
eastern tent caterpillars, which
few other birds do. Irruptions of
these destructive foliage eaters
may attract orioles, temporarily
increasing their local populations. Orioles also consume many
other insects, plus spiders and
snails. Buds, flower nectar, fruits,
and some seeds are frequent food
items, as are garden peas, mulberries, shadbush berries, and
blackberries. These birds relish
orange slices at yard feeders and
also visit hummingbird feeders.

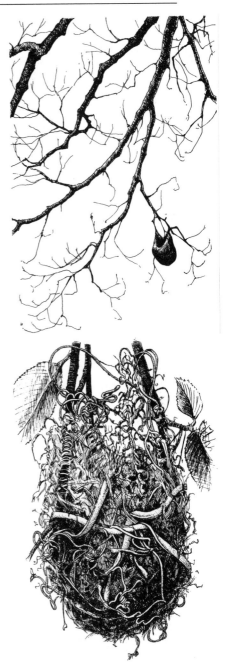

*Baltimore oriole nests hang at the
outer end of drooping branches (top),
becoming conspicuous after leaves
drop in the fall. The nest itself
(bottom) is a flexible, intricately
woven bag.*

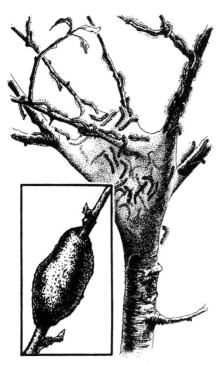

*Web nests of irruptive eastern tent caterpillars (*Malacosoma americana*) attract orioles, which forage in the webs. Numerous egg masses of this moth, seen on twigs in the fall (inset), may forecast next year's local abundance of orioles and cuckoos.*

Some researchers believe that yard feeding accounts for the increasing winter presence of orioles in the United States. Winter range foods include caterpillars, beetles, winged termites, and cecropia fruits.

Competition between Baltimore and Bullock's orioles is difficult to judge. Both are currently expanding their ranges at each other's expense in certain areas. Plumage and adaptive variations—such as the Baltimore's tendency to suspend its nest from thinner branches, possibly a defense against more numerous squirrel predators in the East—distinguish the two species.

Baltimore predators include screech-owls, American crows, and red and gray squirrels. Baltimores seldom tolerate brown-headed cowbird parasitism, rapidly ejecting cowbird eggs from their nests.

Focus. The word *oriole* stems from the Latin *aureus,* meaning "golden," first applied to the unrelated Eurasian golden oriole (*Oriolus oriolus*), which resembles a large goldfinch. New World orioles, though more orange than yellow, were named after their supposed resemblance to this bird. Thoreau called orioles "golden robins." Pioneering naturalist Mark Catesby named the Baltimore for its fancied resemblance to the black and orange livery of Maryland colonist George Calvert, Baron Baltimore. But modern ornithologists have vacillated to a more than ordinary degree over this bird's rightful name. In 1973, data seemed to indicate that Baltimore and Bullock's orioles were actually a single species, so taxonomists officially lumped them together as two subspecies of the northern oriole, a new designation. This was because landscape alteration in the western United States had brought the two into contact, and they hybridized. But the hybrid population, it was discovered, soon melted away, and Baltimore and Bullock's maintained their separate identities in the border zones—"an excellent example of evolution in action," as one observer noted. Selective pressures, obviously, were operating against hybridization in this case.

The initial lumping into a single species had seemed gratuitous at best to many birders—and was roundly cursed by baseball fans of the Baltimore Orioles. Twenty years later, armed with new data, scholarly opinion was swinging back. By 1995, Baltimore and Bullock's orioles were again officially classified as two separate species, and northern orioles, so briefly among us, were suddenly defunct. Maryland dwellers, who never considered renaming their state bird in the first place, thus remain on track.

FINCH FAMILY (Fringillidae) • Subfamily Emberizinae • BLACKBIRDS

Common Grackle (*Quiscalus quiscula*)

Our largest northeastern blackbird, at a foot long, is marked by a "striking yellow eye amidst a sea of iridescence," as one observer described. Its long, broad-tipped tail and stout, sharp-pointed bill are also distinctive. Males have shiny iridescent purple, blue, or green heads and deep bronze or iridescent coloration on the back; females, smaller than males, show less iridescence and browner plumage. The song is a discordant creak—"like a great rusty spring," wrote Thoreau—accomplished with effortful fluffing and hunching; loud, croaking "cack" notes are also common.

Close relatives. The seven *Quiscalus* species all reside in the Western Hemisphere. Only the common grackle, one of three North American grackles, breeds in the Northeast. The boat-tailed grackle (*Q. major*) mainly inhabits southeastern coastal marshes, the lower

Mississippi valley, and the arid Southwest; great-tailed grackles (*Q. mexicanus*) also reside in the Southwest.

Behaviors. The grackle seldom hops, but walks. A long-tailed bird strutting in stately gait across your lawn, or uttering harsh, unmusical squeaks that sound as if its syrinx, or "song box," needs oiling, is this familiar blackbird. Unlike their red-winged blackbird relatives, which undulate in flight, grackles fly evenly with steady wingbeats. Males often crease their tails lengthwise, forming a keel, when in flight or on the ground.

Grackles are frequent predators on nests of smaller birds, consuming eggs and nestlings, often decapitating their victims. They habitually dump the white fecal sacs of their own nestlings in water, often birdbaths. Some grackles also dunk food items in water before swallowing them. Another common grackle habit is anting—picking up ants, which release formic acid, and rubbing them into their plumage. Grackles anoint themselves with other aromatic items as well, presumably as antiparasitic insecticides; mothballs, marigold flowers, and walnut hulls are favorites. Gregarious at all seasons, grackles frequently mix and roost in large flocks with other blackbirds and European starlings after the breeding season.

Lawn-foraging grackles are common sights, especially in spring, when they consume many root grubs. (From The Atlas of Breeding Birds of Michigan.*)*

Common grackles breed throughout most of eastern North America east of the Rockies and south of the arctic tundra. Northern and central continental populations migrate.

Spring. Grackles usually occupy their breeding range by early to mid-March. Adult birds likely return to previous nesting sites or areas, though pairings with prior mates are probably infrequent. Song is hardly territorial in this species; flocks of up to twenty birds may chorus in a tree, creating a cacophony of rasping "scoo-de-leek" notes. Grackle song is a strenuous, full-body exertion that finally produces an anticlimactic noise. Both sexes sing, often alternatively when paired. Small groups of interchangeable males often follow single females about, gradually decreasing in number as pairing occurs.

Both sexes carry long grasses to the chosen nest site, an activity that may continue for several weeks before the female begins building in earnest by late April or early May. Even then she may abandon one site and rebuild in another. Nesting is often loosely colonial, with a few or many pairs residing within a tree grove; a pair's defended territory usually consists of only a few yards' distance surrounding the nest site. Grackle night roosts become smallest in size at this season, when only unmated birds and paired males—leaving their incubating partners on the nest—inhabit them. During incubation, many male grackles opportunistically mate with females other than their original mates.

EGGS AND YOUNG: typically five; eggs greenish white with brown spots and blotches. INCUBATION: by female; about twelve days. FEEDING OF YOUNG: by both sexes if male remains after incubation, by female if not; insects, other invertebrates, eggs and nestlings of other birds. FLEDGING: about twelve days.

Summer. Most females raise only one brood. Parent grackles— or just the female in some cases—feed their young for only a few days after they leave the nest. You can often see one or more large fledglings begging, following, and being fed by adult foragers on the ground at this time. Soon the fledglings achieve independence and form large flocks that feed and roost together. Adult grackles also consolidate into flocks that roost communally at night in shade trees, usually in habitual sites throughout the year. Flocks wander and feed at widely separate locations during daytime, then fly to the roost before dusk. A seemingly endless line of grackles passing overhead in the evening is always roost-bound. As summer advances, roosts grow in size. Grackles gradually molt into new plumage in August and September; juveniles lose their dark brown color and acquire full adult plumage. A fork-tailed grackle flying overhead indicates a beginning tail molt, when the long central rectrices drop first.

Fall. Roosts become largest in late summer and fall, with thousands (sometimes millions) of grackles plus red-winged blackbirds, brown-headed cowbirds, European starlings, and American robins. Most grackle migration occurs by day; northern populations have largely vacated their breeding range by early November.

Winter. Grackles winter on this continent, most in the southern United States from Texas eastward. Year-round resident populations may remain as far north as the lower Great Lakes and southern New England; single birds or small flocks sometimes winter even farther north. The amount of snow cover may be a crucial factor governing their northern distribution in winter. Grackle existence remains entirely flock oriented through this season. Huge roosts of up to ten million birds may assemble, mainly south of latitude 38 degrees and east of longitude 100 degrees. Individual grackles shift among roost sites, displaying no constant fidelity to a given site. Migrants begin moving northward in late winter; in southern Michigan, vanguard grackle arrivals often coincide with those of red-winged blackbirds in late February.

Ecology. Common grackles fare well in a variety of open-woods and edge habitats. Originally they probably inhabited wetland areas almost exclusively, and many still nest and feed in marsh, swamp, and shoreline areas, sometimes wading into shallow water. Today they also frequent residential areas, parks, orchards, plantations, and hedgerows. Flocks often feed in fields

The bulky mass of a grackle's nest often contains mud reinforcement. Nests may be renovated for use in successive years.

and along roadsides. Roosting habitats are generally the same as for European starlings.

Grackles frequently nest in colonies of twenty to thirty pairs, often in dense groves of conifers. Blue and Norway spruces, white pine, and red cedars are common sites; marsh vegetation, low shrubs, orchard trees, climbing vines, and tree and building cavities are also used at times. The birds favor sites near water, but many nest far from water as well. Nests are often placed near the tops of trees, up to sixty feet high or more but usually much lower, two to twelve feet being typical. The bulky nest consists of coarse grasses and weed stalks, often reinforced with a middle layer of mud and lined with finer grasses and plant fibers. A pair of grackles—though not necessarily the same pair—has nested in a white cedar tree in my yard for many years, probably in the same annually repaired nest located three feet from the top.

Grackles forage in trees, on the ground, and at all points between. Local nuisance flocks of grackles have aroused the enmity of farmers for their food habits. Flocks especially relish

corn in the preripened milk stage, sometimes stripping husks to devour just a few kernels. Sprouting wheat is another favorite. Almost half of the grackle's annual diet consists of grain, much of it gleaned from farmyards and fields. Ragweed and smartweed seeds also rank high, as do blackberries and mulberries. Favored fall items include corn and acorns. In contrast to most blackbirds, grackles' *abductor,* or jaw-closing, muscles are stronger than their *depressor,* or jaw-opening, muscles, and they are not strong gapers. A prominent lengthwise ridge in the upper mandible of the bill enables them to crack acorns with ease. During the breeding season, animal matter dominates the diet. Bees, beetles, grasshoppers, and crickets are favored items, as are cutworms, noctuid moth caterpillars that ravage grain sprouts, perhaps accounting for some grackle damage in pulling up shoots. Grackles

The hard ridge inside the grackle's upper mandible enables it to crack acorns and other nuts.

also forage extensively on lawn grubs, especially those of the destructive Japanese beetle. In addition to a variety of insects, these omnivores consume many spiders, earthworms, snails, and crayfish. They are adept at catching emerald shiner minnows in shallow water. They are foremost predators on American robin eggs and nestlings and aggressively rob foraging robins of their earthworm prey, an action easily observed on lawns where both birds are feeding. At other seasons, however, robins and grackles often roost together.

Often the more adaptable the species in terms of nest sites and food, the less competition it faces from other species; this generally

holds true for grackles, as their
abundance attests. Occasions
may arise when a limited food
resource, such as acorns or small
fruits, which are consumed by
many bird and mammal species,
leads to brief episodic competition. A marsh-nesting grackle
encounters competition from different sources—red-winged blackbirds, for example—than a yard
grackle competing with robins for
earthworms. Grackle size and
aggressiveness make them win-
ners in most conflict situations.

Grackle predators include
owls, accipiter hawks, and falcons, which attack mainly at
roosts. Nests are sometimes
raided by bullsnakes, American
crows, blue jays, and squirrels.
Brown-headed cowbird parasitism is rare in this species, per-

*Japanese beetles (*Popillia
japonica*), seen here in their
adult stages, ravage the foliage
of many plants. Grackles and starlings consume these pests as lawn
grubs.*

haps because of its semicolonial nesting habits.

Focus. The name of this bird derives from the Latin *graculus,*
which was used to refer to several black birds, including cor-
morants (*Phalacrocorax*) and the jackdaw (*Corvus monedula*), a
Eurasian crow whose calls the word *grackle* supposedly echoes.
Crow blackbird, as Thoreau called the common grackle, remains a
frequent vernacular name. Until several decades ago, this bird was
classified as two species: the bronzed grackle, inhabiting New England and westward, and the purple grackle, of Atlantic and Gulf
coastal distribution. These are now classified as subspecies that
show minor differences in plumage coloration. At least one leg-
banded grackle survived to age twenty-two, but average longevity
is certainly far less.

Iridescence, so plainly seen in grackles, some waterfowl and gamebirds, hummingbirds, starlings, and a few others, is a pattern of structural colors, as is blue.

Iridescent colors are as much the work of our own eyes as of feather structure and light, for these colors vary as our angle of vision to the feather changes. Twisted, highly modified feather *barbules*—tiny branches that normally interlock and hold the feather *vane,* or web, together—cast differential reflections of light, and our eyesight does the rest. Iridescent feather barbules, unlike most barbules, do not interlock; hence these feathers are relatively weak.

Immense communal roosts of grackles and other blackbirds sometimes annoy human residents, especially in urban areas. Aggressive efforts to wipe out the largest roosts have somewhat reduced grackle populations since the 1970s, but grackles remain abundant on their seasonal ranges.

FINCH FAMILY (Fringillidae) • Subfamily Emberizinae • BLACKBIRDS

Brown-headed Cowbird (*Molothrus ater*)

This seven-inch-long blackbird has a thick, sparrowlike bill. Males are black with clove brown heads; females are a uniform gray-brown with no distinctive markings. The male's song, a liquid, squeaky "glug-lug-glee," sounds as if he is swallowing his own notes. A long, squeaky whistle is also common. Females often utter a series of chattering notes similar to those of house wrens or eastern meadowlarks.

Close relatives. Of the five other cowbird species, only the shiny cowbird (*M. bonariensis*) of the Southeast and the bronzed cowbird (*M. aeneus*), a southwestern desert dweller, reside in North America. The rest are South American species, only one of which, the bay-winged cowbird (*M. badius*), is not a brood parasite and raises its own young.

Behaviors. Note the cowbird's habit of uptilting its tail when (like most blackbirds) it walks. Cowbirds are highly gregarious for most of the year, associating in large flocks with other blackbirds and European starlings.

All brown-headed cowbirds are stepchildren, having been raised in nests of other species—"the ultimate form of day care," in the words of one researcher. Cowbird nestlings often coexist with host nestlings, but often too they supplant them by more rapid hatching, growth, and aggressive begging behavior, resulting in starvation or crowding out of the host nestlings.

Cowbird numbers relate directly to habitat. Originally a Great Plains species that associated with bison herds, giving them the vernacular name buffalo bird, cowbirds have extended their range eastward since agriculture cleared ample new habitats for them. As a result, several eastern passerine species, especially certain warblers, are today seriously threatened by cowbird brood parasitism. Some birds, including blue jays, American robins, gray catbirds, brown thrashers, and Baltimore orioles, have learned to recognize cowbird eggs and eject them from their nests. Other species abandon parasitized nests. One theory even attributes the evolution of blue egg color, as in robins, catbirds, and chipping sparrows, to defense against cowbird parasitism, enabling the blue-egg hosts to discriminate the cowbird egg from their own and eject it from the nest. But most eastern passerines have not yet evolved defensive behaviors and thus, on occasion, may raise more cowbird young than their own.

The cowbird female is an opportunistic egg layer in open nests, but rarely in cavity nests. She shows little discrimination in nest choice and will often deposit eggs in nests of inappropriate species whose type of nestling food will not sustain young cowbirds. Nest accessibility and timing of host presence at the nest are the key factors in choosing where to deposit her eggs. Of some two hundred twenty host species recorded, about one hundred forty-four are successfully parasitized and fledge cowbird young.

Cowbirds expend a huge amount of energy to reproduce themselves. Although only about 3 percent of cowbird eggs laid result in adult cowbirds, this percentage produces enough cowbirds to threaten the survival of several host species that are already threat-

A cowbird egg in the nest of a red-eyed vireo is larger and will hatch sooner than the vireo's eggs; the cowbird nestling thus gains a head start on the young vireos.

ened or endangered, such as Kirtland's and prothonotary warblers. This is because, as one researcher writes, "each pair of cowbirds replaces itself with an average of 1.2 pairs—which will double a cowbird population in eight years." Population numbers of the most common victims, however, seem little affected by cowbird parasitism, though as cowbird numbers increase, this could change. Red-eyed vireos, song and chipping sparrows, American redstarts, and yellow warblers, though most frequently and successfully parasitized, show stable or increasing abundance in most areas. Cowbird parasitism ordinarily affects host bird populations only when other factors—often human-induced habitat changes—lead to cowbird overabundance. We have strongly invited cowbirds to succeed—and they have.

Several other North American bird species, including cuckoos, pheasants, and a few ducks, occasionally dump eggs in nests of their own or other species; such occurrences are fairly common among several passerine species as well. But the cowbird is our only *obligate* brood parasite—it *must* parasitize nests for its own survival. Worldwide, obligate brood parasites include the European cuckoo (*Cuculus canorus*), the honeyguides (*Indicator*), and several weavers (Passeridae). Thus brood parasitism is not an anomalous or abnormal biological situation, but a complex, highly evolved reproductive strategy.

Brown-headed cowbirds breed throughout North America, except for peninsular Florida, from mid-Canada into Mexico. Northern populations migrate, but the birds occupy a large, year-round midcontinental range from New England and the Great Lakes southward.

Spring. Northern cowbird populations usually arrive on their breeding range in early spring, often mid-March. Males usually appear before females. Studies reveal that of all blackbirds, yearling cowbirds are least likely to return to their birth sites in spring. Until egg laying begins in late April, I often observe the birds in trios of two highly attentive males to one female, the males perching and singing wherever she perches and following wherever she flies. Also conspicuous is the male topple-over display as he fluffs, arches, spreads wings and tail, tips forward as if about to fall, and creaks out a song.

More than for most species, cowbird courtship and territorial behaviors are keyed to their habitats. In eastern North America, females are the territorial sex, defending areas of ten to fifty acres from other female cowbirds. Territories often overlap, however, which may be why some host nests receive multiple cowbird eggs. Cowbirds are generally monogamous and sometimes retain the same partners over successive years. Courting males may wander in and out of several female territories until a female pairs with one; the chosen male then follows and guards his mate from invading males but does not defend her territory. At certain times of day, territorial boundaries lapse, and all cowbirds in an area may gather to forage gregariously in prime feeding spots. Midwestern farmlands, where host species and their nests are scattered over much wider distances, present a different picture. There males tend to group in small, loose flocks and remain in areas of twenty to one hundred acres. The females establish no territories, wander widely in search of host nests, and mate promiscuously with dominant males of a flock wherever they can.

Having mated, a female cowbird searches out a host nest by three main methods: by perching in silent observation, by walking on the ground while watching for birds in the vicinity, and by raising a ruckus—noisily rummaging on the ground and in tree foliage as if trying to flush out hidden potential hosts. She usually selects a nest in which at least one host egg is already present. If she finds more than one, she often removes one of the host eggs the day before laying one of her own. She never lays more than one egg at a time in a given nest, though another cowbird female may repeat her performance in the same nest. This operation is performed quickly, usually in seconds, often just before dawn when the host bird leaves its nest to feed.

EGGS AND YOUNG: Female cowbirds often lay an egg a day for five or six consecutive days, quit for a few days, then begin again (some sources say a female lays an average of forty eggs per breeding season, others say up to forty); eggs grayish white, brown dotted, especially at the larger end. INCUBATION: by host species; ten to twelve days (about the same period as that of the smallest passerines), the egg often hatching the day before the host's eggs hatch, thus gaining the cowbird nestling a head start. FEEDING OF YOUNG: by host species, though there have been rare observations of female cowbirds feeding nestling cowbirds in host nests; food consists of whatever the foster parents feed their own young, in most cases insects; cowbird nestlings may starve without a high-protein diet. FLEDGING: ten or eleven days.

Summer. Female cowbirds continue laying at progressively less frequent intervals until about mid-July. Thus, as the season advances, many later- or repeat-nesting species escape cowbird parasitism. Cowbird nestlings, often growing much larger than their foster parents, receive the most attention and thus most of the food brought to the nest. The foster parents also continue to feed fledgling cowbirds from two weeks to a month. Marked behavioral differences between host and parasite species sometimes become apparent during this period. Researcher Harry W. Hann, describing the behavior of cowbird fledglings from ovenbird nests, noted that their tendency to fly up to a perch was "quite disconcerting to the foster parents, which like to keep the young on the ground." Soon the juveniles disperse to nearby areas.

Do cowbirds have the avian equivalent of an identity crisis? Having supposedly become imprinted on a host species, how does a young cowbird achieve cowbirdhood? And does having a particular species as foster parents result in an adult cowbird's favoritism toward that species as a future host? Researchers continue to grapple with these and other puzzles posed by this intriguing bird. As the season advances, young cowbirds, resembling female adults, seek out their own kind, joining also with other blackbirds in foraging and roosting flocks.

Adult cowbirds undergo their annual plumage molt in late summer and early fall.

Fall. After the breeding season, cowbirds might almost be said to lose their social identity as a species. They blend into a larger entity, the blackbird flock, mixing with other blackbirds as if these were their true siblings. Huge mixed flocks of red-winged and rusty blackbirds, common grackles, and cowbirds—which may constitute only 1 to 3 percent of the flock—move southward from their northern ranges mainly in October. Flying by day, they forage in fields and spend nights in transient roosts, often marshes or conifer groves. Northeastern cowbirds may travel five hundred miles or more to their wintering areas.

Winter. Researchers long believed that young male cowbirds learned and developed their species song from older males during winter, when the birds are associated in roosts. Recent work, however, suggests that they learn their song by female feedback—that is, the wing-stroke reactions by a female to a song she "likes" may "teach" a male his song even if he has never heard another male cowbird. Most cowbirds winter from New England, the southern Great Lakes and Great Plains, and California to the Gulf and into Central America.

Ecology. Cowbirds were originally native to the short-grass plains, which they still inhabit and where they associate with grazing cattle, horses, and bison. They began expanding their populations both east and west concurrently with land clearing and cultivation. Their feeding association with grazing mammals was seen to be unnecessary to their survival and reproductive success. It took them more than a century, however, to span the continent. Optimal cowbird habitats in the East include open forest and edge mosaics amid plenty of open land for ground foraging. Residential areas and farm country with woodlots, hedgerows, roadside vegetation— almost any landscape with a tree-shrub-field mix—serve cowbird needs. Because of these habitat preferences, most cowbird hosts are edge-dwelling species. Yet this is changing. Forest fragmentation has increased the vulnerability of many interior woodland birds to cowbird parasitism. Since cowbirds often penetrate woodlands several hundred feet—and occasionally much farther—from their edges in seeking out host nests, virtually every nest in a fragmented stand may become accessible to these parasites.

Cowbirds construct no nests of their own, though ancestral cowbirds probably did so. How and why the parasitic nesting habit evolved in these birds remains a subject of endless theory and speculation. Likely it had something to do with the birds' transient lifestyle as they followed the bison herds.

Cowbirds often feed adjacent to grazing mammals, but the association is obviously not necessary to cowbird success.

Primarily insect eaters during the summer, cowbirds consume many leafhoppers, beetles, and caterpillars, but almost half their insect food consists of grasshoppers. From the farmer's point of view, the cowbird's consumption of destructive insects makes it a beneficial bird. Spiders, snails, and eggs from host nests are also eaten. Early observers, watching cowbirds perch on the backs of cattle, believed that they benefited grazers by feeding on the animals' skin parasites. Perhaps they do to some extent, but probably the association is mainly *commensal*—that is, cowbirds capture insect food stirred up by the grazers, which neither benefit nor suffer. About 75 percent of the cowbird's annual diet consists of weed and grass seeds; ragweeds, knotweeds, foxtail grasses, and crabgrasses rank high, as do corn, oats, and wheat. Since cowbirds feed mainly on the ground, most of their grain consumption is harvest waste.

Probably the cowbird's foremost competitor is itself, especially in host nests where two or more large cowbird nestlings must contend with each other for food. They also compete against high statistical odds: If the host bird does not eject, bury, or abandon the cowbird egg, and if, once hatched, the cowbird nestling receives enough protein food and does not fall victim to a nest predator, its chances for survival to adulthood are good. But only a small percentage of cowbirds make it that far.

Though many host species show hostility to adult cowbirds in or near their territories, few succeed in driving the silent female stalkers completely away. Cowbird eggs and nestlings are vulnerable to any host nest predator, and flock roosts may be raided by owls. Hawks and falcons also capture cowbirds.

Focus. Thoreau sometimes called this bird the "cow troopial" (troupials are related to South American orioles); cow bunting and cow blackbird were other common names. Audubon and other early naturalists misidentified the juvenile cowbird, naming it a separate species, the "ambiguous sparrow."

Brown-headed cowbirds have been known to live for almost sixteen years; average longevity is probably half that or less. Researchers estimate that twenty to forty million cowbirds currently inhabit North America.

In areas managed for certain host populations threatened by cowbirds, trapping and killing the parasites has provided at least temporary relief for the victimized. Yet these birds, posing as many problems as they do for bird conservation and research, offer a wealth of interest. And their gamble on the successfulness of deceit reminds us of the endlessly variable survival strategies evolved for living on Earth—that nature's "agendas" far transcend the values of human community. For that reason alone should cowbirds intrigue us.

Closer look. Friedmann, H. *The Cowbirds: A Study in the Biology of Social Parasitism.* Springfield, IL: Charles C. Thomas, 1929. An old but basic reference.

Index

Illustrations indicated by page numbers in italics

DATE